RENEGADES AT SEA

The Adventures of Chas From Tas

RENEGADES AT SEA

The Adventures of Chas From Tas

by

Juliet Prentice

and

Charles Blundell

With much gratitude to Douglas Hawkins for the cover and maps.
Doug taught drawing, sculpture and ceramics at the National Art School,
Sydney. He also works for public and private collectors worldwide.
Contact: salgoud08@gmail.com

Many thanks to Jack Hawkins for computer graphics,
winner of Young Architect of the Year, 2014.
Contact: jackllhawkins@gmail.com

Thank you to Ranchor Prime for his line drawing illustrations
Contact: ranchorprime@gmail.com

published 2015 by Shimran
Suite 10 Lauder Court, Milborne Port
Sherborne
Dorset DT9 5EL
UK

ISBN 978 1 910819 30 2

Printed by IngramSpark
Distributed worldwide by
Filament Publishing Ltd
www.filamentpublishing.com

Dedications

To my wonderful father who introduced me
to the freedom and beauty of the ocean
Fruity

To my dear mother and for the sea,
which has given me so many magical
moments and adventures
Chas from Tas

Contents

Foreword by Sir Robin Knox Johnston

How often do we hear people say that you don't find characters today the way you used to. Well, Chas from Tas proves that they still exist! He is not a world-renowned racing skipper, or millionaire who can afford to hire the best crews available, he is one of the unsung heroes of yachting without whom the boats could not safely put to sea, who sailed with the best in many of the big races. He moved around from owner and skipper, from boat to boat, playing his part and watching and picking up the incidents that are an inevitable part of our sport and making friends.

Chas is not just an interesting personality, he is a fount of useful knowledge picked up over the years from his experiences at sea over most of the world's oceans. Apart from being a great companion to share a few beers with when the opportunity of finding ourselves in the same place at the same time occurs, he is a most amusing storyteller, using incidents from his own experiences and telling them in a way that always brings a grin to one's face.

For those who want to know what goes on behind the scenes, this is the sort of book that shows you how it really is, in life as in sailing. The fun and dramas that don't make the newspapers, which bring so much enjoyment to those of us who share our sport are all a part of the stories that miss the headlines – in many cases, thank goodness! It is also about friends made over the years, and Chas has many scattered all around the globe.

Masefield said it all. He must have had Chas in mind for the third line:

I must go down to the sea again, to the vagrant gypsy life

Renegades at Sea

*To the gull's way and the whale's way, where the wind's like a
    whetted knife
And all I ask is a merry yarn from a laughing fellow rover
And a quiet sleep and a sweet dream when the long tricks
    over.*

There is no better fellow rover than Chas from Tas.

Sir Robin Knox Johnston

Foreword by Sir James Hardy

Day after day, day after day,
We stuck, not a breath nor motion;
As idle as a painted ship
Upon a painted ocean.

Water, water everywhere
And all the boats did shrink,
Water, water everywhere
Nor any drop to drink.

The Ancient Mariner

Like Samuel Taylor Coleridge's Ancient Mariner, Chas from Tas has many times held me spellbound with stories from his life at sea in all of the globe's oceans on offshore races and countless delivery voyages he has made ferrying yachts between venues. Chas tell his stories because he loves the sea, its elements and the boats and characters who sail it. He has not kept me from a wedding feast, as the Ancient Mariner did, but he has delayed my progress to many a yacht club bar to get the next drop to drink.

Chas, like the Ancient Mariner, is a compelling story teller. He has much to tell, from dodging pirates in Asian waters and typhoons across the Pacific, escaping from Simon Le Bon's maxi, Drum, when it capsized in a Fastnet race, to escapades ashore that I am not about to reveal here.

Like the Ancient Mariner he has a strong affinity to the sea and its creature, although fortunately never shot an albatross, which was the Ancient Mariner's undoing. I suspect Chas is more at home at sea than ashore where he usually totes most of his possessions around in two sailing gear bags between yacht clubs and airports.

He became interested in ocean racing after an encounter with Don Mickleborough at Constitution Dock after a Sydney to Hobart race.

Mickleborough recalls: "This fifteen or sixteen-year-old on the wharf said, 'Can I come on board your yacht and have a look around'? I replied 'Yes, if you take the empties ashore'. The deck was littered with empty long-neck bottles from the lengthy post-race celebrations on Southerly. Chas duly disposed of the bottles, came aboard and said 'This ocean racing is alright' and stayed for two and a half days."

Chas's long career as a professional sailor began in 1971 when he served six months on the Fyfe 86 Carlina in the Mediterranean. Then he joined Sir Max Aitken's Gurney 63 Crusade on a Transatlantic crossing and afterwards raced and delivered for more than thirty years on many notable yachts including Phantom, Windward Passage, Sorcery and Nirvana from the USA; Yeoman XXI, Yeoman XXII, Rothmans and Mistress Quickly from the UK. The Yeomans were owned by Robin Aisher whom I raced against in the Mexico Olympics in 1968 and who became a good mate. Other yachts included were Hitchhiker, Sweet Caroline and Magic Pudding from Australia, and Lady Fling and Bimblegumble from Hong Kong.

The races and events he has sailed multiple times include the Southern Ocean Racing Circuit and the Newport-Bermuda race in the States; the Fastnet race and Admiral's Cup in the UK; the Pan Am Clipper Cup in Hawaii; the Sydney-Hobart race and Hamilton race week in Australia; and the Hong Kong Manila race and the Kings Cup in Asia.

Although a serious leg injury in 2000 put him ashore for a long recuperation he is still delivering boats regularly to major races and events. Recently his mission has been collecting yarns of his experiences into this book, which I am sure will be as compelling to readers as the Ancient Mariner's tale was to his listeners.

Sir James Hardy

Acknowledgements

To my friend Juliet Prentice, aka Fruity, without whose help writing this book and encouragement it would never have seen the light of day.

To all my generous friends who have supported and tolerated me over the years, and to the ones who have joined the squid in Davy Jones locker, or are having a rum and dancing with the girls at Fiddler's Green and won't be around for these reminisces, thank you.

I have tried to make this book as accurate as my memory allows, if I have failed please forgive me.

Chas from Tas

Preface

I am so glad I have been able to tell this story. I remember when I first heard Chas recount one of his wild trips at sea thinking that it might be an idea to one day chronicle his adventures and write of a time we will probably never see again. The stories of an ocean-going vagabond and a cast of renegades and buccaneers who all share a passion for the world's oceans, fine sailors one and all.

My father was a great sailor, he adored the sea and just before he died he held one last memorable farewell party attended by many of his friends that he had sailed with during his life. It was during this occasion that I decided to take a shot at the book and finally the project started in Australia, one dark and stormy winter's night over some whisky in the local pub. In fact shortly after this I decided to stock up on quite a lot of good whisky thinking it would most definitely be needed!

Chas was still covering twenty thousand miles a year at sea and his stays on land were brief, so locating the old seadog was often elusive. I remember being grateful that my father had been a code-breaker and hoped I had inherited some small part of his ability in trying to piece the jigsaw puzzle together from scraps of paper and notes that were more often than not scattered in chaos amongst beer bottles and shrouded in clouds of cigarette smoke.

I would often be astonished that Chas could recall his early career nearly fifty years ago and remember journeys that amount to the same distance as travelling to the moon and back one and half times.

Writing the book, this one being the first in a trilogy, has been an adventure in itself. I am so grateful to many dear friends for their support along the way, for Jessy and her unwavering faith and enthusiasm, to Susan and Clare for all their kindness and for believing in the book, to Ranchor for his great editing, design and drawing skills, to Doug who always held true in stormy weather and for his cover artwork and lovely paintings, to Captain Tits and Blowie for their much appreciated help, to Butch for his encouragement, to Chas's brother Richard for always being there with a helping hand, to Ian for arranging the first launch in Hong Kong, to Don who lent us his glorious classic old boat *Southerly* as an office and which was conveniently berthed outside the Sydney Cruising Yacht Club bar, to my late father John, a supporter of the many mavericks of the maritime world he loved so much and wherever he may be he would be pleased this book came to fruition, to Robin, Jim and Simon for their forewords thank you. And lastly I want to thank Chas, for his unique and wonderful adventures.

Juliet

Lotus Outreach

A percentage of proceeds from this book will be donated to Lotus Outreach.

Founded in 1993 by Buddhist Lama Khyentse Norbu to serve the most neglected and forgotten peoples, Lotus Outreach's mission is to ensure the education, health and safety of at-risk women and children in the developing world.

Trafficking is inextricably linked to poverty; for that reason Lotus Outreach considers all of its programs to be preventative in nature. Their work is to support families in dire poverty so they don't put their girls into child labor, to reduce violence to women and prevent abuse and exploitation. For those who are survivors of violence Lotus Outreach has programs that provide trauma therapy, social services and economic empowerment.

Lotus Outreach is a non-profit organization and invests in initiatives that improve earning potential and livelihood for individuals, families and communities. Through the provision of skills training, small business grants and the establishment of community-led savings and loan groups Lotus Outreach ensures communities can meet their own needs, such as food, healthcare and education without continued dependence on development and relief organizations.

www.lotusoutreach.org

Introduction

Chas From Tas,
A Seafaring Legend

H E CAME INTO THE BAR OF THE ROYAL WESTERN YACHT CLUB, a raffish-looking wild man from the sea and his voice, hoarse and unrepentantly Australian, whiplashed the reefer jackets with scorn and challenge.

"I'm Chas from Tas," this refugee from the Fastnet gale announced, eyes like gimlets, glaring red down a broken beak-nose. "Charles P Blundell from Hobart, Tasmania."

It took several gulps before the venerable club members could fully comprehend the apparition before them: matted, sun-bleached hair, flaring mutton chops, a twist of leather around his neck, tattered woolen jacket and salt worn jeans. As piratical a seadog as ever had walked into the RWYC in its 152 years of history.

Then a remarkable thing began to happen. Men came out of the smoke in amazement and began clapping Chas on the shoulders, shaking his hand. One of them a Swedish millionaire, another a British industrialist. Soon a whole troop were listening avidly as Chas, unabashed by any sense of modesty, recounted his latest adventures.

Chas not only looks the part, but already had become a seafaring legend among the men who take yachts out to sea in the big international events. He roams the seas of the world, hiring his skills plus

Chas from Tas

keep…or nothing, if the challenge is big enough.

Not having lived anywhere for more than six months, Chas has sailed more miles to the moon one and half times and back, a feat which even the greatest seadog of them all Sir Francis Drake would regard with envy.

Chas is seldom on land for long. It is just as well, for ashore he is an unmitigated disaster, requiring constant care and attention. His friends gently navigate him from bar to taxi to station or airport and when the trip is over more friends are there to take over. On land he is absolutely hopeless, but at sea it is another matter entirely.

Chas has never lost one of the hundreds of boats he has delivered for owners who want them expertly set up in some distant port. Such is his reputation that he usually steps off a boat, catches a plane somewhere across the world and steps on board another yacht. He carries all his worldly possessions in three small sea-bags. He owns nothing else.

"All I own in the world is me," Chas says.

It is a statement no one is prepared to dispute, because it is so obviously true.

He has friends all over the world, men he's sailed with on the seven seas, and as a young man swore never to take a job ashore again. It's a promise he has kept.

There will be plenty of wild stories to tell, whether you meet him in a bar in some far flung port, or read about his adventures in the pages of this book.

With thanks to Philip Cornford

I would rather be ashes than dust,
A spark burnt out in a brilliant blaze,
Than be stifled in dry rot.
For man's purpose is to live, not to exist;
I shall not waste my days trying to prolong them,
I shall use my time.

Jack London (1876-1916)

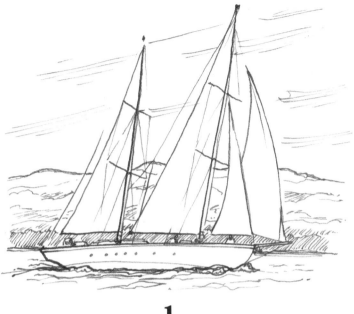

1

The Asinara Falcon

Thus I reclaimed my buzzard love, to fly
At what and when and how and where I choose.

John Donne

A T THE TAIL-END OF THE SIXTIES, not long after the first man walked on the moon, I decided that sitting on my arse in an office for the rest of my life was not an option. On the back of this realization I strode into a Melbourne travel agent and bought a one way to ticket to England. I was in my early twenties, and with adventure on my mind and just a few dollars in my pocket, I boarded the *Northern Star* about the time the North Vietnamese leader Ho Chin Min died, Colonel Gaddafi barged into power and Richard Nixon was inaugurated as the next US president.

During a six-week voyage, Northern Star travelled eastwards across the Pacific and I lived like a lord on three free meals a day, plenty of duty-free grog, and best of all the single female passengers outnumbered the men three to one. From the ports of Papeete to Barbados and Balboa I ran into a bunch of seafaring gypsies living the dream, and by the time I disembarked in Southampton the seeds of a life spent sailing the world's oceans were firmly planted in my mind. But first things first.

By Christ, England is bitterly cold in January and I nearly froze my balls off standing on the station platform waiting for the old British Rail rattler to show up and take me to London. The train trundled along through the snow-covered countryside past fields that from an Australian's perspective didn't look much bigger than snooker tables. Staring out of the window at the bleak scenery I decided that although I needed to make some money during the next few months to keep my ribs apart, future stays in the northern hemisphere would most definitely be limited to summers only.

Within a few days I scored a job with the House of Dunhill situated on the corner of Jermyn and Duke Street in the West End and I'll never forget the interview. A dapper chap trussed up in a pin-striped long-tailed suit looked up from his desk after he'd finished sifting through my references, raised his eyebrows and announced:

"Most impressive, you certainly have packed a lot into your life so far, young man. I'm assigning you to the pipe and tobacco section with old man O'Connor. I don't think your fishing experience will be of much use around here, but welcome aboard anyway."

He stood up to shake my hand on the deal and went on to speak in a hushed conspiratorial whisper:

"You're the first Australian we've employed here and I should warn you that a band of notorious fraudsters known as the Kangaroo Gang, led by one of your fellow countrymen King Arthur Delaney, has raided Harrods of Knightsbridge and more recently Fortnum and Masons across the road. Scotland Yard has been after them for months to no avail, and I believe they may attempt to rob Dunhill's, so if you see anything suspicious I would appreciate it if you let me know immediately."

The decrepit old Irish codger O'Connor I wound up working with had been in the pipe and tobacco game all his life. He plastered his wispy grey hair with Brylcreem and swept it back over his head teddy-boy style ending with a greasy duck tail at the back, had a pair of enormous ears hanging on the sides of his wrinkled face like a couple of dangling bats, and wore a pair of round glasses with lenses as thick as the base of a Coca-Cola bottle.

"You'll have to keep an eye out for any likely IRA parcel bombs in the shop," he drawled in a thick Dublin accent, leaving me wondering if working at Dunhill's might be more fraught with danger than a walk through the snake and spider infested outback Down Under.

For the time being, however, the establishment wasn't raided by crooks or blown up by terrorists and I found myself looking after a wide variety of customers. We often got good-looking Scandinavian au-pair girls dropping in to pick things up for their employers, and one day the actress Britt Ekland walked in wearing a long coat and bright yellow rubber boots and needed a lighter fixed. I thought her the finest looking au-pair girl I'd ever seen and asked her out for a date and who could blame me. She giggled over my proposition and mentioned something about filming in Switzerland, but she did give me her phone number, and it was only on the way home I realized who the hell she was when I saw her beautiful face splashed across the Evening Standard.

Sammy Davis Junior rocked in dressed in a sharp suit, wearing a bowler hat and wielding a fancy ivory-handled umbrella. He jived around the show-room whistling Pop Goes The Weasel and pointing his brolly at whatever caught his eye. It was quite an act until he waltzed out of the door in the direction of his chauffer-driven Rolls Royce and fell flat on his face where he sprawled on the pavement until some big fella tossed him into the back of the Roller. Yul Brynner, the bald-headed movie star, would come by pretty regularly too, and spend a fortune adding to his already vast collection of pipes.

And then there was one day when a couple of coach loads of Japanese tourists burst through the doors and swarmed all over the shop buying up a shitload of cigarette lighters. The bloke that had employed me strutted around like a magpie selling to all and sundry when suddenly he waved me over with an anxious look on his face.

"I think I may have spotted King Arthur Delaney and some of the Kangaroo Gang," he gasped nervously.

"Where, mate?" I asked looking around over the top of the crowd of diminutive Japanese customers.

"Look, over there by the Meissen porcelain counter. Try and keep him occupied and hold the fort while I call Scotland Yard," he instructed.

As soon as I saw the bunch of Aussies I recognized one of them, in his early thirties, tanned and fit, and the last time I'd seen him was in Tasmania playing a tennis exhibition match with Lew Hoad. In fact it was Ken Rosewall, known affectionately back home as Muscles because he didn't have any, and on this trip to London he ended up playing against John Newcombe in the singles final at Wimbledon.

"You'd better call off Scotland Yard mate. These blokes aren't the Kangaroo gang, they're some of our finest tennis players," I called out to O'Connor who was hovering nervously in the back of the shop.

There was no way in the world I was going to stay in the pipe and tobacco business for longer than necessary, shit, I only got half a Saturday and Sundays off, and what could I do with that? Dunhill offered me a job looking after their joint in Beverly Hills, Los Angeles, which I promptly turned down, and anyway I wanted to explore Europe for a while. So I hit the frog and toad and jumped into an MGB with a mate who was so tall he barely fit in the small car and took off for Spain to chase good-looking women.

In Greece I came to the conclusion that Greeks weren't all about fish and chip shops and after a few months adventuring ended up fishing and farming out on the Isle of Muck in Scotland, where I discovered not all Scots wear kilts and play bagpipes.

I didn't get back to London until March, the day that Smoking Joe Frazier stopped Mohammed Ali in the fifteenth round during the fight of the century at Madison Square Gardens in New York. Not long after getting a job painting walls for a company that imported Peruvian fish meal in the Baltic Exchange in the East End, I dived into the subterranean depths of the London underground on a dark and gloomy day and picked up a tattered copy of The Times newspaper left lying on the seat beside me by some bowler-hatted brief-case baron.

Turning the pages I arrived at the employment section to find an advertisement looking for crew on a yacht called Carlina setting off in May for a three month adventure in the Mediterranean. The weather was still shit in England, especially for an Australian, and I was dreaming of the sea, yachts, sunshine and women – the time had come to haul up anchor and get out of town. The dice rolled in my favour largely because I showed up for the interview in Belgravia Square a week earlier than requested, and within a few days I found myself southerly-bound on a BEA Trident headed for Malta and arrived in Valetta marina on a blazing hot afternoon.

I spotted Carlina, a glorious 86' ketch constructed of the finest timber and eyed up her perfect sheer line from the tip of her bowsprit to a double-ended stern and the two spruce masts that towered above her decks. Built in Scotland by Jason Miller in 1939, the classic yacht was tied up to an old stone wall, and a regal Afghan hound lay growling at the top of the gangplank guarding his floating home. His name was Shibumi and he would later become the finest of shipmates.

Henry 'Mitch' Mitchell Jnr, the ketch's owner, was a distinguished-looking Englishman who had served in WWII as a spitfire pilot. His family once owned the Mitchell & Butler brewery and made the famous beer Brew XI which had the logo 'For Men of the Midlands' plastered across the bottle's label. The company eventually got swallowed up by Bass in 1961 and Mitch inherited a small fortune. He had a taste for both fine classic yachts and beautiful women, and Jackie, his second wife, was a tall graceful dancer from Sacramento. They were an elegant couple. The rest of the crew showed up over the next few days. Janine, an Australian girl engaged to some bloke in Sydney that she was saving herself for, Jane, a pretty freckle-faced American who came to tutor Jackie's daughter Holly, and Yarpie Don, a young engineer who had escaped South Africa hounded by the authorities for sympathising with apartheid.

Malta is full of fascinating and often bloody history, much of which is due to the strategic position it holds bang slap in the middle of the Mediterranean. Battles raged between the Turkish Corsairs from the Ottoman Empire and the crusading Knights of St. John, who desperately defended the island, and the thirty-foot high and forty-foot thick walls around the waterfront are testament to the struggle. And Nelson and Napoleon fought a hard naval scrap over the place in nearby Egypt. Nelson fucked the Frogs and in 1800 the Union Jack was raised in Malta five years before the battle of Trafalgar.

For me it was a nostalgic visit to where my father had been posted as an RAF flight engineer with two hundred and fifty people under his command at the height of WWII. At the beginning of the war the island's air defence consisted of six Gloucester Sea Gladiators, three of which remained in packing cases while the other three, 'Faith', 'Hope' and 'Charity', successfully defended the island against an Italian invasion until the British and Commonwealth forces arrived with reinforcements in the shape of Hawker Hurricanes, Spitfires and Flying Boats. Malta was under siege, German U-boats ran amok and it was near impossible to bring supplies in.

My old man told me that caves were used as aircraft hangers and most of the running repairs were carried out largely on improvisation and ingenuity. Almost brought to its knees, Malta was nearly out of fuel when the the the SS Ohio, a US oiler manned by a British crew, half of whom were dead, was towed into the grand old harbour in an almost unrecognizable state by a couple of Royal Navy escorts, the sole survivors of a convoy. Things still hung in the balance but the defence forces, along with the resilience of the Maltese people, were able to grimly hang on through over three thousand air raids until the British navy broke the blockade and Montgomery, with the aid of American-built tanks, overpowered Rommel, turning the tables.

Not long before we set sail Susanne, one of Mitch's daughters, showed up out of the blue. Looking like a young Rita Hayworth with a cascade of rich red hair tumbling down her back, green eyes and a body to die for, she spilled the wind right out of my topsails. One evening not long after she arrived I was about to set off for a pint or two at the closest watering hole, a pub called The Britannia, and to my surprise asked if she could tag along. The bloke that owned the joint was a patriotic, pot-bellied Brit with a corkscrew-shaped nose and known locally as Barnacle Bill because he was more or less permanently glued to a bar stool from where he barked orders to a couple of broad-beamed cockney bar maids who poured copious amounts of beer for the local wharf rats. Although on frequent occasions they served up one of Bill's other tipples, he had become renowned for a blinding mixture of opium, chalk and brandy, which he swore cured an ailment referred to locally as the Malta Dog.

In the early hours I rolled out of the boozer and my hot red-headed companion seduced me in a wild frenzy on a swing in a park on the way back to the yacht. By the time we finally arrived on board Carlina, she lured me into her cabin for more. Terrified of being caught by her father I decided to make a dawn escape, and as I clambered skywards through the heavy teak and bronze hatch the damn thing fell on me with a resounding crash and the catch went right through one of my fingers. In agony I staggered on down the deck leaving a dripping trail of blood behind me – it hurt like hell, but Susanne had been worth it and promised all the excitement of a secret romance.

Mitch and Jackie knew some interesting people on the island, among them a beautiful girl engaged to a Knight of Malta who lived with his mother, the Countess della Catena, in a faded tumbledown estate. We were all invited to a party one evening and I ended up getting into a rap with the countess, a great old broad with a shock of white hair and piercing eyes.

"And where are you from, Chas?" she asked.

"Oh, I'm a Taswegian from Down Under," I replied.

"Is that so? I spent my childhood in Australia. When I was a young girl my father became Governor of Tasmania in 1904 and later took up the post of Governor of Western Australia, New South Wales and Norfolk Island before coming back here to Malta where he got appointed Prime Minister. Come with me and I'll show you his smoking room," she offered.

I grabbed Susanne's hand and followed the grand dame up the sweeping staircase.

She led us through a heavy door and into a room stuffed to the gills with so much paraphernalia, it made for a poltergeist's paradise.

"That's my father, Lord Gerald Strickland," she said pointing at a large painting and leading me over to a bloody great blackwood desk. She picked up a dusty brass plaque.

"And this was a gift to him from the people of Tasmania."

"What's behind those big curtains over there?" I enquired.

"Oh, that's the library," she explained, pulling the heavy drapes to one side and taking us further into the lair, a room crammed full of faded leather-bound books. "Shakespeare's over there, and here are various rare editions, and this is a map of how the world looked when I travelled with my parents as a child – all the areas marked in red cover the British Empire as it was then. Now I must get back to my guests, but do stay and look around if you like."

The library had a musty smell but Susanne's perfume cut through it like a dose of aphrodisiac smelling salts, and before I knew it she'd ripped my clothes off and set about ravaging me on an acre-sized antique Persian rug. She was so bloody beautiful I almost forgot where we were until we collided into one of the bookshelves and nearly brought the bard's entire collection of plays crashing down on top of us. And I nearly jumped out of my skin and lost my grip of the situation when a monstrous-sized antique grandfather clock struck a series of sonorous booms.

"Jesus fucking Christ, Susanne, we've gotta get out of here before the ghost of the Contessa's father shows up," I said, hauling on my trousers and grabbing her discarded Ossie Clark silk dress off the top of an old brass telescope.

And with that we belted back down the grand old staircase, hijacked a bottle of wine from the butler on the way out of the castle, and headed for the safer confines of Susanne's bunk on Carlina.

By the beginning of June, fully provisioned and having cleared customs, we cast off the dock lines as the first shards of sunlight skimmed over the tiled roof tops of Valletta and spilled down towards the waterfront, chasing away the last of dawn's shadows. The six-cylinder Gleniffer donk rumbled away until Carlina made it out past the headland.

We rumbled on past a bunch of little luzzus, the lateen-rigged traditional Maltese fishing boats with their brightly-painted double-ended carvel-planked and proud flared bows decorated with a lovely pair of eyes. Soon we had the sails up and were on our way to the small island of Comino where we anchored in the blue lagoon to celebrate Susanne's birthday. Long after everyone had gone to bed she and I stole away in a dinghy to a beach in the bay for a moonlight swim armed with a bottle of rum and what was left of a damn good cheesecake. The early morning warning of a tinted scarlet sky greeted us the next day, and without further ado we set a course for Cagliari in southern Sardinia.

"I've just listened to the weather report from Valetta on the radio and they reckon it's going to be great for the next couple of days," Mitch said tapping the face of the barometer. "Yep, fine and fair," he confirmed, and settling back behind the helm lit up his briar pipe.

Cat's paws broke the water's glassy surface as a light breeze sifted its way down through the copper-coloured hills and over the clifftops, mixing the scent of rosemary with the sharp salt of the sea. By noon it was hot as hell and only the sound of the engine ghosting along broke the silence of a stultifying heat. We entered the straits between Sicily and Tunisia where conditions began to change and Carlina began to bounce over short, rough waves. I heard Donald shout out,

"What are those things in the sky that look like railway lines?"

"What colour are they?" Mitch called out from down below where he sat at the chart table.

"It's difficult to tell, I'm colour-blind," he squawked.

"You're what?!" Mitch bellowed, clambering up the gangway.

"I can only see in black and white," Donald mumbled back.

"For Christ's sake, how the hell are you going to handle the night watches and identify ships, or any other hazards for that matter?" Mitch asked in exasperation.

"Well the South African defence forces didn't seem to give a shit about it when it came to conscription. As long as I could tell the difference between black and white they were quite happy to put a gun in my hand and send me off to some god-forsaken outpost near Mozambique," replied Donald.

"Jesus, don't tell me you were using a gun with this condition!" exclaimed Mitch.

"Well no, I didn't have to in the end as I managed to get a deferment to continue my studies at university," said Donald.

"Well it's too late to worry about it now. Come to think of it, I remember a couple of recruits in the RAF who were deployed into aerial reconnaissance on Beaufort bombers and Sunderland flying boats where they distinguished themselves detecting camouflaged artillery," he said, pausing a moment to pat Shibumi who'd padded up onto deck to see what the fuss was about. "Maybe we can turn this disability into an attribute; you never know, you might be able to detect unlit markers against a night sky," Mitch pondered.

By this time the sun had been swallowed up in a veil of haze, and a mackerel sky of pink, white and grey began to advance like a huge flock of Australian galahs.

"I've seen shit like this before in the Bass Strait and it blew like a bastard a couple of hours later," I muttered.

"The Arabs called the island of Pantelleria in the Straits of Scilly 'Bent el Riah', daughter of the wind. There's often a bit of breeze around here but I doubt it will blow more than twenty-five knots," Mitch said cheerfully, and with that took off for a siesta.

11

When he reappeared a while later I told him I'd bent on the spitfire jib and reefed the mizzen.

"What the hell for?" he spluttered.

"I've got a bad feeling it's going to blow, mate," I explained.

By midnight Mitch changed his tune. A solid forty-knot gale had enveloped us, the white crests of the steep waves turned to spume and Carlina's decks were awash with rushing water. He looked haggard and pale in the dimly-lit pilothouse; the two of us were taking turns to steer now, the auto-pilot was fucked and we hung on hard to a starboard tack and headed for Tunisia, riding up and over the bucking rollers. Mitch threw up a pretty good dinner out of the side door, and turning to me afterwards mumbled,

"My God, Chas, you must have cast iron guts. You were right about the weather, dammit, it's a bloody majjistral, the Maltese mistral. You don't often get them this late in the year. I reckon there's a low pressure system somewhere between Sicily and Sardinia, and a high over North Africa, and the two systems are spinning like roulette wheels – this nor'wester will be a combination of the two of them."

"What do you want to do, Mitch? The storm's pushing us further and further south!" I yelled out as we crashed down the far side of another roller.

"Get the hell out of here and hope we can hang on till dawn! I'm worried about Lampione, that damn rock Cyclops cast into the sea. It stands thirty-six meters high and isn't lit. If we miss that we can head back towards Malta," he hollered.

During the night we sagged off to leeward like a polar bear on ice with its claws lopped off. Dawn sprang on us none too soon. A several hundred-meter high tower on the west side of Lampedusa island revealed itself and we were forced to put in a couple of tacks to clear the hazards, which involved a two-man job to release and secure the pair of six-foot long bronze high field levers that operated the running backstays. Somewhere around the bottom of the island the VHF crackled into life and the coastguard called to see if we were all right.

"Sure, it's rough out here, but we're ok. Is that a new tower you've got there?" Mitch asked.

"Yes, we've almost finished building the new Loran and Omega station. We have had to abandon the old one in Libya thanks to Gaddafi," the voice came over the radio.

Is that an American accent you got there? What are you guys doing over here?" Mitch enquired.

"Yeah, this is a US-manned station. I'm from Pittsburgh and looking forward to getting back home," the caller replied.

We lost contact with them when we rounded the other side of the island, and with the wind on our quarter and our tails firmly between our legs, we set off towards the small Maltese island of Gozo on a thunderous blast reach. Not far from the town of Mgarr we anchored Carlina in an isolated cove to the sound of distant explosions and gunfire rifling down through the valley. And then came the booming of bells echoing off the steep oystershell-tinted and hollow-cheeked limestone cliffs above us. It was out with the old guard and in with the new— Dom Mintoff and his socialist party had stormed into power.

Over breakfast the next morning Mitch caught sight of the white spiralling volcano smoke rising from distant Mount Etna on the northern horizon.

"You know, I've always wanted to hike up to the top of Etna," Mitch mused. "Yeah, let's go. Haul up the anchor and put up the red duster, Chas," he said referring to the British flag in a defiant tone.

Sicily's Catonia harbour was a dismal, dirty place but it didn't deter the Mitchell's enthusiasm for their volcanic excursion in the least. With customs formalities completed, Mitch, Jackie and the girls piled into Carlina's tender along with Shibumi and Don the Yarpie.

"Isn't Susanne coming?" Don shouted up.

"No, she's got a migraine and isn't going ashore," I called back.

Left in charge for the day I had some work to do. The head up forward needed fixing, so I pulled on a boiler suit, grabbed a toolbox and began grappling with the plumbing.

"Hi sailor, can I take a shower?"

I turned around to see Susanne standing in the doorway not wearing much.

"I thought you were crook. Are you feeling better?" I asked, the adjustable spanner shaking in my hand as she took off the little she had on and eased her naked body under the shower and turned on the tap.

"Oh, I've never felt better, but I've had enough of volcanoes for a while after taking too many magic mushrooms on Grande Soufriere in Guadeloupe not so long ago."

"Oh shit," I whispered, pointing above my head in horror.

The sound of paws and claws followed by the dull thud of footsteps across the deck could only mean one thing.

"Christ, turn off the fucking tap, it's your father!" I yelped.

Quick as a flash Mitch walked through the saloon and aft state room, and by the time he reached the head I'd positioned myself across the doorway, flat on my back with a plumber's wrench in my hand.

"I've forgotten my bloody driving licence," he explained. "How's the plumbing coming along?"

"Ok, I'm nearly finished," I mumbled, terrified he'd see his daughter looking like something off the cover of Playboy magazine in the shower, all lathered up in soap.

"Well remember to put Vaseline on the O rings before you put them back on. By the way, have you seen Susanne?"

"Oh no, she must be still in her bunk," I stuttered, thinking I was a doomed man.

"I won't disturb her, but here are some fresh pastries from town to eat later," he said handing me a paper bag.

I propped myself up as he shoved the bag in my direction, and to my horror caught a glimpse of Susanne in the mirror above me. At which point Shibumi saved my arse and, inquisitive as always, barged his big body past Mitch and in the process pushed the door up against the shower unit, blocking Susanne's reflection.

"What's up, Chas, you're looking a bit pale?" asked Mitch.

"I'm feeling a bit dizzy, it's very hot in here," I groaned.

"Better get some fresh air then," he advised, adjusting his shirt collar in the mirror. "I've got to dash, see you later."

And with that he took off leaving me near a heart attack.

A couple of days later we left Catania and travelled up through the Straits of Messina and sailed through spinning whirlpools stirred by sirens of the deep. In the Tyrrhenian Sea we picked up an Easterly breeze which carried us to Capri and anchored in the little harbour next to the island's bustling port overshadowed by the steep hill one had to climb to get up to the town. The island was wonderful in those days, and unspoiled, with small cafes and restaurants that served up delicious pasta, crisp white wine and sun-ripened Mediterranean fruit.

After a rocky start in my relationship with Shibumi, where he made it difficult to get around the boat with his uncanny sense of always placing himself under one's feet, everything changed when we started to go out on morning walks together. Susanne had left and I was sad to see her go, but our affair had been a great initiation for a young guy like me into the age-old seductive combination of women and boats! Shibumi remedied my loss and became a great ally for meeting women. He adored them and they made a great fuss of him with his flowing Afghan coat and aristocratic ways. Unlike the rest of us, Shibumi only ate on board Carlina, and his supplies consisted of half an ox carcass stashed in a separate deep freeze, an antique wooden sea-chest stuffed with cans of English dog tucker, and a bin loaded with hard biscuits. Jackie saved the elongated paper bags we bought baguettes in and used them to wrap up 'Shibumi's Mr Biggs' as she called it. Together the hound and I would amble along until he found a secluded spot, then I'd beach the dinghy and take him ashore for a shit. But it wasn't as simple as it seemed. The Afghan was a pernickety bugger and he'd scout around for ages, a full ritual of shilly-shallying about, sniffing, scratching and pissing, before he settled on the precise spot to take a crap.

Now all this took up quite a bit of time and Mitch gave me some extra advice.

"Whatever you do, Chas, particularly after a two-day voyage, never goad or taunt the old bastard. Those biscuits he has when he's sea-sick constipate him and if you upset him he'll get the collywobbles."

"What the hell are collywobbles?" I asked, confused with the complicated issues of canine welfare.

"They're his nerves. Once he loses his self-confidence his bowels tense, his sphincter muscles seize up and he goes into a shattered state of total lock-down," he explained.

"Jesus Christ, what do you do when that happens?" I asked in alarm.

"The only option is to dose him with castor oil, otherwise the biscuits bind him up and he shits grapeshot that looks like the fodder they used to feed Nelson's cannon with in the Napoleonic wars."

"Bloody hell!" I exclaimed "How do you prevent him from going into meltdown?"

"Something you should be good at, Chas! Settle yourself down somewhere near him and light up a smoke, then imagine you're sitting on a river bank fishing with a good-looking woman you want to go to bed with, and as you patiently fish, tell her how beautiful she is and anything else that relaxes her. If you do this softly but loud enough for Shibumi to hear, he'll take a shit without a hitch."

I took this advice very seriously, and by the time we got to Ischia I began to get the hang of things. I'd sit down, light a cigarette and coax him along with my latest repertoire. He seemed to enjoy it and would applaud my efforts with a cacophony of loud farts and then deliver his morning consignment. Apart from the paper bags from the bakery, I'd always arm myself on these excursions with a newspaper, a putty knife and some gaffer tape.

One morning he'd snapped off a firm, well-granulated turd the thickness of a ship's cable and the length of a good-sized banana. With steam still rising from it I laid out the opened newspaper and using the broad end of the putty knife's blade pushed it into the middle of the newspaper, then rolling up the paper I folded the open ends and sealed them up with the tape and shoved the package into the baguette bag. Shibumi shook himself down and started dragging me down the beach towards town at high speed until, exhausted, I decided to take a rest on a bench where a bloke the size of a walrus plonked his arse beside us at the end of the seat. I'd just put the paper baguette bag down beside me along with one of my favourite hats I'd got in Barbados which had 'Cockburn's Rum Breakfast for Champions' emblazoned across its peak, when Shibumi spotted a poodle bitch, gave a terrific lurch, yanked the leash out of my hand and escaped at high speed towards his quarry.

I jumped up and in full pursuit took off to recapture him. Things weren't looking good, the two most probable outcomes being a fuck or a fight – the latter being the only one I might be able to prevent. Luckily the poodle was in a mean mood and so was its owner, a feisty old Italian lady who turned on both Shibumi and me with a tirade of furious insults. Hastily retreating back to the bench with the wayward hound I sat down, heaving a sigh of relief, only to find the baguette bag and my hat had disappeared and so had the fat fella. The baguette bag had still been warm with dog shit and he was about to find out that breakfast wasn't quite what he had in mind when he made off with the bag.

After a week or so of cruising Carlina around a few bays and islands we set sail for Barcelona and ran slap bang into a building westerly gale in the Straits of Bonifacio, which separates Corsica from Sardinia.

Falling away to leeward on a starboard tack, and after a long night, we fetched up on Sardinia's most north-western point Cape de Falco and found shelter behind an off-lying island called Asinara. Once we'd struck the anchor Mitch, Shibumi and I went ashore, and no sooner had we hit the shingled beach than the Afghan dashed into some coarse undergrowth, flushed out a wild hare and shot off after it at full tilt. Mitch yelled to the frenzied dog to come back to absolutely no avail, until the disturbance brought two uniformed guards belting towards us on motorbikes.

Unbeknown to us we'd landed on a penal colony which was strictly off limits unless authorised, and none too friendly the officers barked various hostilities at us in rapid-fire Italian. Unperturbed Mitch stood his ground. He had a reasonable grasp of the lingo, and by the time a somewhat dishevelled Shibumi re-emerged from the scrub the heated exchange had been defused and the topic of conversation had turned into a negotiation of bottles of whisky for sacks of vegetables. Low on fresh provisions, Mitch sent me off to the penitentiary with the guards and I clambered on to the back of one their bikes; and clinging on for dear life to the warden's coat tails wound up a narrow, steep hill at full tilt. At the top of the rise we joined a broader dirt road that levelled out, and we were soon hurtling along leaving clouds of dust in our wake. Either side of the road gangs of prisoners were wielding farm implements and toiling away in the hot sun as we rattled on towards the entrance of the penal settlement. I staggered off the bike, dusted myself down, and looked up to find the head honcho standing in front of me with a stony expression. I mumbled a few words of introduction and he broke into a horse-toothed grin when he heard we had whisky on board the boat. He promptly warbled out some orders and dispatched a couple of men to gather up some victuals.

Over the next couple of decades the island would become a maximum security prison for members of the Red Brigades and various high profile Mafioso, although even the current guests of the establishment had me feeling pretty nervous.

"Many of zese men are here for making ze kidnapping, but zere is no problema for your safety, Señor," the Captain reassured me when he saw me tentatively eyeing up a few of the burly crims prowling around nearby.

The two convicts fetching the vegetables shuffled back carrying little more than zucchinis and potatoes, and to my surprise clutching a wild and handsome falcon which they forced into my hands.

Unable to refuse, and by this time wanting to get the hell out of the place, I gathered the sack of food and the bird and climbed back on the motorbike for another hairy ride. My new-found feathered mate wasn't keen on the trip either, squawking all the way as we pitched and rolled down the road at Italian breakneck speed. Not daring to announce the falcon's presence to Mitch, I wrapped him up in a T-shirt, which had the added advantage of protecting my hands from his razor-sharp talons and knife-like beak, but even so his presence didn't remain a secret for very long. When I climbed on board Carlina Shibumi picked up the falcon's scent and went bloody beserk. The bird managed to break loose and took off, skimming over the water for fifty meters or so before crash-landing in the sea. I managed to rescue him before he drowned and Jackie persuaded Mitch to keep him until he grew his feathers back and learned to fly. And that was that: we had another crew member. We christened him 'Asinara' and before long the falcon and the Afghan became fascinated with each other and established a firm friendship.

Asinara was fed on a diet of pork and lamb chops. After being picked clean, the bones would be pushed down the air vents into the engine room, driving Don the Yarpie crazy when the debris dropped on his head and littered his working space. We figured out later that the bird was simply following an old instinct, for wild birds of prey toss the bones left over from their meals out of nests built high up in mountain crevices and throw them down the cliff faces.

After a while Asinara insisted on sitting on my shoulder like a pirate's talisman, or on top of my head while I was on watch in the wheelhouse, and he kept an eagle eye out on the action; and a few hundred sea miles later he'd settled in as an inseparable companion.

In Barcelona we secured a berth next to a floating pontoon in Port Vell, located in the old part of town. The Mitchells decided to travel overland to Portugal for a while, leaving me and the Yarpie with a maintenance list a fathom deep and up to our necks in work. The heat of the Spanish summer was intense, so we rose early to beat the heat and at night camped out on deck, grateful for the cool evenings. The eccentric Asinara took to sleeping by my side, and when dawn broke and the first slices of silver light hit the deck he'd raise his slender gun-

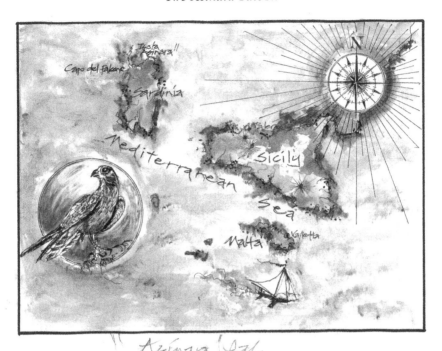

Setting for the Asinara Falcon adventure
map by Douglas Hawkins

smoke grey wings and let out a shrill series of cries and peering at me with his magnificent deep yellow and jet black eyes tell me it was time to get up and feed him.

Late in the afternoons, when the last of the sun shone down in hazy ribbons, I'd wrap some chamois leather around my wrist and take the falcon out for a stroll along the waterfront and visit some of the local bars. At that time of day old men with weather-beaten and creased faces would wake from their siestas, many of them bearing missing limbs and vivid scars, souvenirs and legacies from the past civil war, and head to their favourite watering holes. They'd gather in groups and sit on oak stools around tables laden with bottles of rough local brandy and red wine, the surrounding nicotine-tainted posters plastered on the walls of these joints depicting bull fights and famous matadors, from Manolete to Domingum and El Cordobes. The old boys would engage in fiery debate about this and that as they reminisced, spinning tales, shuffling their feet and spitting into the sawdust-sprinkled floors

19

in a world of their own, until they set eyes on Asinara perched on my shoulder; and a hush would come over the bar before they'd begin rhapsodizing about the falcon. He adored coming on these outings and would fly into a rage if I did not take him along. I carried many a scar from his persuasive argument until he became a permanent fixture on the trips ashore.

One day we decided to visit the famous Copito de Nieve, or Snowflake, a fully-grown albino gorilla with bright blue eyes who had been captured as an orphan in the Western equatorial lowlands of Spanish Guinea. Hoofing it over to the local zoo we passed through the neighbourhood where Picasso grew up and did his first sketches before pissing off to Paris. We trekked on through the Parc de la Ciutadella, and after visiting Snowflake found the zoo's aviary where I got into a rap with the head avian, a charming and helpful fella who got quite excited by my description of Asinara. He assured me without doubt that he was an Eleanora Falcon, named in memory of the fourteenth-century heroine Eleanor of Arboca, who during her life had managed to secure equal property rights for women and also established full protection for all falcons in Sardinia. And he went on to say that the Eleanora Falcons migrated huge distances to Africa. It's since been discovered with the aid of satellite tracking that these wonderful birds fly across the Red Sea down to Somalia and on to Madagascar, where they winter before flying back to Europe, covering distances of eighteen thousand kilometres. They fly alone and can travel up to one thousand kilometres in twenty-four hours, probably navigating by the earth's magnetic fields when flying these vast distances overland and crossing big expanses of sea whether during the light of day or pitch dark of the night.

I explained to the keeper that we couldn't keep Asinara with all the travelling we did and that he desperately needed a home.

"Si, Señor, we would be delighted to look after your falcon," he agreed.

And so when Jackie returned we took him up there, although not without further incident. Crossing the park and nearing the zoo entrance we came across a Barbary ape being led on a silver chain by a hefty Spanish woman. The mischievous beast spotted Asinara, jerked himself free from his owner's grasp and leapt up towards my arm to grab at the falcon's striped tail feathers. Our brave bird was having

20

none of it. Jumping into the air he lashed out with his strong legs, striking a couple of lightning blows on the ape's face, who let out a terrified howl and retreated out of harm's way in a flash. The aviary keepers gathered to watch, and enthralled by Asinara's performance took a great shine to him and not only gave him a wonderful home but also provided him with love in the form of a female mate.

The time had come to set sail for the Balearic Islands. Susanne's younger sister Gayla arrived, a ravishing flame-haired beauty, and fashion designer Ossie Clark's favourite model, and who used to knock around with Jimi Hendrix in London before he died. I fell hopelessly in love with her at first sight. They didn't call her child of the moon for nothing; her eyes were like lagoons, so enticing I could have drowned in them and my heart would palpitate like an out-of-tune glockenspiel. And Sir Winston Churchill's daughter Sarah joined Carlina's floating caravan. Sarah carted a ton of luggage on board and we headed out to sea.

The islands were wonderful in those days, the harbours, beaches and bays deserted, and apart from the locals in the small fishing villages only a handful of hippies floated around. It was the middle of a glorious Mediterranean summer and the sun beat down on a deep blue sea day after day. On America's Independence Day, while Jackie and the girls whipped up lunch, Mitch turned on the radio to catch the BBC news. Jim Morrison, the singer from The Doors, had overdosed in Paris the day before. Nothing was said for a few moments, it felt like we'd been hit in the guts by the hoof of a phantom horse. But then again, perhaps we should have been getting used to it. Musicians who had lit the world up with their music, like Janis Joplin, Brian Jones from the Rolling Stones and Jimi Hendrix, had been snuffed out like candles in the space of less than two years while still in their prime.

We pushed on for Mallorca and sailed around Cap de Formentor, passed under the towering lighthouse built on top of the steep cliffs hundreds of feet above and finally reached the southern part of the island where we anchored off the beach close by a pretty 58' ketch, built in 1929 called Nitchevo.

"That's Peter Ustinov's yacht," called out Mitch. "I'll call him up on the radio and see if he can make dinner tonight."

The famous raconteur and actor was an old friend of the Mitchells and he and Sarah were great friends too. The morning before we left

Mallorca I took Sarah and Shibumi ashore to say farewell to her old mate.

"Peter is in-between his second and third marriage," she explained on the way. "He has a passion for wine and owns a vineyard. Nitchevo largely serves as his floating wine cellar!"

"What does Nitchevo mean?" I asked.

"It's the Russian word for 'nothing'," she laughed.

We hauled the dinghy up the beach, padded over the sand and spotted a small café where we found Ustinov. The great bear of a man hauled himself up to greet Sarah and lowering his six-foot, two hundred-pound frame to Shibumi's height gently patted him.

"And you must be Chas from Tas, this fine hound's mate," he said turning to me. "Sarah's told me something of your exploits with Shibumi in Italy, and I hope you don't mind but I've developed my own story out of the incident with the baguette bag."

He plonked himself back down in his chair and glugged back his morning coffee.

"Oh, what's your version Peter?" Sarah asked him.

"Well," he said rubbing the bridge of his angular nose, "I've portrayed the villain of the piece as an Italian naval captain on leave from his ship in Genoa. His son had just announced his engagement and he thought he should visit his future daughter-in-law's family on their island home of Ischia. He telephoned them from the ferry terminal before he left to let them know what time he would be arriving and they apologised they didn't have a car to collect him, but could he please pick up a loaf of bread on the way to their house. By the time he'd got off the ferry the captain was feeling a bit tired and sat down on a bench to take a breather. Already running late he thought it would take too long to go to the village bakery to get the bread and then spotted the baguette bag beside him. Deciding his need was greater than its current owner he left a five hundred lire note in its place, picked up the bag and went across the street to meet his son's mother-in-law. You can guess the rest," he laughed.

He shot the breeze for a while, amusing us with his great repertoire of stories, and walked back down the beach with us to the dinghy, said his goodbyes and embraced Sarah saying,

"Always remember hell is a place where you would find Italian punctuality, German humour and are served English wine."

We eased on west up the southern coast of Spain to our last port of call before heading for northern Africa to the little port of Motril, which lies between Almeria and Malaga at the foot of the Sierra Nevadas. We pulled into the harbour under billowing clouds of smoke pouring out of the local distilleries that knocked out Ron Palido rum. Mitch decided to travel inland and visit Grenada and we drove north up the steep winding roads through the rugged countryside, past small whitewashed villages and orange groves and went to explore the red fortress Alhambra. Moorish poets describe the great palace as 'a pearl set in emeralds', and we strolled through the ornately carved column arcades and beautiful gardens full of fountains and running water in a world of our own. And when the sun dipped over the horizon and dusk came we headed on to Sacramonte on Valparaiso Hill to explore the old caves which had been made into houses and been a great centre for Gitano culture. Drinking the rough red local wine we listened to the gypsies play their haunting music and watched them dance flamenco with passion and fire. It was a magical evening in an old and true Spain.

A couple of evenings later we pointed Carlina's bow towards North Africa. Approaching the Straits of Gibraltar the sails filled with the first gusts of the damp, dew-dripping levanter, a local wind that rolls in from the east and funnels out through the Pillars of Hercules into the deep Atlantic. Mitch and I shared the graveyard watch as we crossed the busy outgoing steamer lane.

"That's the light on Cap Spartel," Mitch explained pointing towards the faint flashes illuminating the north-west tip of Morocco. "It's not far from the Grothes d'Hercules, the caves where Hercules rested for a while after he dug out this trench of water. Legend has it that once the two pillars were one rock and he tore them apart to get to the western seas on his way to fulfil one of his ten labours," he ended with a chuckle.

"No shit!" I exclaimed, while trying to dodge the oncoming shipping traffic.

"Yeah, the Straits have been of strategic importance for hundreds of years," he continued. "In fact the name Gibraltar was derived from Gebel-al-Tarik, the hill of Tarik. Jebel is the Arabic word for mountain and Tarik was the North African Moorish leader who invaded and conquered Spain in 711 A.D."

The moon rose like a rusty coin corroded by Africa's red dust, the warm levanter wind gathered a few more knots and Carlina kicked up her heels and bounded along in a Force 4 on a broad reach. An hour or so later Sarah showed up in the pilothouse carrying a couple of cups of coffee and began to tell us of her times during WWII when she served in the WAAF, the Women's Auxiliary Air Force, and where she gained a reputation for photo reconnaissance.

"Apart from that, my father insisted I accompany him as an aide on his war-time conferences abroad. He hired a brilliant pilot called Vanderkloot to fly us to various locations for secret meetings," she said.

"Of course, I remember now, that guy published a book at the end of the war which became a bible on aviation navigation. He was an American, wasn't he?" Mitch asked.

"Yes, that's right. My father called him over to Admiralty House and told him he needed a pilot to fly him out to see Stalin. I remember Vanderkloot saying he would but only if he could fly out of England in the worst possible weather so we stood less chance of being shot down. We travelled on an American plane, a Liberator B-24, code-named Commando. For our mission the bomb racks were removed and on doctor's orders the interior fitted with a pressure chamber in case my father needed it. Gibraltar is quite a nostalgic place for me and I remember taking off from here on that trip with four Beaufighters as escort in case we encountered enemy aircraft. They accompanied us as far as Morocco, and when we reached the Sahara peeled off and left us to fly on until my father bellowed out from the cockpit that he could see the silver reflection on the Nile which led us to Cairo."

I was enthralled listening to her recollections from that remarkable period of Churchill's life. And she talked about Sir Winston's appointment of Field Marshal Montgomery as commander of the Eighth Army.

"You know, Chas, in his younger days Montgomery spent eight years in your home land Tasmania where his father had been the bishop of the colony at the turn of the century," she explained.

And by the time we sailed past the blinking beacon on the breakwater wall at the Port of Tangiers, we'd been introduced to Chang Kai-Shek, the war lord ruler of China, and Soong May-Ling, his Christian wife, who had majored in English literature in the American south and acted as her husband's muse, eyes and ears much to the delight of President Roosevelt. Sarah had been the only other woman present at this historic pow-wow in Cairo and she went on to describe the subsequent meeting between Stalin, Roosevelt and her father in Tehran.

We berthed Carlina in the horseshoe-shaped harbour amidst the hustling life of the working dock and hundreds of Arabs scrambling over the construction of a new breakwater wall. Tangiers was still a big spice capital in those days and populated with French and British colonists and Muslim, Christian and Jewish communities. Occupied by the Phoenicians in the early 5th century, who dedicated the place to the Berber goddess Tinga, it was later taken over by the Romans and became part of the Byzantium Empire for a while. In the 16th and 17th centuries the Barbary Coast was crawling with pirates. The Barbary corsairs and the likes of wild sea rovers like Barbarossa caused havoc in the Mediterranean, attacking and looting European ships and carrying off thousands of Christians to be sold as slaves. For just over a decade in the forties the city became an International Zone and served as a playground for eccentric millionaires and secret agents, crooks and gamblers. And later, great writers like Paul Bowles, William Burroughs, Tennessee Williams, Allen Ginsberg and Jack Kerouac and various musicians and artists made it home for a while.

After a couple of days in port Mitch decided we'd better hire a night watchman to guard Carlina.

"See if you can rustle up a few contenders, Chas," he instructed.

"Good idea mate, we need some protection, the officials are so crooked here they use corkscrews as rulers," I mumbled.

A lot of guys showed up for the job and it was a game of Russian roulette choosing one; half the papers they produced were forged and it was anyone's guess as to whether we could trust them or not. In the end we went for a lumbering, heavy Moroccan who looked like his nose had been hit by a knuckled kebab. He produced a mile-long list of credentials, all bullshit of course.

"You and Don had better sort out a twenty-four hour rotation watch between you Chas, just in case," Mitch sighed.

We ended up watching the fat bastard of a watchman watching us and thus began our stay in Tangiers.

For the most part Shibumi loved everyone, particularly women, but he developed a total aversion to Arabs after a couple of days listening to them wailing to Mecca out on the sea wall. He decided the target of retribution for the insufferable noise would be the night watchman.

25

Each evening the Moroccan would stumble on board stoned out of his mind, and before long took to plundering the ship's supply of brandy. After a few hours steady drinking he'd inevitably pass out and Shibumi would wait patiently until he started snoring and then choose his perfect moment to cock his leg and piss on him.

Mitch and his entourage of women spent their days in Tangiers touring the surrounding country and in the evenings watch the buttered sun sink down over the Atlantic from the cliff-top terrace of the Café Hofa. Drinking mint tea with fat cats dozing on the straw-matted floors they would shoot the breeze with the likes of Paul Bowles and his friends before going to dinner at the Guittas restaurant where writers, musicians and artists hung out.

For the most part I stuck to exploring the medina where I came across an Arabic crypt dedicated to Ibn Battuita, a fourteenth-century Islamic scholar, who by way of foot, hoof and boat covered more miles than Marco Polo in his thirty years of wanderings. And I spent many an hour lost in the labyrinth of the Kasbah with stoned westerners, snake charmers, gamblers and madmen. In the maze of streets around the fortress white-robed men with red fez caps tried every trick in the book to lure you into the back of their shops and fleece you, while old men wearing leather slippers and long striped djellabas sat around the archways of dimly-lit doorways playing chequers and draughts amidst clouds of smoke which drifted through the honeycombed alleyways from their water pipes filled with hash brought down from the Rif mountains.

One night I ambled into a faded, dusty cinema where a French version of the Jerry Cotton movie 'L'homme a la Jaguar Rouge' was playing. Packed out on a Friday night it was toking in Tangiers as joints and clay pipes were passed up and down the crowded rows of seats for the entire movie. The clouds of smoke were so thick in there it resembled an Australian bush fire, and before long I was as stoned as the rest of the audience and completely enthralled with the movie, riveted to my seat that had become the seat in the red Jaguar. After what felt like an interminable age the show finished and by now, completely disorientated, I tried to navigate my way back to the harbour through the snaking streets.

The levanter rolled in like a wet blanket shutting out the heavens above and by this time I was hallucinating so much I felt like Sinbad

26

the sailor escaping from a flock of Rocs, the mythical bird from the Arabian nights that fed on giant serpents and fully armoured knights on horseback. With wingspans of thirty paces and feathers of ninety spans they laid eggs as big as castles, and I thought perhaps they were hovering overhead in the dark night sky ready to swoop on the very soul of Tangiers that night. In my stoned paranoid state it never occurred to me that I may be the more likely target of a blade-wielding thief who'd carve me up like a roasted goose for the few shackles I had in my pocket.

Before things got totally out of hand the master of arms and a bunch of naval ratings from a visiting navy mine-sweeper appeared in front of me and, with a sigh of relief, I followed them back to the safety of Carlina where I passed out in the scratcher, still dreaming of Sinbad's adventures for a few hours, before staggering out of the pit the next morning to pull up the anchor and leave for Gibraltar.

Once there we berthed in the old submarine pens, and it was here I first met the infamous Charlie Rodriguez with whom I'd form an alliance for many years to come. Charlie ran the show down that way, an amiable, burly rogue who supplied anything you could possibly imagine to yachtsmen and chandlers alike. Every sailor that ever hit Gibraltar knew Charlie. The moment a yacht appeared at the breakwater wall he'd jump in his dilapidated old truck and bump and grind down the road at high speed to see what was cooking. Perched on his balcony, the ever watchful Charlie kept a look-out for incoming prey with the eyes of a sea eagle and would be at the dock before his quarry to grab the lines as the yachts pulled into the sub-pen. No one else would ever be there to greet you, but that fucker was every time. He'd accept payment for his wares in just about any form going, from cabbages to gasoline. The only thing he never supplied was whores.

The Mitchells came to Gibraltar on an annual pilgrimage to restock Carlina's comprehensive booze cellar which was stashed beneath her heavy teak floorboards. Charlie had a memory like an elephant, remembering what they'd bought on the last visit and what to add to the collection. To his best customers, a category which Mitch definitely qualified for, he'd donate several gallons of original Pusser's navy rum. The final blend was vatted in the Royal Clarence yard in Gosport, England, before free issue of rum to the Royal Navy ceased in 1970. However, Sir Frank Twiss passed a bill allowing petty officers to get hold of the brew and somehow Charlie had managed to hijack an almost inexhaustible supply of the rare barrels of Black Tot Consignment rum. I happened to know Sir Frank Twiss when he was Second Sea Lord, and before he became the Black Rod I shared a couple of black tots with him at Admiralty Arch in London and he told me about the difficulty he'd been placed in recently to pass the bill without instigating a mutiny in the navy!

The big wooden kegs of 'Nelson's Blood' were kept inside a bonded warehouse deep within the heart of the rock of Gibraltar, and Charlie siphoned the rum off into wax-sealed and corked wicker-covered glass demi-johns. Despite being distilled from molasses and blended from five different West Indian rums, the lethal brew had characteristics not dissimilar to Scotch. That stuff was hundred-and-ten percent proof and so damn strong that after a couple of shots you'd be on your arse, and if you put a match anywhere near, it would ignite like rocket fuel. I bought the last of Charlie's supply ten years later on my way to Porto Cervo in Sardinia for the World Two Ton Cup. A few demi-johns were enough to get a hundred sailors stoned at a party put on by Phil Wardrop, aka The Nudger, president of the IBNA, the International Brotherhood of Nautical Associates. He called it the 'Chas from Tas Look-a-like Party'. Everyone did a fair job impersonating me, old mates showed up wearing tattered salt-worn rags with beer cans stuffed into every pocket, cigarettes hanging out of their mouths and smoking so much they looked like walking bonfires, drawling yarns in Australian accents and waving their arms around. Baron de Rothschild and Prince Harold of Norway showed up for the shindig too. The Prince did a fair impersonation of me by shoving a battered old floor mop on his head, and the two men made fine allies, their presence insuring no complaints were made over the bacchanalian chaos that ensued. But that's another story for another time. And in case you're wondering, the King of Norway's get-up didn't cut the mustard, I won the Chas from Tas look-alike competition!

When I wasn't loading Charlie's hefty consignments on board I'd hoof it over to the local seaman's mission, The Flying Angel, for a pint or two and raid the small library they had there or amble on over to The Angry Friar, Lord Nelson or Lotties in Engineers Lane for a game of pool and an ice-cold Heineken served by a buxom bar maid. Not that there were any good-looking single women around, and to rub salt in the wound we had the most sensational girl on the boat, pretty enough to turn my knee-caps to jelly. I had a secret crush on Gayla and how could you blame me? I couldn't bear the thought of her catching me with some undesirable wench so I kept my powder dry. I would while away a few hours reading a sensational book Gayla and Sarah had bought me on the great Ernest Shackelton by F.A. Worsley, describing his heroic journey into the Antarctic. The girls had written a thank you inscription that ended: 'if you're ever passing through you've somewhere to stay and we will show you the bright lights of London'.

The last night in Gibraltar, before Sarah and Gayla left for London, Mitch took his posse of women out for dinner and a flutter at the casino. Dressed up to the hilt Gayla looked simply stunning with her flame-coloured hair tumbling in waves down her back and wearing a black silk dress that opened to her waist. Carrying her shoes she paused at the gang plank and I suggested she put them on before walking on the dusty dock. She flashed me one of her dazzling smiles and handed me the vertiginous red Manolo Blahniks. If she'd asked me, I'd have done a Sir Walter Raleigh and laid a cape down on the ground if I'd had one. I carefully slipped her shoes on her, and adjusting the straps around her slender ankles I looked up to check out her perfectly formed arse.

"You look so beautiful you make me feel funny, if you know what I mean," I murmured.

"I can only imagine," she giggled before sashaying down the gangplank as if she were on one of the catwalks she trod.

I didn't get up off my knees until she was out of sight so she didn't see the roaring horn in my pants, and to make it worse 'Where do you go to my Lovely' warbled out of the radio. I eased on over to the centre cockpit and sat down, crossing my legs in an attempt to alleviate the situation, and picked up the Shackleton yarn. My mate Shibumi joined me and lay at my feet while I read about Sir Ernest and his men in the Antarctic, huddled up in their twenty-two foot double-ended and carvel-planked James Caird. It was the second night of April 1916 at 58 degrees south in the stormy 50s. Captain Worsley manned the helm through rearing mountains of freezing water in a south-westerly gale and dared not look back as he charged down the foaming crests of a monstrous hissing sea. Reading his descriptions got rid of my hard-on as good as a cold silver spoon.

Autumn approached rapidly and the time came to set sail for Ibiza and shore Carlina up for the winter. Her journey nearly at its end, I began to contemplate horizons anew and where the future would lead me. However, no ending is ever predictable and none more so than in this case.

On a moonless night in early September I steered slightly north of east past Cape de Gata and altered course for the final run across to the Balearic Islands with the lighthouse in sight and the loom of Almeria's lights hanging over the distant landfall like a smouldering camp fire. To the east the sea had turned from indigo to Indian ink and the stars cast dancing reflections on the dark mirror calm of the sea. Spotting a small flotilla of Spanish fishing boats dead ahead, Mitch decided to shift a few degrees to port and slide through on the inside of them. It was a bloody hot night, and leaving him to it I went to sleep in a bunk where a cooling breeze swirled down though the open hatch and drifted into a dreamland sharing the good times with wild women and Bengal tigers in some far-off place.

Suddenly all damn hell broke loose. A hideous gut-wrenching crash ripped through the night and we lurched to starboard with a heart-stopping jolt. The sound of shattering glass in the wine cellar was deafening and the splintering of timbers horrendous, then with one more colossal crash the engine died and the mortally wounded Carlina came to a grinding halt.

With a thunderous roar water poured into the boat and gushed into the cabin with a hell of a force. For a brief moment I contemplated grabbing my passport and wallet from the hanging locker at the foot of the pipe berth, but to my horror saw the whole lot had been swept away along with my sea bag.

"All hands on deck!" Mitch yelled above the din of his precious yacht breaking into pieces.

"Jesus Christ, it's a holocaust!" I shouted scrambling out of the hatch with Yarpie Don right up my chocker.

"What the hell have we hit?" Mitch frantically cried out from the pilothouse. "Is it a fishing boat?"

Like a crab I scuttled up to the bowsprit and peered down into the dark depths.

"We've hit the wreck of a fucking freighter and it's torn a hole through the port side!" I hollered back.

We were sinking fast and about to founder.

"Get the life-raft out!" Mitch's urgent commands rifled out from the pilothouse.

I rushed over to release the raft's canister and brushed by Yarpie Don as he stooped over the guard rails shaking the contents of his pillowcase overboard, leaving a trail of his weed stash and blonde buds on the water's surface.

Pandemonium broke out in the cockpit as we prepared to abandon ship, and amongst the chaos I heard Janine's muffled screams for help coming from below. Hurtling down to her cabin I found the refrigeration system torn from its fastenings and toppled over, blocking her escape. The only way out was the half-ajar heavy hatch above and I shot back up on deck to see if I could pull her out. The hatch was a dead ringer of the one that I'd clambered out of that had bloody near severed my finger after screwing Susanne and I knew its mechanisms well. Looking down into the cabin and seeing Janine already waist-deep in water the adrenalin kicked in; at this rate she only had minutes to go before drowning. The mainsail halyard winch, a lethal bit of kit if operated by inexperienced hands, was one of my responsibilities, and when making a passage I used to stow its very large handle in the dorade ventilation box a few feet away from the hatch. I grabbed it and jammed it hard under the hinges like a burglar's jemmy-bar and levered the hatch open until it broke loose. Janine leaped on top of a locker and reached upwards so I could haul her to safety. She fled for the life-raft and I belted behind her with Mitch following as Carlina's bow pitched forward and began her descent into Davey Jones' locker. Neither of us had lifejackets on and together we were sucked helplessly into the turbulent water like rats in a drain pipe; everything went black and it was like being in a washing-machine tumbling over and over. I had the life-raft's trip-cord wrapped around my fist and when it reached the end of its tether somewhere above the canister exploded and the raft inflated and yanked me to the surface. I burst into fresh air gasping for breath to the sound of Jackie screaming.

"Mitch, Mitch, where's my Mitch?"

For what seemed like an eternity we anxiously waited until with a great whoosh he broached the surface like a seal exhaling spent air. I grabbed him by the shoulders and between the two of us we managed to climb into the raft with Jackie, the rest of the crew and a very dis-gruntled Shibumi, who looked less than happy about his late-night swim and near drowning. White as a ghost, Mitch hauled himself over the side to safety and collapsed exhausted, wretching up a bucket of seawater.

"Where do you reckon we are, Chas?" he gasped, slowly catching his breath.

I looked skywards to get my bearings and found the constellation Ursa Major, the Great Bear or Plough. To some it resembles a saucepan with a curved handle and if you follow the outer edge of the saucepan you find the two stars Merak and Dubhe, and continuing on this angle it will lead to Polaris, the North Star. The star was directly above the blinking lighthouse on Cape de Gata and I remembered Madrid and Hobart have almost the same latitude on opposite sides of the equator, so tossing a few marbles around in the back of my head, forty degrees north seemed like a good number. The lighthouse sat about a hundred feet above sea level, which made another nice round number. Making a monkey's fist out of my hand and cocking my thumb at right angles it spanned about fifteen degrees at arm's length. Positioning the heel of my hand on top of the lighthouse it worked out around two handspans in the night sky away from Polaris.

"I reckon we're a few miles from the lighthouse but maybe the shoreline in the west is closer," I replied.

"Can you hear those fishing boat engines out there? Maybe they'll give us a hand," Mitch said hopefully.

We loaded the Varig pistols and fired off some flares and waited. After a while it became obvious none of them were about to give any assistance, which seemed unbelievable at the time, but we weren't to know they were a bunch of smugglers from Palomares just up the coast that had been picking up a load of contraband from a steamer bound for Marseilles in France.

"Nothing doing, Mitch. Maybe we can make it to shore on our own, but we've got no oars," I sighed.

Out of the debris and remains from Carlina, Holly's small Por-tuguese guitar floated close by. Yarpie Don plucked it out of the water.

"Try this mate, it's better than nothing," he said.

And so using the guitar, the skipper's cheese-cutter cap and a bailer, we started paddling and several hours later made landfall on a deserted beach just as dawn broke, a weary band of shipwrecked castaways.

"You'd better go and try and find some help, Chas, I'll stay here and look after Jackie, Holly and the girls. This is swamp territory so mind how you go," instructed Mitch, dragging the life-raft further up the sand.

The only person with a pair of plimsolls left, I set off on a winding track, dodging around brackish pools of stagnant water and thick clusters of rushes and reeds. After an hour or so wading through thick mud I stumbled across a couple of men slashing away at the vegetation and wielding scythes that glinted in the early morning sunlight. Wearing brightly-coloured bandannas wrapped around their heads and baggy pantaloons, sweat glistened on their swarthy backs as they toiled.

"Ola Señor," one of them called out as I emerged from the undergrowth plastered in mud and looking like a swamp rat.

"G'day mate," I replied. "Do you know where the nearest road to town is?"

Neither of them replied. Shit, I mumbled to myself, they don't speak English. The pair of them stood looking at me expectantly.

"Buenos dios," I tried again and promptly ran out of Spanish vocabulary.

From there on I relied on sign language and gesticulating. In response the men caught the drift of my problem and volunteered a guide, a small urchin of a boy who tended to a white pony and a half-filled dray of reeds, who showed me the way along a small path that led to a dirt road. Waving goodbye he disappeared back down the track and I set out in the hope of finding a ride into Almeria. Before too long I heard the spluttering of an engine and looking over my shoulder saw an ancient motorbike weaving precariously up behind me. I waved the driver down and an old man with a battered face and a gammy leg pulled up beside me. I scrambled on to the back of the dilapidated vehicle and hoped for the best. We trundled on past the remnants of what looked like a town out of the American wild west. I later learned this was where they'd filmed the sequel to 'The Magnificent Seven' starring Yul Brynner, who used to come into Dunhill's in London when I worked there, and also that some parts of the 'Guns of Navarone' had been filmed near the lighthouse. A few miles up the way we hit a road-block operated by the local Guardia who refused to let us past and ordered us back to the beach.

By the time we'd bounced over several more miles of back-breaking stony road we arrived at the same spot I'd started from that morning, to find Mitch and the girls surrounded by several Vespa scooters, a VW combi-van, a beaten-up Citroen sedan and half-a-dozen more Guardia clad in pea-green uniforms and armed with semi-automatic rifles and thirty-eight calibre hand guns stuffed into their hip holsters. Hell-bent on proof of our identities, Yarpie Don had to accompany several Spanish navy divers down into the depths to try and retrieve the yacht's documents and our passports. By the time they got to the wreck, Carlina had been pillaged by smugglers, but fortunately they hadn't managed to break into the safe, and Don salvaged its contents. By some miracle he spied a glittering golden piece of jewellery amongst the debris which turned out to be the Mitchell family crested ring. Back on the beach our skipper was brought near to tears when Don handed it to him, along with a precious bottle of Remy Martin Louis XIII cognac.

By this time the acting British consul for Madrid had arrived thanks to a message the lighthouse keeper had sent. The girls, Don and I stayed at the Grande Almeria hotel and the consulate put the Mitchells up at his residency. Shibumi was overjoyed with the arrangement when he found a good-looking Alsatian bitch in the house and she got the full treatment from the Afghan hound. If you go to Almeria today you may well find some descendants of the passionate union – if Shibumi is anything to go by it will be a great lineage.

The following day we all trekked over to the courthouse for a meeting. We weren't on our own. The captain and crew of a sixty-foot power boat also attended – apparently they had suffered a similar misfortune and struck the same wreck the day before us. But if the port captain had been negligent in his duties of marking the wreck he certainly showed no signs of it, adamantly claiming that he'd placed a danger sign there weeks before. Flanked by the chief of Franco's Andalusian police armada it became clear that these guys were not about to tolerate anyone who fucked them around. At the end of the heated hearing they gave Mitch a brutal deadline of seventy-two hours to salvage his beloved Carlina before they brought in a navy demolition team to blow the whole bloody thing sky high. With a useless communications system and telephones that took hours to connect to Madrid and beyond, Carlina's rescue was impossible. Mitch had to walk away heartbroken over the loss of his beautiful boat.

Not surprisingly, my passport was never found at the bottom of the ocean so technically I was a stateless person. The consul gave me a 'London brick', which was ten pounds sterling, and along with half a smoked ham and a goatskin pouch of wine they bundled me onto a train bound for Madrid. I spent a bitch of day at the embassy explaining my plight and was finally supplied with the papers and funds needed to fly back to London. A stunning green-eyed ticket agent at the airport gave me the last seat on the plane, 13F, and to this day if I happen to be in a casino I play that number in roulette with quite a high success rate.

When I arrived at Heathrow the customs officer asked me where my luggage was. I pulled a toothbrush out of my back pocket and told him I'd barely escaped shipwreck and lost everything.

"You'd better get yourself over to the British Embassy, son, they'll sort you out from here," he said, casually screwing up my Madrid papers and throwing them in the bin.

Waiting outside the terminal I found the fabulous Sarah and Gayla who whisked me off to Sloane Square, and that was the beginning of another story and the start of some serious ocean racing.

2

Crusading for
Rumbullion and Racing

A wet sheet and a flowing sea,
A wind that follows fast,
And fills the white and rustling sail,
And bends the gallant mast.

Allan Cunningham (1784 – 1842)

WITH *CARLINA* A FOND BUT FADING MEMORY I reckoned it was time to find out what ocean racing was all about. In England the centre of the sailing world is southwest of London by a hundred miles or so, on the South Coast. I headed for Cowes, a small town on the Isle of Wight, a postage stamp-sized island, situated across a stretch of water known as the Solent. This small outpost is where much of the action takes place and the site of the world's greatest annual yachting festival, Cowes Week, which started its first race in August of 1826. The quaint old town is steeped in seafaring history, where for hundreds of years, ships, yachts and sailmaking trades have flourished.

My lovely mother originally came from the Isle of Wight. As a child I remember her reminiscing about times spent sailing with famed naval architect, boatbuilder and sailor Uffa Fox. My uncle Bobby Lowein lived in Cowes. In his early fifties his swarthy, weather-beaten face bore the hallmarks of a life spent living for the sea and racing boats, for which he'd been awarded the 'Yachtsman of the Year' title during his younger days. In '71 he helmed Lord Beaverbrook's yacht, an Alan Guerney design called *Crusade*. In the fall the 60' yacht was being readied for a trip across the Atlantic to the States, where she would take part in the Southern Ocean Racing Circuit Series, and I had been invited to go with her.

Crusade was a handsome yacht, with a cutter rig. Her hull was painted midnight blue and her decks a rich burgundy and the internal overhead wooden beams were all visible and cold-moulded in Douglas Fir. Before leaving she needed a few alterations in order to rate less on the I.O.R. (International Ocean Racing Rules), so she was pulled out of the water at Souter's yard in East Cowes to have her stern shortened. Too big to fit into any of the sheds, the work had to be done outside and due to the notorious vagaries of English weather the glue and epoxies took forever to dry, when what had been a glorious Indian summer turned to hard raw rains heralding a cold northern hemisphere winter.

Bobby took me under his wing and taught me how the capricious currents and mercurial winds played their tricky games in the Solent, which little did I know then, would become useful knowledge in the years to come. None the less I was champing to get going and every day I would go over to the yard to see how the work on *Crusade* was progressing – I was land-bound for those long weeks and a desperate man.

Finally the last of *Crusade's* alterations were completed. A bitterly chill front came belting through the Solent and we hoisted the storm sails and took the yacht out for a test drive to see how the new stern handled, beating up to The Needles in fifty knots of wind and freezing sleet. Christ, it was cold!

Crusade beating up the Solent under a cutter rig, high-cut yankee and low-footed staysail. Photo: Beken of Cowes.

After a final leaving party a bunch of shivering cold well-wishers gathered on the dock to see us off, and we kicked over the traces and headed out to sea. The Squadron Yacht Club canons fired off a booming farewell salute and *Crusade* took off down the English Channel in a blistering Nor'easterly like a scalded cat.

We shot down past the Lizard and sailed to the south of Bishop's Rock Lighthouse, its mournful horn moaning eerily through the swirling mist of a gloomy dawn, serving as a grim reminder of past shipwrecks that have met their ruin in the Scilly Isles' graveyard over the centuries. Pushing on into the North Atlantic, the wind shifted and we peeled off on a reach towards Madeira and stood well out from Cape Finisterre before setting a course to clear the coast by a hundred and twenty miles or so. If you're in a big westerly, which we were, it's foolhardy to go straight down towards Ushant – it's real easy to get trapped in the Bay of Biscay in those conditions, especially if a winter depression comes through and then you've got a shitload of problems with the lee shore, the shallow water and surging seas where many a good boat has been snared by the whirling scurrilous cauldron of Spain's infamous bay, and gone down. *Crusade* rolled on into huge swells, so big it made it near impossible to see a bloody great passing oil tanker when it ploughed into deep ravines and disappeared behind high walls of green and grey water in tempestuous weather created by an intense low south of Iceland. I've seen it like that a thousand times since, but it was a big experience for me in those early days.

We had a crew of about ten on board. Skipper Russel Anstey, a burly cheerful man with a mountain of sea-faring experience under his belt, Australian George Waring, who'd been sailing with Alan Bond's *Apollo*, and Geoff Swaine, an experienced dinghy sailor and marine biologist.

And then there was the great Teddy Hicks, an outstanding navigator, a skill for which he was famous. Teddy was a wonderful man with deep, crinkled laughter lines etched into a face sculpted by many a sea-worn mile. He had been a classical and mathematical scholar at St. Catherine's, Cambridge University, and was at the forefront of British mountain climbing when he wasn't chasing wind and tide. During the war he was in the Light Infantry. Captured at Dunkirk he spent the remainder of the war in a succession of prisoner-of-war camps, where he was a constant thorn in the side of his captors. There's a wonderful recollection of how Teddy filled his time as a prisoner repairing over a thousand watches, but when prisoners from the Dieppe raid came handcuffed into the camp, he found a method to unlock all the handcuffs with an adapted sardine-tin opener.

I thought the world of him. He was a marvellous mentor for a young twenty-four year-old like me and taught me the art of steering down-wind when the boat was tearing up the highway with the spinnaker in full flight. When we set sail on this trip he was in his later years. His heart occasionally played up, and when we got down to the warmer weather and into the Trades his feet would swell up like balloons, so I'd scoop up seawater in a bucket for him to cool them down in. Perhaps most touching of all, for the last years of his life when he went to sea he always carried an extra British ensign in his bag, so if he died out there he could be wrapped up in his favourite blue duster and cast overboard.

Celestial navigation is a dying art. Teddy was a master and patiently taught me as much as he could of a lifetime's worth of accumulated knowledge. I was fascinated by his wizardry and the old instruments which adventurers and sea rovers have used for hundreds of years to explore unknown oceans. The only other form of navigation on the boat was a big radio direction finder, so with sextant, sun, stars and moon we guided *Crusade* ever closer to our destination in a steady 20 to 25 knots of wind, and made landfall in Grenada in time to celebrate Christmas.

Long before the days of mass tourism, the Caribbean in those days was a paradise. While we sailed I dreamed of days gone by, of a kingdom still haunted with the seafaring exploits of many a privateer, pirate and buccaneer. Buccaneers had originally been a small, rough group of hunters who chased wild pigs and cattle. Their name came from 'boucan', derived from the Caribbean Arawak word 'buccan', a wooden frame for smoking meat.

The Buccaneers hated the Spanish and never more so when their enemy killed off their animals and food supply to drive them out of the islands. Nevertheless, the buccaneers realized that Spanish treasure ships offered a more likely source of wealth than selling cured meat. And so the hunted became the hunters and turned to piracy. Attacking Spanish galleons and sloops, they set to seas to roast a prey of another kind. Buccaneers initially attacked the Spanish in small boats, often at night, stealthily climbing aboard before the alarm could be raised. They were expert shots and would quickly kill the officers, so gaining a reputation as cruel pirates. Joined by fugitives from passing slave ships and many a runaway sailor who could no longer bear the harsh discipline of navy life, these pirates did much to diminish Spain's grip on the West Indies, and in a consequent irony made the way easier for the French, Dutch and English to stake a claim on various islands.

And then came the legendary characters of piracy from Henry Avery, 'Calico' Jack Rackham, Henry Morgan, 'Black Bart' Bartholomew Roberts, Jean Laffitte and Captain William Kidd, sailing in ships that would become as famous as their captains, Blackbeard's *Queen Anne's Revenge*, Edward England's *Pearl* and Samuel Bellamy's *Whydah*. A certain Philip Adams was captured by pirates in 1722 and didn't particularly enjoy the experience, although he escaped to record the following:

"I soon found that any death was preferable to being linked with such a vile crew of miscreants, to whom it was a sport to do mischief, where prodigious drinking, monstrous cursing and swearing, hideous blasphemies and open defiance of heaven and contempt of hell itself was the constant employment, unless when asleep something abated the noise and revelling."

The revelling in part was far from surprising considering that rumbullion, the demon offspring of rumfustian, was a great pirate drink. Brewed in huge vats and filled with molasses, overripe fruit and sulphuric acid, only the most foolhardy drank more than one mug.

For me, pondering the secrets of buried pirate treasure became something of a lifelong interest, of which the trail to Captain Kidd's lost fortune surfaced in a strange set of circumstances years later; but I am getting ahead of myself.

After briefly stopping in St. Thomas to take on water and food we journeyed on north across the top of the Bahamas where we ran into rough weather and a cold front winging its way down from Florida. Even with a reduced headsail we damn near lost the staysail. A slamming wave tore across the bow and pulled the sail overboard, ripping out all the stanchions on one side of the boat. Although luckily, still hanked onto the headstay, it couldn't go anywhere, but it was a hell of a job pulling the thing back on board in big seas—saltwater-soaked sails weigh a bloody ton.

My first voyage across the Atlantic reached its destination and the faithful *Crusade* made her way to Bob Derecktor's boatyard in Fort Lauderdale. With no other plans I had just enough money in my pocket to buy an airfare back Down Under, when one of Sir Max's professional paid hands, Mike Butler, showed up at the dock suggesting I stay for an extra couple of days to catch the big Super Bowl. The Miami Dolphins were playing the Dallas Cowboys, which he reckoned would be a hell of a game. It seemed like a good idea: the beer was cheap and a rollicking good party cranked up for the match. The Cowboys scorched home triumphant winners, much to the disappointment of the Miami locals. The festivities left me nursing a crashing hangover and slowed down my efforts at hauling my arse out of town. Half way through packing my shit into a sail bag, someone knocked on the hull of the boat. I leaned over the side to find a big, bald-headed guy.

"Are you Chas from Tas?" the fella asked.

"Yeah," I said. It was a question I came to know well over the years, and I came to recognise was usually portent for the beginning of an adventure of some kind.

"My name is Butch Pliske. I'm taking *Phantom* down the coast. The guy that was meant to show up has disappeared and I can't wait any longer, can you come instead?"

"Sure," I replied, and within a short time was heaving halyards and pulling up sails on the brand new C & C 50' red sloop just arrived on a truck from Toronto. Amongst the crew were well-known delivery skipper Mike 'Captain Smoke' Clancy and Tommy Coyne, the navigator, who'd been in the US navy on board an aircraft carrier. *Phantom* arrived in Tampa just before the SORC started and at the beginning of a pre-series race that was to end up in Venice, fifty miles down the coast from St. Petersburg.

As fate would have it a lot of the crew didn't make the start, delayed by a blizzard up in New York. Consequently the boat's owner Ralph Ryder was short-handed and asked me if I would stay for the race. *Phantom* was a fast boat, and on a rip-roaring ride she creamed through the fleet to take first prize. With the main series about to kick off Butch put up a proposition.

"We've got enough crew for the rest of the racing, Chas, but would you like to stay on the boat as a paid hand?"

By now I had begun a long love affair with fast racing sea-horses, yachts that came to be etched into my heart and soul for the rest of my life. Time spent on land would become merely brief and, more often than not, quite drunken interludes between riding the great oceans until my blood ran with salt water and the forever horizon of sea and sky had its way with me.

I told Butch I wasn't interested in hanging around unless I could sail competitively. Five minutes later he came back with another offer, saying Ralph had agreed I could join the race. A luminous crew gathered for the fray. *Phantom's* designer George Cuthbertson, Bruce Kirby, a Canadian ex-Olympic sailor who later designed the brilliant Laser dinghy with Ian Bruce, and Olympic gold medal winner Gene Walet, a former sabre jet pilot who was also two-time Martini award winner, the US equivalent of the Yachtsman of the Year. We careered around Key West and into the Gulf Stream on the four hundred-mile race to Fort Lauderdale, beating into a hard northerly in rough conditions, but the nature of the race was about to take a different turn for me. Navigator Al Dahms went into the head to take a crap and jammed it up. He pumped the handle like fury to try to clear the problem, which had the undesired effect of blowing a pipe, and Christ knows how much shit exploded everywhere, all over the ceilings and walls, accompanied by an unbelievable stench.

"Can you go in there and sort it out, Chas?" Butch asked.

"Oh fuck!" I sighed.

I stripped off and dived into the sewage. It took two monstrous

43

hours to clean the bloody awful mess, while I was bounced around like a fucking jack-in-the-box in 35 or 40 knots of wind and fifteen to twenty-foot high seas.

At the end of the race I emerged looking like a dung beetle and smelling like a skunk. Ralph eyed up my appearance, and keeping a safe distance called out,

"Listen son, you've got a job as long as you want it. I'd like you come to Bermuda and then on to Spain. Anyone that can get in there and handle that kind of shit under those conditions without getting sea-sick, I'd like to see on my boat."

As far as rites of passage go that was one of the most foul. However, the result of the crap-cleaning exercise wedded me to *Phantom* for the time being.

Amongst the people I met at the end of the race in Miami was Eric Tabarly. Eric was a smallish man but hard as bloody nails and as tough as a plank of Rangoon teak, cunning as a Bengal tiger and a damn famous sailor; a pioneer who set the bench-mark for the future generations of French men and women who became well known for slogging around the world trying to break speed records. He had brought his 57' sloop *Pen Duick III* over from France to do the SORC after finishing the Middle Sea Race in Malta, sailing out via the Canaries, through the West Indies and sliding up between Cuba and Haiti. On the northeast Cuban coast Eric got hauled over by the Cuban military. Armed with machine guns the patrol stopped *Pen Duick* in her tracks and ordered Tabarly and his crew into port where they were interrogated and the boat searched. After two days and a lot of political pressure applied by the French, who are fond of their sailing heroes, Tabarly was released and made it into Tampa Bay, sailing right into the dock with empty fuel tanks and only twelve hours to spare before the race to Fort Lauderdale started.

About the same time as I had been fixing the shit-house on *Phantom*, one of Taberly's sub-mariner crew was aloft in the mast fixing halyards when he lost his grip, bounced off the spreaders and landed on the deck like a hundredweight coconut falling out of a tree. Luckily the fall didn't kill him, but it left the guy with a badly broken leg. In true French Legionnaire tradition Tabarly simply strapped him up with sail batons and a couple of meters of duck tape and carried on racing. The wounded man sat in the cockpit cranking winches and swallowing pain killers for the rest of the race, sweating with the agony and apologising profusely to Tabarly for the fuck up. They got him to the hospital in Miami, put a cast on the leg and he went straight back to grind the winches on the next race. That's how tough those guys were.

Phantom had an average result in the Miami to Nassau, but found her stride in the final race, coming over the line second in the fleet and winning the final race of the circuit, 'The Governor's Cup', which boosted morale considerably. The evening celebrations got under way at the presentations, although not without further calamity.

Lynn Williams and I left the prize-giving and set off for the infamous 'Baccarat' party George Coumantaros threw each year. I must have been looking unusually flash that night, dressed up in my favourite, in fact only, silk shirt I'd bought from Jermyn Street in London. In those days I used to wear a gold ring. Lynn had claimed a silver medal in the Tokyo Olympic games, was as tall as a lamppost and hailed from the windy city of Chicago. On the way down the road he stopped at a bar to take a leak and while in the pisser left me temporarily without a bodyguard. His absence turned out to be the beginning of an absolute holocaust. In a New York second I was shanghaied at knife-point by two raggedy and menacing Bahamian guys and thrown into a beat-up old sedan waiting in the street outside the bar with the engine idling and a driver attached. Trussed up like a turkey in the back seat, with a mean-looking knife-blade sticking into my ribs, the car took off at high speed down some back streets, across the bridge, past the casinos and screeched off towards Paradise Island. It was far from a paradisiacal situation, however, and by the time the runaway car, which was shot to shit, ground to a halt out in a no man's land of isolated sand dunes, it occurred to me I might be in serious trouble.

The hijackers hauled me out of the car, frisked me down, stripped me of money and threatened to cut my finger off to get the ring. In the shakedown they found a bunch of traveller's cheques I had in my jacket along with one of Baron Bic's ball-point pens. In a moment of desperation I held on to the pen and ran it along the side of the clapped out vehicle in the vain hope of being able to identify the bloody thing again if I managed to survive. In the process the pen was destroyed and to the bandit's fury too fucked up to be able to sign the cheques. It was probably just as well. If I had signed them the odds on chances were that the bastards would have beaten me up and left me to die in the dunes, but as fate would have it, after a furious argument, they threw me back in the car and set off in search of another pen. Just after the bridge the frenzied driver crossed half of the highway and for a few precious seconds the car slowed down in the middle of the road. Seizing the moment and with all the force of a desperate man I jammed my elbow into the guy holding a knife in my side, pushed him out of the way and grabbed the door handle, flung myself out of the death trap and rolled into the road, battered and bruised, but still breathing.

Before they could snare me again a motorbike came steaming down the road and I frantically waved him down. It was a young guy from *Celerity*, the smallest boat in the race, who thankfully assessed the situation in a flash, recognised me and ground to a halt. I hurled myself onto the bike and we roared away, tearing off down the road with the once fond silk shirt flapping and slashed to ribbons. I reckoned if we made it to George's baccarat party just down the track, a half-a-mile from the Mermaid Tavern, we must just be all right. The Harley screeched into the car park with the banditos still in hot pursuit and came to a tire-burning standstill smack bang in front of a Bahamian steel band who were hammering the shit out of 'Yellow Bird' on the tops of 44-gallon drums. Thankfully Big Jan Piper, who stood just under seven foot tall, with shoulders as broad as the Sydney Opera house and flowing, long hair that had him resembling Tarzan, was standing out in front of the party. He had been a mercenary along with Mad Max Hoare in Mozambique and was ridiculously strong; so strong, in fact, he'd ground the clue out of the lovely sky-blue 12-meter *Weatherly's* No 1 and No 2 headsail, which takes some doing. Quick as a flash he thundered over to help out. My potential assassins took one look at him, and with the tables well and truly turned they screeched out of there like scalded hyenas.

It took me a year to get the refund on the traveller's cheques. American Express were reluctant to cover the costs until the cheques showed up, and it wasn't until I got back to Florida and the bank made me swear on a bible the bad signature on the cheques wasn't mine. Usually mine are written in a scrambled scrawl, but these signatures were so neat they were barely recognizable. Anyway the whole incident saved me twelve hundred dollars – I would have only blown it in a casino or somewhere along the line.

George put on a bull-roarer of a party. He was a shipping magnate and owned a pearly white 73' Sparkman & Stephens ketch, planked with gorgeous teak decks, called *Baccarat*, a name dedicated to his favourite game. The man was a big-time player and used to gamble for high stakes, the biggest gambler I've ever seen anyway. Each year he funded a formidable piss-up for boat owners and crews taking part in the SORC. This shindig was no exception and I threaded my way over to the nearest drinking station, which was being looked after by Flea Man, a bantamweight wiry chap and his king-sized cheerful mate Congo Man.

"I hear you got rolled tonight," rumbled Congo.

"Did you lose much?" Flea Man piped up.

"I'm still alive, fellas, but it was nearly a fatal fiasco," I answered, downing the rum brew they handed me in one gulp.

"You'd better have a couple of bodyguards to get you back to the boat tonight in one piece, Chas," said Congo pointing towards Finger Man and his old buddy Tito Teichosky.

Tito was a bushy-bearded concrete construction workhorse in the ordinary world. He had a few years on the young guns, but his muscles were as hard as the steel drums the band were playing. He looked like he'd just fallen out of the movie 'Deliverance' as he blasted away on a harmonica, whilst Finger Man swayed back and forth beating the shit out of a drum trying to keep up with the band, the pair of them three sheets to the wind.

Like the Aussies say, a party's not a party unless there's a fuck and a fight, and this one included the essential ingredients needed to qualify with a massive amount of drinking out of ten-gallon containers filled to the brim with rum, flocks of willing women and topped off with a fight between the Messenger brothers, a pair from Salcombe in Devon. It was a full-on belter of a night, added to which I was celebrating still being alive. And so my initiation into racing hard and playing harder kicked off and would continue in a rollercoaster of a wild ride for many years to come. As the old saying goes, sailing for me has always been like sex: when it's good it's very good, and when it's bad it's better than none at all.

With the racing finished, the crews flew out, and Butch and I with a couple of guys were ready to take *Phantom* back to Miami. The crew came in the form of Richard Grossmiller, otherwise known as Finger Man, Tito and Freddy Blackwell. Freddy was from the Bronx and a dead ringer for Sylvester Stallone. He looked like him and talked like him, except instead of being a movie star he shovelled snow for a living, and when things started turning to slush in New York and business was slow he'd come down to sail in the SORC and get warm. He was brilliant on a boat and mischievous as hell.

"You see that steel drum over there?" Finger Man asked me over breakfast at the pilothouse next morning. "I want one of those bastards. It's called a Sparrow, the best you can get, and named after the drummer from Trinidad who wrote 'Yellow Bird'. The song must have done something for him, Christ knows how many wives he had, and between them they knocked out forty or so kids, which he attributed to some weird aphrodisiacal ammunition he used to take."

"What the fuck are you going to do with the drum?" I asked.

"Shove it on *Phantom* and take it back to the States," he said slurping down the rest of his coffee, and took off to thrash out a deal with one of the guys from the band who'd played at George's party.

While Finger Man loaded his cumbersome new acquisition onto *Phantom,* Freddy started chatting up a girl, who told him she was having a problem flying off the island.

"How would you like to make the trip to Miami on a racing boat with me?" the horny New Yorker hustled, his sights set on his buxom prey.

"Ok, but I need to pack and have someone pick up my suitcases," she said, eyeing up the predatory Freddy.

"Where are you staying?" he asked Sharon, who came from a town near Chattanooga at the foot of the Racoon Mountains.

"Up at the Princess Hotel," she replied.

"Right, I'll send my limousine over to collect you and your gear in half an hour."

I was listening with idle curiosity. There was no way in hell Freddy had a limo, but the voluptuous Sharon, who was built like Dolly Parton on steroids, bought the bullshit and he duly arrived at the hotel to pick her up in the limousine he'd promised her, which in fact was a very small, very dilapidated Mini-Moke.

"I'm sorry, the limo broke down," he told her with a wolfish grin.

Sharon threw a considerable amount of garish-coloured luggage covered in Tennessee stickers into the diminutive vehicle and together they rattled down the road towards the boat. I'm not entirely sure how

Phantom C & C 50 1972 racing in the Bahamas.
A flanker and Banana staysail. Photographer not known

much she enjoyed either being bounced around in the Mini-Moke or, for that matter, the trip on *Phantom*, which was a stripped-out racing boat and far from being a luxury cruise liner. Within hours of leaving the Bahamas Sharon's mascara and makeup melted in the sweltering heat and ran down her face like ice cream, and in the time it would have taken the Chattanooga Express to pull into Nashville she turned a searing scarlet that perfectly matched *Phantom*'s bright red hull, and she arrived in Miami looking like a Maine boiled lobster with one of the worst cases of sunburn I'd seen in a long time. Freddy's goose was cooked. There was no way Sharon was remotely shaggable in her blistered condition.

Finger Man enjoyed himself steering the *Phantom* up and over the beam seas, rolling along the Gulf Stream in a steady twenty-knot Sou'wester. Off the bow ahead the gloom hanging over the Florida coast began to dwindle when dawn broke in the east behind us.

Tito sat near the helm and finished cleaning his false fangs in saltwater, and wiping them across his shorts popped them back in his mouth.

"Where's Freddie camping?" he asked, armed with his chompers again. "I haven't seen him for a while."

"He's roosting down below suffering derailment blues after failing to hitch a ride on the blistered Tennessee rattler," Butch replied, appearing on deck with a few cups of coffee and looking up at the white mare's tails streaking across the sky above us.

"Looks like a front coming down from the north, fellas. Maybe it'll start blowing tonight," Finger Man mused.

"Yeah, we'd better shorten the sails," Butch replied.

"Nah," Finger Man reckoned looking over the horizon, "we haven't got far to go and it won't freshen till we're back in port."

Butch and Finger Man went back a lot of sea miles. They'd raced on the wooden classics *Ticonderoga, Bolero, Escapade, Windigo,* and *Figaro* with the legendary yachtsman Bill Snaith, when Finger Man got washed overboard in the Irish Sea during the Fastnet Race. Thanks to some damn good seamanship and a lot of luck he lived to tell the tale, but since then he moved around the decks of a boat with one hand for the ship and one for himself, with his feet glued to the decks like rivets.

"What's on the cards when you get to Liquordale, Dick?" Butch asked, referring to Finger Man's real name.

"I've got a bit of a problem with Lady Finger," he answered. "She's all bent out of shape about my current lifestyle, says I spend way too much time sailing and drinking firewater so she's gone back to Arizona and I've gotta bunk up on a trawler in front of Fowler's joint on the canal."

"What about Sister Finger's place?" Butch enquired.

His question fired the Finger up.

"Jesus, holy mackerel, you've got to be fucking kidding! I burned my bridges with her a long time ago," he groaned.

"How did you meet your old lady?" Tito asked.

"Well, when I got called up by the army I specialized in codes. A guy called Bob and I became close buddies, his father was a full-blooded Navajo Indian and one of the original 'Code Talkers' in the Pacific fighting the Japs. A dictionary was created with all the military terms written in Navajo and the Japanese never managed to break it. But the Navajos could encode, transmit and decode a three-line English message in twenty seconds compared to a machine that took thirty minutes."

"Holy smoke, that's some difference," Tito murmured stroking his beard.

"Yeah, it sure is," agreed Finger Man. "Bob's father was one of the best code talkers, although the poor bastard took a bullet in the Guadalcanal assault, but his son followed in his footsteps when he enlisted. Matter of fact, I'd planned to do a bit of gold prospecting with him this summer. Anyway, somewhere along the way I got to meet Bob's half-sister, the current but nearly ex-Lady Finger!"

"Have you still got those gold stocks you told me about?" Tito butted in.

"Bloody hell, I do!" exclaimed Finger Man. "I bought a load of them at standard value just after I got out of the army and Nixon freed up the price last year. The shit's worth double that now and the broker reckons it'll do way more than that in the next years – that'll be the retirement fund, fellas."

Not to be outdone, Tito had his own story of treasure and gold at the ready. He pulled off his glasses and cleaned the salt tracks off the lenses with his shirt and rubbed his deep blue eyes with one of his bear-sized paws.

"Well that sounds pretty good, man. Once the nest-egg hatches you'll be sitting on a small fortune and you'll be able to change your name to Gold Finger."

Sliding his hand into his pocket he produced a pouch, and undoing the leather drawstring tipped out two large coins. On one side they were pitted with blemishes and the other side gleamed silver and bore the mark of a cross.

"Shit, aren't those pieces of eight?" spluttered Finger Man.

51

With only the sound of the sea rushing past us and the whistle of the wind through the rigging we waited with baited breath for Tito's story.

"Come on, you old bastard, you've got us by the seat of our pants!" piped up Butch.

"It was a bit over a year ago," Tito reminisced. "I was on one of Betchell's tug-boats and we'd just finished hauling pipe up from Alabama to the Bahamas. On the way back a storm came through and we pulled into Key West till the weather settled. I ended up in Sloppy Joe's, that joint Hemingway used to drink at years ago, and ran into a couple of divers operating for Mel Fisher, the treasure hunter. It turned out they had a problem with a blown head gasket on an engine so I cut out a new one for them on the tug-boat. They were real appreciative, especially as I wouldn't take any money, so instead they gave me a couple of pieces of eight in gratitude.

"Keep going, Tito," Butch urged, taking another turn on the winch while he listened intently to the unfurling yarn.

"Well here's where it gets interesting, fellas. These Spanish coins were minted in Mexico in 1713 and came from some wrecks carrying what's known as 'The Silver Plate Treasure'. One of the guys was Fisher's son and he told me their dream was to find a fleet of Spanish galleons sunk during the 1622 hurricane in the Keys. One particular galleon, the *Nuestra Senorade Atocha* went down with a massive haul, referred to these days as the 'motherload'. Fisher himself had gone to Seville, and after paying a hefty bribe got access to the archive records and various ship logs to help him track down his quarry of a hundred or more tons of gold and silver. I was so impressed with what these guys were doing I invested a few grand into the hunt."

"Well, old salt, you never know, maybe this will turn out to be your Eldorado," I said.

And sure enough, Tito's hunch turned out to be right. In 1980 Fisher discovered the *Santa Margarita* galleon, which in itself turned out to be quite a treasure trove, but in 1985 he found the *Atocha*. It dwarfed his previous expeditions and he dragged up from the deep forty tons of gold and silver, along with countless emeralds that originally came from the Muzo mines in Columbia. The State of Florida and the Federal Government tried to fleece Fisher out of his prize, and for seven years the court case raged until finally the Supreme Court awarded him his rightful conquest. The expedition's private investors made an absolute killing on the returns, which in the end was valued at 450 million dollars. Hopefully Tito made out like a bandit and lived long enough to spend the loot like a king.

Apart from a forlorn and frustrated Freddy, we arrived in Miami after a pretty good trip and left him to load Sharon's heavy suitcases into a truck and, resigned to defeat, take his tomato-red companion to the airport. Departure, however, was delayed when blasting gun-fire shattered the evening calm and police sirens wailed and howled in the park by the marina, a place that turned into a jungle at night-time and became a notorious hangout for jackals and hyenas.

"Jesus Christ, a war's broken out!" I yelled, diving for cover.

"Goddammit!" swore Freddy as he pulled the screaming Sharon back out of the truck and shoved her down below decks into relative safety.

After a furious shoot-out, a gang of Hispanic guys were on the fly and speeding their truck like bats out of hell in a flurry of burning rubber down to the nearby Chalk Airlines flying-boat terminal to escape the cops who were hot on their trail. The fugitives grabbed some unsuspecting, terrified hostages off the dock, and under a captive human shield seized a flying boat and took off for Havana with sacks of cash from a bank they'd just robbed; which was a fucking weird way round as most people were trying to get out of Cuba at the time. Castro probably thought it was Christmas time when those guys arrived.

There were quite a lot of other racing boats coming in to the marina after the SORC finished, to stay for a couple of months while the weather settled down, before travelling on north. Amongst them was *Aura* from Chicago, owned by a guy called Wally Stenhouse. Wally had ordered some new sails from North Sails in San Diego, and Aussie Johnny Bolton, who also went by the name of the Fat Rabbit, went out to the airport to pick them up. On board the same plane as the sails was an Indian elephant which had been transported over from San Diego to the Miami zoo for mating purposes.

Nature did not intend elephants to fly, and this poor animal got so stressed on the trip he suffered a bad case of diarrhoea on the way over. An astonishing amount of crap poured through the hold, and *Aura's* brand new sails ended up plastered with elephant shit and stinking to high heaven. It was way before the days of Kevlar or Mylar and the sails were made out of Dacron, which meant Fat Rabbit never did get the stains out, and the boat sailed around looking like a skewbald steer. For weeks afterwards in amongst the salt and brine we'd always know if *Aura* was upwind of us when the unmistakable and strong aroma of Punjab elephant shit wafted across the water.

About three weeks before we headed north and up the Eastern seaboard to Long Island Sound, a race was organised from Fort Lauderdale to Cat Cay and a bunch of celebrities were showing up to take part. Joe Naymath – 'Broadway Joe', the quarterback from the New York Jets and member of the Super Bowl winning team – was assigned to *Phantom* for the trip. The starting gun was due to fire off at midnight, after a big party to launch the affair. We waited and waited until the last moment for Broadway Joe to show up, until Ed McMahon, Johnny Carson's sidekick, climbed aboard *Charisma* lying alongside and told us Joe had pulled a couple of women and was last seen buggering off in the opposite direction with a girl on each arm.

Minus the philandering quarterback, we raced into the Gulf Stream towards Bimini in the moonless dark, and booming drum rolls of storming thunder began to shake the night sky. By the time dawn broke we were sailing under a brooding steel-grey cloud shaped like a cigar, which began to rent its fury on whoever dared pass below. Lightning shot out from the underbelly of the heavy awning and pierced the sea with strike after strike, while a southerly buster marched towards us in a line squall.

"Get the spinnaker up!" Jim's son Skip hollered out, barely audible over the din.

The wind came belting in and we hauled up the smallest, heaviest spinnaker in our arsenal, a flanker, which is similar to a star-cut and weighed about 2.2 ounces. It wasn't great timing. A solid fifty knots hit hard and fast, knocked *Phantom* flat in the water and threw us into a vicious Chinese gybe. The spinnaker pole snapped like a twig and all hell broke loose. Needless to say, by the time we'd sorted out the fiasco we were as good as buried as far as the race went. Torn and frayed, we limped into Cat Cay and took shelter while the storm played itself out. All was not lost, however. I met Lori, a long-legged part Cherokee beauty who loved sailing, and by the time we left for the States *Phantom* had a good-looking extra passenger on board. After we arrived in Miami, her home town, she would drive down to the boat in her canary-yellow mustang each night, pick me up and whisk me away to wonderland. She kept me happy for a couple of weeks.

Spring was upon us, and with hurricane season hot on its heels the time had come to kick over the traces and sail *Phantom* to New York for the beginning of the Onion Patch Series. I waved the lovely Lori goodbye from the dock and Butch set a course for the north with Finger Man, Captain Smoke and a young German guy called Juergen on board as crew. Freezing fog has a damp, bone-chilling cold all of its own, and we ran into a thick, blind wall of it off the New Jersey coast. Just after Cape Hatteras, the wind died and the world turned a dull, sodden grey. Pulling into Ocean City to top up with fuel we eased past the breakwater wall where a couple of lone fishermen stood casting their rods into the harbour.

"How's Governor Wallace?" Finger Man yelled out.

"Wallace lives!" the reply drifted over the water. The night before someone had tried to assassinate the guy and shot him down in Alabama.

Fog obliterated the sun all the way to New York. It was damn near blind sailing all the way up the East River and on to Larchmont, which lies at the beginning of Long Island Sound at the top of the river. With only a few hours to spare before the race to Martha's Vineyard started, and little sleep under our belts after days of tense navigation, a bitch of a race began. Cold as hell and with a howling forty-knot gale blowing, the crews on the two hundred and twenty competing boats almost froze their balls off.

Phantom scorched through the tough conditions and won her class on corrected time, coming in fifth in fleet under a spinnaker finish. She only just made it in one piece. Seconds after crossing the line the steering broke, and then the mast, which had spent most of the race precariously inverted. We were due to meet up with the spar's designer from C & C yachts to fix the problem, but it turned out he'd just died through some misadventure, so we diverted and made for Marblehead, Massachusetts, where Ted Hood's yard would build us a stronger mast with a longer boom and supply the new sails needed to fit the alterations.

The small town of Marblehead is a rocky promontory nestled amongst the granite coves and ledges of the Massachusetts coast, which peers out over the stormy Atlantic. The place was first settled as a plantation in 1629 and originally known as Masebequash, named after the river which ran between there and Salem and the land's first inhabitants, the Naumkeag Indians.

Immigrants from Fowey in Cornwall called it Foy, and a Captain John Smith called it Marvell Head, but in the end the seafaring town got stuck with the name Marblehead when a group of white settlers mistook its granite ledges for marble. There's a heap of folk history, and tales of pirates, sailors and scoundrels abound, but the town became rich and affluent just before the Revolution when locally financed privateering vessels raided the surrounding trade routes carrying bounty-laden European ships.

These days the town is one of the yachting capitals of America, tucked into the harbour's edge and built on bedrock which sticks out all over the small town between weather-board houses lining narrow lanes. Three hundred or so of the oldest houses were constructed before the American Revolution, and the locals reckon – although there is some argument over this – that the area is the birthplace of the American navy; but either way, through all its history Marblehead has always been a place whose heart belongs to the sea.

With one of the oldest lighthouses on the East Coast towering overhead on the high cliffs, we sailed around the corner into the picturesque harbour and dropped *Phantom's* anchor amongst a group of classic, timber yachts, and for a brief, nostalgic moment the place reminded me of my Tasmanian roots in Hobart, where the converted buildings at Salamanca Place and Battery Point and the bars and restaurants line the stone wall waterfront. It wasn't long before we found ourselves in 'Maddy's', the oldest bar in town, a converted sail loft and now a well-known yachties' watering hole. I also found a smoking hot French teacher and ended up staying in her house, happily whiling away the cold nights in her warm bed until *Phantom* was ready to roll once more. She soon realized her efforts to teach me some of her native language were futile, but found a willing student in other areas which has left me with an appreciation of French women ever since.

The yard did a great job with the new mast, and on a tight schedule to make the start of the Newport to Bermuda race we hoisted the new sails and took off, making our way down through the Cape Cod Canal and across Buzzard's Bay, the scene of many a great dinghy racing championship, and on to Rhode Island through mile after mile of ghostly, swirling, heavy sea mist. Arriving in Newport, with just over a day to go before the racing started, both the town and marina were buzzing with activity and full of crews from all over the world rushing around preparing for the fray. There was a big fleet competing, and reflecting back on it there was an interesting statistic which I am sure was unique to those times. Out of the one hundred and seventy-eight yachts competing, I don't ever remember race gatherings since which included so many family dynasties. On *Fjord VI* from Argentina there were four Frers, including the great Papa Frers, the legendary designer and his son German; from the well-known American sailing clans there were on *Thunderhead* four Hoffmans, on *Carina* three Nyes, on *Prim* four Gibbons-Neff, on *Pageant* four Pages and two Loomis, from *Surprise* four Mculloughs, and on the 50' ketch *Adele* seven Burns. And interestingly on *New World*, the John Spencer-designed schooner, both future great designers American Doug Peterson and Kiwi Ron Holland were sailing, just before their careers catapulted them to fame.

On June 15th, the day before the start of the race, weather guru and navigator Jan Hahn of Woods Hole Oceanographic Institute gave the forecast in a detailed presentation, describing the position and shape of the Gulf Stream, which paves the way to Bermuda, basing the information on his own air-sightings from two days previously. There was also a report made a week before by the Navy, which of course in those days we relied on, as not even weather faxes and most certainly not satellite images were available back then. The forecast indicated a distinct parabolic meander astride the rhumb line with its high at 38 degrees, 20 minutes north. The difference in positioning of the two reports showed an eastward drift, and if this was presumed to continue at about five miles per day, those entering on or west of the rhumb line could encounter an unfavourable meander, leaving the logical place to enter the current about 20 miles east of the line.

Phantom had a crew of eleven experienced guys on board. Finger Man was still part of the picture, navigator Al Dahms, helmsman Skip Ryder and his father Dr. Bill Smoke, and of course Butch along with Bob, a burly Yankee and a hell of a good helmsman, and tall lanky Mal, a Canadian mainsail trimmer. An adrenaline-charged start kicked off the game in fifteen knots of breeze, and densely-draped curtains of fog lay low over the water and made for lousy visibility. We charged down the line and bore away to weather of most of the boats around us and roared along hard on the wind on starboard tack. By the 17th June, at about 1800 hours on the second day out to sea, the weather cleared and a welcome new breeze came in from the south-west. *Phantom* neared the Gulf Stream on a close reach under a blue sky scattered with lamb's wool clouds and a sea full of dolphins, whales, flying fish and strewn with golden Sargasso weed and streams of Portuguese Men O'War with their blue and purple sails up and long tentacles drifting behind as they hitched a ride on the serpent's back of the sweeping current.

The great snake of the stream travels and weaves its way across the ocean and curves its way across a boundless seascape. Eddies break away on the ninety degree angles where the current curves from side to side and these are crucial to avoid when racing, for the chess match can be won or lost on the way one steers around them. It's not easy to do. Eddies invariably drift a few miles each day, those west of the main axis normally spin in a clockwise direction and those to the east counter-clockwise.

The water is at its warmest in the core of the Gulf Stream and can be as much as 80 degrees Fahrenheit. It's vitally important to keep taking the water temperature at half-hour intervals so you know what part of the stream you're in, and then make the exit at the appropriate point where the current is in your best favour. Modern-day satellite technology and infra-red show up this information, but in those days the only tools we had were a thermometer, a sextant and a constant dead reckoning. By now Al was operating on information three days old, and the whole process involved a fair bit of luck and considerable navigational skills. In order to monitor the temperature a thermometer was kept in the head, and the closer we got to the axis of the stream the higher the mercury rose. By midnight it read 76 degrees and by six the next morning it was up to 80; and then started dropping to 74, so we knew we'd crossed the centre point by about fifty miles east. Hanging on to the starboard tack we put up the staysail when the breeze lifted and then tacked over when it shifted into a south-westerly. When Al took the noon shot we were in fact ninety miles east of the line and able to steer a course that lay quite easily around 170 degrees, which put us in good stead and able to make St. David's Head two hundred and fifty miles away.

We sailed on into a night crowned by a full moon surrounded by an ominous-looking halo which is omen for one of two things. Either it's going to rain like a bitch or blow like a bastard, and sometimes both. By noon on the 19th, *Phantom* was a hundred miles from Kitchen Shoals Buoy and reaching along like a bat out of hell, with two reefs in the main and a blast-reacher up as the weather began to close in. Picking up Bermuda radio the forecast came over loud and clear. A depression and storm were about to hit the island. After a tropical storm you're usually looking at a hurricane developing; the sea began to rumble and fifteen and twenty-foot high waves began to rear like wild mustangs.

By afternoon a hard rain hit and the wind was up to 40 knots. *Phantom* had a double-grooved headstay, but you couldn't swivel it, which makes it hard to change the sails, so we had to do a bald-headed change, shifting down a gear to the No 3 headsail, and for the first time in my life I ended up using a safety harness. It was getting harder to see, rain squalls were sweeping through and the visibility was almost zero, while rain stabbed our eyes like marlin spikes. Many of the boats were in dire straits. Three of them had lost their masts and were in danger of being blown onto the reef, forcing the British Naval ship *HMS Berwick* to abandon its position at the finishing line and take off to search out and assist the disabled yachts. The rest of the race committee up in the lighthouse with the keeper Vic O'Connor had their hands full, unable to see a bloody thing.

About 45 miles out our Brooks and Gatehouse radio direction finder was hurled off the hook, hit the bulkhead and smashed when *Phantom* slammed into the wall of a wave with all the force of a sledge hammer hitting a rock face. The cord broke and the instrument tumbled into the bilges, rendering it waterlogged and useless. So we had no vital navigational tool which would give us a radio bearing and our dead reckoning was off because the very strong current was setting us down. The pounding of the sea meant there was a thirty degree difference between all the compasses during the worst of the storm and we were sailing stone blind, rolled like dice in a tumbling sea while the wind bellowed and hurled us around.

Finally we got soundings, which meant *Phantom* was horribly close to the reef, and in fleeting moments you could just make out the flashes of tearaway white water and hear its baritone roar when it crashed onto the jagged, rocky death trap. Skip Ryder tacked the boat around head to wind and the headsail was dumped in exchange for a storm jib. Working on the foredeck was like clinging to a deck chair on the *Lusitania*. *Berwick* was rescuing *Nepenthe*, who had a broken mast, *Sorcery*, *Safari*, *New World* and *Windward Passage* had suffered damage to their rigging and sails and were on a hard beat, all of them ending up west of the rhumb line, ploughing into forty miles of shit and fury.

Every time *Phantom* registered a twenty-fathom sounding we had to tack her back out again or we'd have been pulverised by the reef, until finally the light flashing on Kitchen Shoals buoy gave us our bearings so we could crack off the sheets and reach down to St David's Head to lay the finish just after four in the morning. The cat and mouse game of darting in and out of the soundings of about 25 fathoms on the edge of the reef had probably cost us around forty minutes, and with *Berwick* no longer in position we all had to guess our own times and take a stab at guessing the moment we crossed the finishing line. *Phantom* edged precariously through the narrow gap which leads into St. George's harbour on the north end of the island, on a hairy ride amidst breaking water crashing against the sides of the small channel, before finally rafting up next to *Sorcery* and *Yankee Girl* who pulled up alongside twenty minutes later, congratulating us and reckoning we might have won the race. In fact, we finished third and *Noryema* won the day, the first British boat to do so. Teddy Hicks collected the silver trophy and it was a wonderful sight to see the great old sea dog holding the prize, with his blazer and Brenton Red pant cuffs billowing in the breeze.

The storm eventually ran out of steam and exhausted itself, disappearing out to the north. Butch and I holed up in St. George's with our hands full and up to our necks in yacht repairs. Bermuda is a picturesque place and St. George's a pretty spot, decorated with painted, shingle-roofed cottages and many a small and friendly pub to ease our thirst after the long days spent working in the hot sun. I felt right at home here and quickly cemented long-lasting friendships with the locals who were all curious and eager to know about life Down Under on the equally small island of Tasmania. Tex Houseman and his family more or less adopted me and gave me a roof over my head and home-cooked food, so I managed to keep out of trouble, which if I'd been hanging out in Hamilton down the other end of the island where the rest of the yachts were berthed I would have doubtless been tangled up in. I also spent some time with the Loader brothers, Charlie and Sonny, two fine and well-known shipwrights, who showed me the beautiful local Bermudian dinghies made out of rare and much prized cedar wood. Uffa Fox designed *Victory*, the most famous champion of the class, and it was a sad day several years later when a fire swept through and burned many of these glorious boats to a cinder.

Finally, departure day dawned for the start of the Race of Discovery, a Transatlantic race which celebrates and commemorates Christopher Columbus's journey on *La Pinta*, the fastest of the ships to return to Europe after his first transatlantic voyage in 1492. The two thousand seven hundred-mile race would take us from Bermuda and around a mark off the Azores before finishing the steeplechase in Spain. The marathon attracted a fleet of over fifty boats, with more than twelve countries represented. *Apollo* from Australia, Tom Clarke's *Buccaneer* from New Zealand and other famous contenders included *Windward Passage*, *Ondine*, *Blackfin* and *Sorcery* from the States.

The last of the crew's sea bags were stowed on *Phantom* with enough food on board for six hundred meals, which would supply ten of us for twenty days. It sounded like way too much at the time, but turned out to be a fortunate case of over-provisioning. Little did we know that the upcoming voyage would last a lot longer than anyone imagined. With a flotilla of local boats trailing us out to the cut in the reef, our faithful red yacht set sail under a blue sky scattered with cumulous clouds, the starting gun fired her salvos and we hoisted the spinnaker and were off and running towards the Azores.

Finger Man was to be *Phantom's* weatherman for the trip, Franz Schneider the navigator, and included in the team of merry men were Freddy Blackwell, a fella called John Steiner known as Clever John, and William Acton, known as Willie Walker, which was his former DJ name when he'd spent a couple of years on Radio Caroline during the Sixties and helped rock the pirate radio boat stationed in the North Sea.

Freddy had a way with unusual but inventive innovations, and his ability came in damn handy when he knocked up a horseshoe-like ring that had roller-skate wheels attached to it and slid along the spinnaker pole so a bosun's chair could be fixed to the end and meant we could peel the spinnaker. And he also drummed up a ratchet made up with a hook on the end of it which joined to a cable that wrapped round a drum. With a couple of grommets stuck into the headsail, you could pull the outside sail down on an inside out change. The following year a new head-stay design evolved and had swivels placed on the bottom which made things a lot easier.

The main challenge of the Transatlantic race is figuring out the weather patterns and how to get around the big high pressure system which sits between Bermuda and the Azores. Some years before, Finger Man had been called up for Vietnam and got posted to Honolulu to operate Morse code radio, and what he learned while there turned out to be pretty useful. The sea buoys and light ships out in the Atlantic gave out coded weather reports. Finger Man used a pilot chart for the whole of the North Atlantic, put on some headphones and listened for the signals on *Phantom's* single side band sailor radio so he could interpret and draw the weather maps on to a big piece of plastic he laid over the map. Technology was pretty basic in those days, but in a way it made things more interesting, for one had to be ever resourceful and make the most of whatever was to hand. It took Finger Man a few hours to do, but the end result gave us the valuable twice daily information needed, enabling us to go over the top of the high pressure system and keep ourselves a hundred and fifty miles to the north of it and, as a result, a hundred miles in front of the rest of the fleet. It was pretty good going considering *Phantom* was 50' long compared to the 70' maxis she was playing against, the majority of which followed each other one by one straight into the high and ran out of wind.

While the Ryders were sleeping, the larrikin watch had taken over. A sail appeared on the horizon out of bloody nowhere moving on a reciprocal course to *Phantom*. The white-hulled yacht closed in by the hour and we could see she carried racing numbers on the mainsail and a self-steering vane so figured she was competing in the single-handed race from Plymouth to Newport, Rhode Island. We yelled out an 'Ahoy!' to no answer.

"Maybe the helmsman is taking a nap," I mused.

"He might be. Hey Chas, have you got any of those Tom Thumb rags on board?" Willie asked me, referring to a filthy New York comic.

"Yeah, they're around somewhere," I replied.

He disappeared down below to raid Clever John's none too erudite library and climbed back up through the hatch with a big grin on his mischievous face.

"Pull up as close as you can to that boat, Freddy, the postman's about to deliver his mail out in the middle of the Atlantic," he chuckled.

Freddy manoeuvred *Phantom* to just a boat length apart from the mystery yacht and Willie seized his moment. With a throw the legendary cricketer Viv Richards would have been proud of, he bowled a large, worn red woollen sock with two Spanish onions jammed into the foot and the comic sticking up between them into the passing yacht's cockpit, where it landed with a thud. God knows what the sleeping sailor made of Tom Thumb and the phallic sculpture when he found it.

We covered around a hundred and seventy miles to two hundred miles a day over the next forty-eight hours and our strategy worked fine until the high pressure began to edge north in our direction. For some reason the Ryders stopped listening to Finger Man's instructions while on their watch during a six-hour reach, and sailed us bang slap into a cul-de-sac. The wind died and the barometer steadily rose higher and higher, until it read about 1044. The sea turned to a glassy calm and the heat of the sun near baked us alive. After a tactics debate we managed to crawl out of the windless zone. Way to the south the rest of the fleet were wrapped up in a much worse predicament and barely covering forty miles a day. Caught like rats in a trap, the maxi yacht crews began to run low on food and water, having only provisioned enough supplies to handle what should have been a ten or eleven-day race.

About the day we should have been arriving on the Spanish coast had the weather not been such a bastard, Clever John developed a problem. John was built like a lumberjack, had colossal hands and feet, a pronounced Roman nose, dark brown eyes that peered out from under a set of extraordinarily long eyelashes, a protruding set of front teeth, and dark hair that tapered into a mane down the back of his neck. The combination of all these features made him look not dissimilar to a draught horse. A true Caulkhead, he hailed from the Isle of Wight and was a rigger – and a damn fine one at that. Whether a tail of Samson braided sheet needed splicing into a galvanised wire or the head of a damaged sail required intricate stitching with a palm and needle, or indeed whatever the task he turned his skills to, you could count on him. Armed with a leather sheath carrying a marlinspike, a pair of pliers and a razor-sharp buck-knife strapped onto the navy surplus belt which held up his baggy pants, the big Clydesdale of a man would never complain but just keep plodding along.

While whiling away the calm *Phantom* was caught in, I was off watch and lying in the bunk closest to the galley when Clever John lumbered past to talk to Butch, who was cooking breakfast.

"Morning Butch, I've got a problem," the big man said.

"Ok John," he replied, "I'm half way through rustling up some scrambled eggs, give me a few minutes and I'll be right with you."

John waited patiently in the stifling heat, the sun beat mercilessly down onto the deck and the gas cooker fully fired up made for an inferno down below. Ten minutes later Butch turned to John, who by this time looked distinctly uncomfortable.

"What's up mate?" he asked.

"I haven't been able to take a crap since we left Bermuda," Clever John replied.

"Jesus, John, that's nearly two weeks! I hope to hell you don't have an obstruction, we're a bloody long way from land!" Butch exclaimed, then wiping the sweat from his brow with an old towel, he turned to me with a wink and resumed. "I'll see if I can brew you up the remedy my Polish grandmother used to give my grandfather for the same affliction."

I watched with curiosity while Butch rummaged around in the ship's stores for a bunch of herbs and spices, mixed up a paste, threw in half a bottle of castor oil, topping off the witch's brew with some iced tea, and dug out a couple of garish-coloured yellow pills from the medical supplies.

"OK mate, give this a whirl and with a bit of luck your troubles will be behind you," he said handing the gruesome cocktail over to John.

"Cheers Butch," John spluttered, knocking back the shit-kicking mixture. "Fuck, that's the foulest stuff I've ever tasted!"

Halfway through the morning while Clever John was winding the spinnaker trim on a winch, he unleashed a series of explosive farts and yelled over to me:

"Quick Chas, grab the sheet, I've got to go!" and bolted down the hatch headed for the forward head.

Christ knows what Butch had given him, but whatever alchemy he had employed worked wonders. John sat on the shitter like a shag on a rock right through the afternoon, and was there so long he ended up repairing sails while glued to his perch.

It was a trip of extremes, for no sooner had we managed to escape the grip of the high pressure system than a series of thunder storms and rain squalls came busting down the line. *Charisma* appeared on the horizon and for the next one hundred and eighty miles we were boat for boat and battling it out until another gusting squall shot through. *Charisma* caught the best of it and screeched ahead and out of sight, leaving *Phantom* helpless as a sitting duck in a cascade of torrential rain.

Becalmed or not *Phantom* was still in the game. Lady Luck threw a squall in our direction and this time we were on the right side of it. Lo and behold, as the Azores loomed we found ourselves beside *Charisma* once more. Boat for boat we raced around the Flores mark, the most western island of the Azores, hardened up and set off on a beat, trying to make for a favourable wind around a low pressure system which had formed further north. Two days later we stumbled on Dick Nye's swift raven-black Mcurdy & Rhodes designed *Carina*, and every time we came in on a tack for the next five hundred miles the three boats would cross within a mile of each other in a hard-fought ocean-going duel.

Nature's elements can throw the well-laid plans of yachts and men into disarray in a split second. *Phantom* ground to a halt when the low pressure system ran out of steam and the rest of the boats, led by the maxis three hundred miles behind us, went further east and picked up a southerly breeze, and slowly but surely their fortunes changed, enabling them to lay a direct course for Baiona. The whole fleet crossed the finishing line within forty hours of each other after nineteen and-a-half days of tough racing. Weary crews tied up to makeshift docks in the marina by the grand old yacht club and celebratory festivities fired up under a scorching Spanish sun. Baiona was still an undiscovered, small fishing village forty years ago. With close to an invasion of a thousand people, crews, friends, wives, girlfriends and families, the organisers, who hadn't had to deal with an operation of this size before, couldn't keep up with the demand for cold beer. Not that this provided too much of a problem, the kick-ass strong local, rough brandy was poured down thirsty throats instead, cranking the evening up a gear or two and providing fuel for a fiesta which steamed on into the presentation ceremony where *Phantom* was awarded third place in class and fourth overall in fleet.

I don't know how Columbus would have celebrated the return from his voyage to America, but there again, sailors are sailors, and whether the fifteenth century or the twenty-first I reckon the fun and games still run along the same lines as a lawless wild west.

General Franco was scheduled to come over for the presentations, but because of trouble with the Basques, who had threatened to shoot him, he sent in his place the Commander-in-Chief of the Spanish Navy and his wife, who also happened to be Franco's sister. The Commander pranced into the joint decked out in full decorated uniform, and Franco's sister sailed in on his arm looking like an ornate, over-canvassed galleon wearing a frothing long white lace dress, which must have taken a couple of spinnaker's worth of material to make.

Franz was by this time completely shitfaced and desperately needed to take a leak, but he mistook the end of the bar for the bathroom, which in his blind drunk state looked remarkably similar in design. In doing so he pissed all over Franco's sister, soaking her voluminous dress as she stood alongside. My god she was angry! Her furious reaction would have woken the dead; it sobered Franz up enough for him to realise what he'd done. He took off like a bat out of hell. He fled the bar with the Commander's guards in hot pursuit, tripped over the wire connecting the phone to its box while someone was on the blower, ripped the thing out of the wall and crashed headlong down the stairs, before speeding down to the dock where he jumped into a tender piloted by several naval ratings from the Annapolis Naval Academy and went into hiding on a big US ketch representing the States for the race series.

The following morning I was on board *Phantom* nursing a mother of hangovers when a tall, immaculately uniformed American prowled over.

"I'm the Commodore of the New York Yacht Club and I'm looking for Franz Schneider, do you know his whereabouts?"

"No mate, I'm Chas from Tas, I come from Down Under," I replied in my best Taswegian drawl.

"Well, let me know if you hear anything. I need to get hold of him before we have an international incident on our hands."

Franz was safe from the Spaniards' retribution as long as he was on the navy yacht and therefore US territory, but they finally brought him ashore. The Commodore told Franz that Franco's sister was incandescent with rage at being pissed on by a drunken yachtie and that he had ten minutes to get over the border to Portugal and save his sorry arse from the General's revenge.

Franz hightailed it out of town, luckily before Franco found him and put him in front of a firing squad. In his absence the revelry rocked on. Fat Rabbit and the Australians filled a bath with sangria and a blown-up alligator, and the usual chaos ensued until some guy threw up cascading waterfalls of vomit all over the communal apartment's washing lines below and the local Guardia appeared on the scene and threw a bunch of guys in the slammer. The party kept rolling and culminated in an absolute riot when the crews from New Zealand, South Africa, the Yanks and the Poms arranged a jousting competition, charging opponents with flagpoles on the old fortress walls of the town, which two guys catapulted over, ending up in hospital, and duel after duel disintegrated into mayhem.

What with this, the Franz Schneider incident and various other fun and games, the press reported and blamed the uproar on the Americans, but in actual fact only a few of them could be held responsible; they took the rap largely because so many of the racing yachts were carrying US flags. At the end of the roistering shenanigans the show had to hightail it out of Dodge City in a big hurry.

Butch decided to fly over to England for a while to see his wife in the Hamble, and Finger Man and I sailed *Phantom* to Lisbon, Portugal, where the Ryders wanted arrangements made for her to be shipped over to Rio. Well, that was the idea anyway, until they changed plans.

"I've bought a radio station and a boatyard in Miami and I want *Phantom* shipped back to the States for an overhaul," Ralph announced.

The last thing I felt like doing was sweating my guts out during hurricane season up some river in Florida and so I decided the time had come to bid the red *Phantom* a fond farewell and set out for new pastures.

I found myself pitching up on *Windward Passage*, the fastest and biggest maxi around at the time, and the chance to gain more experience and sail on her was an invitation not to miss. It was a beautiful

Windward Passage, 73', the fastest and biggest maxi around at the time, owner Bob Johnson. Built in Bahamas 1962. Designed by Alan Gurney
Photo: Bob Ross

late summer in Portugal and we stayed in the old port of Lisbon, once one of the busiest trading harbours in Europe, where *Windward Passage* was tied up directly under Padrao dos Descobrimentos, a bloody great concrete monument fifty-two meters high and built to commemorate Henry the Navigator. Carved into the prow of a sculpted ship, Henry stands at the head of thirty-two characters, from Ferdinand Magellan, the first man to circumnavigate the globe, to Bartolomeu Dias, who proved Africa could be circumnavigated when he got around the Cape of Good Hope. Then there was Vasco da Gama who discovered the sea route from Europe to India and a bunch of other extraordinary map-makers, cosmographers and navigators.

I spent some time in the maritime museum near by the entrance to Lisbon harbour, which had been built on the site of a hermitage founded by Henry the Navigator. Born in 1394, Henry was quite a guy according to history, the third son of King John I of Portugal, the governor of the Portuguese Knights Templar and largely responsible for beginning European worldwide explorations. He developed a new and much lighter ship known as the caravel, which carried a triangular sail that handled both cross and head winds, and the new design gave the Portuguese considerable advantage over slower and heavier vessels of the day, making it possible to sail further and faster on long journeys during the Age of Discovery. But for all his interests in science, mathematics and astronomy, he exploited other driving ambitions and raided Africa for its gold and justified his capture of slaves in the name of religion, saying he was converting them to Christianity.

Back in present time we decided to do some exploring of our own and rented a couple of cars, which took a fair amount of punishment over the next couple of weeks and were not exactly in the same shape they had been at the beginning of the trip. When the day came to pull up the anchor, a couple of the guys took the by now severely beaten up vehicles into the city, jumped out at a set of red lights and hopped into a tram, leaving the dilapidated wagons in peak, rush-hour Friday afternoon traffic, and then called up the rental company to report the cars had been stolen before leaping on *Windward Passage* as she caught the outgoing tide. Weeks later the rental company called to say the cars had been recovered, apologised profusely to us for the inconvenience, and supplied a few more free of charge, agreeing to deliver them in whatever port we required.

There were seven of us on board *Windward Passage*: skipper Aussie Rex Banks, an affable, wiry, tough guy who'd done a lot of diving in his time and followed the surfing trail from Hawaii to Peru in search of the perfect wave before getting into sailing full time; Curtis 'Cowboy' Jackson, an ex-rancher from California; old Sandie McKenzie who took care of the cooking, Rex's girlfriend Jackie, a petite but well-stacked blond, Mike Farley who was solid as a mountain and previously skipper of *Black Finn*, and Doug Fredericks, a college kid on his way to work for Ted Turner.

After a quick stop to refuel and stock up with my old friend Charlie Rodriguez in Gibraltar, we pointed *Windward Passage's* bow out into the Atlantic on a gorgeous day. A classic thin white cloud crowned the top of the great rock, and a levante, a strong and true breeze, blew straight off the top of the mountains. Hoisting the spinnaker we ran off down the Straights in good shape until damn near running into a Greek freighter. The bloody thing steamed towards us just as a 60 degree wind shift put us bang slap on collision course with the monster and it nearly creamed us. There was no time to drop the sails, so we careered into an emergency single-pole gybe, missed the ship by a few meters and promptly had to veer off on another gybe before hitting the lighthouse. Shaken, but still in one piece, we sailed on past the Barbary Coast and set a course for the Canaries, which *Windward Passage* loped towards in big, easy strides covering a couple of hundred miles a day.

The islands appeared on the horizon a few days later and the sea began to stink of rotten, sulphured eggs, turning a turgid shade of yellow, bubbling away like a smoking saffron inferno. We must have sailed right over the top of some deep, volcanic disturbance way down in the earth's crust. I remember reading in the museum back in Lisbon that such was the belief in sea monsters and dervish-spinning whirlpools during the 15th Century that when Henry the Navigator appointed his most trusted captain, Gil Eanes, to sail over the top of one of these things he had to turn back fifteen times before summoning up the courage to pass through the bubbling water, afraid it was of such an intense heat that he and his men would be boiled alive.

Windward Passage stole on through the next night and Rex and I were on watch about seven miles from Graciosa, a small island north of Lanzarote.

"Fuck, what's that tall, black shape up ahead? Either it's a rock or we're about to sail into a black hole out there!" I exclaimed anxiously, peering across the dark water a few hundred feet in front of us.

"Nah, it's just a real black cloud," Rex replied.

A few minutes later I called out,

"That's not a cloud, it's a bloody rock!"

A thumping big rhyolite stone pillar shaped like Abe Lincoln's hat stood with uncompromising menace two hundred feet in front of us.

"Where are the bloody charts?" I yelled. "Find out what this thing is before we're shipwrecked, for Christ's sake!"

The pilot charts didn't illustrate the lurking hazard, but it turned out to be an isolated piece of granite sticking out of the deep, a sixty meter high lone sentry called Roque del Este. Christ we were lucky we didn't run into the thing, Davy Jones would have claimed too valuable a prize in the beautiful *Windward Passage*, although little did we suspect he was about to take another shot at kidnapping her.

We pulled into Tenerife and anchored alongside fellow maxi-yachts

Jubilee and *Buccaneer*. When the sun set over the yard arm we hooked up with our fellow desperadoes off the two big maxis and snaked up the hill to the local bar. Several gallons of beer and good wine later and half-way through a pile of paella, a half-crazed Spaniard charged into the yacht club. Yelling in unintelligible broken English laced with rapid fire Spanish we got the drift, that all three yachts had broken loose – and worse, were well on their way out to sea.

Rex leaped up to scan the harbour.

"Jesus fucking Christ, the bastard's right, the boats are gone!" he cried out with a horrified yelp. "The anchor lights are nowhere to be seen. What the hell's happened?"

On further investigation it turned out a fisherman had tripped the anchors when he pulled his nets right across the chains, dragging them into deeper water where the old girls went off over the edge.

Soused but sobering up fast, we shot out of the bar at high speed.

"Hold the wine and food till we get back!" someone shouted over their shoulder to the bar's head honcho, and hell for leather we made for the water's edge where we jumped into the club wherry and belted out of the harbour in search of the tearaways.

We got to *Jubilee* first and her captain 'Strings' Schneider swung aboard with some of his crew and the rest of us sped on.

"Hey, I think that's them ahead!" I called out to Rex, pointing at some dim lights in the distance.

The closer we got the more evident it became that the two yachts had tangled themselves together in an unholy cat's cradle, and by the time we got to them the runaways had cantered a mile or so down the track out into open ocean on their own adventure. Finally we caught them, and leaping on board Rex shouted,

"Someone's gotta dive and cut those bloody fishing nets away!"

One of the *Buccaneer* boys strapped on the scuba tanks and grabbed a bunch of knives from the galley muttering, "These bastards should slash through just about anything."

It took a while to fix the diabolical mess, but finally the balls-up got sorted out and we had all three boats back, safely corralled in the anchorage. By the time we returned to the bar things were still in full swing.

"You might find your cooking knives a bit blunter than they were before this screw-up, Sandy," I told the old fella who'd stayed behind to prop up the bar.

"Son of a bitch, those are my best bloody German knives!" he bitched.

"Not any more, mate, they've just hacked their way through a shit load of Spanish fishing nets," I replied, ordering another pint.

"Geez Chas, that was a near one," said Rex, wearily sliding onto the barstool next to me. "That's the first time I've ever seen a cock-up like that. Usually those anchors stick to sand and clay like dog shit sticks to the soles of your boots!"

"Could have been a holocaust, mate," I said, shuddering to think of what might have happened.

"We need some bigger anchors. The folded stainless steel ones we've been using on *Passage* were designed for easy stowage on the Catalina flying boats which used to drone their way across the Pacific, and I acquired some from a guy who used to look after Howard Hughes's fleet of sea planes, including the *Spruce Goose*, the biggest wooden bird ever constructed," he explained; whereupon he jumped on top of the bar, gimbled and rolled his eyes and did the finest impersonation of a shag on a jetty post trying to juggle a fish down his throat.

When the sun rose over the distant volcanic peak on Grand Canary a couple of days later we weighed anchor and pointed *Passage* towards the Southwest, leaving the West coast of Africa in our wake. The sails filled with a strong wind funnelling down off Tenerife's steep headland and we eased the sheets and charged on past Hierro, the most westerly of the Canary Islands, where the breeze died and left *Passage* buffeted by a wicked short sea with a hell of a current to boot. Rex fired up the iron genoa shortly before midnight and we pushed on, but as fate would have it, just before we killed the donk an awful cacophonous crunch followed by an ominous clang reverberated across the boat and the motor seized while still in gear.

"What the hell...!" swore Rex.

"Hang on a moment," said the Cowboy, shining a spotlight over the stern.

"Can you see anything, mate?" I called out.

"Yeah, the prop is snared with bloody miles of quarter-inch blue nylon rope," he groaned.

To add to our difficulties a hot dust-laden wind, not unlike the 'Harmattan' which sweeps in from the Sahara, smothered both us and the boat with a thick carpet of red grime and grit. Heaving to until dawn, Rex put the tanks on and once again had to dive under the boat to free the entangled rope, which by this time had virtually welded itself to the prop shaft and caused some serious damage. A Volvo engine was a twenty year forerunner of the sail drive unit and not the conventional long-shafted drive found on most boats. The gear-box was fucked, which made things damn difficult. With fifteen hundred miles to go before reaching Antigua we found ourselves completely becalmed and trapped in the Horse Latitudes like a fly in a spider's web, and the belt of calm on the northern edge of the Northeast Trades had us by the balls.

The Horse latitudes take their name from the Spanish 'Golfo de las Yeguas' – the Gulf of Mares, so named because of the unpredictable nature of the elements in the area, and thus got compared to the fickle nature of highly-strung Arabian mares. And the name also has another connection. Travelling this route centuries ago, a sailor would sign up for the voyage and then be paid one month's wages in advance, although the money never lasted for long after bouts of excessive drinking and the cost of being entertained by wild women when in port. Once the coins had been spent the ships put to sea and the sailors were left feeling as if they were swabbing decks and hauling halyards for no return, and so began a tradition of calling the first month at sea 'the dead horse month', of which Admiral William Smyth once remarked it was pointless to expect any kind of work from a ship's company during this time. To mark the end of crossing the horse latitudes a celebratory ritual evolved, and a stuffed canvas likeness of a nag was marched around the decks of the old square riggers with great pomp and ceremony, before being hauled aloft to the yardarm and cut adrift while the sailors chanted: "Old Man, your horse must die!"

When *Windward Passage* got to the Gulf of Mares she ground to a halt, the cumulous clouds evaporated and the decks turned to hotplates under a scalding sun. For three days and three nights she drifted help-lessly while we sat on what felt like a burning powder keg and waited. Finally the blue sky began to fill with rain clouds, the sea changed from indigo to abalone grey and pewter and the first squall blew in from the east as the heavens opened, washing away the heat and red dust in rivers of cooling fresh water. We ran up the old three-quarter ounce spinnaker inherited from the famous Herreshoff timber ketch *Ticon-*

deroga, which *Windward Passage's* owner Bob Johnson had previously owned. The aged paper-thin relic kept us shifting for a couple of days, but we pushed it too far when a squall as black as squid's ink suddenly altered course and ran us down. Too late to pull the old kite down, the bitching gust blew the belly of the sail further than her years could bear, until it ripped from the head, down the tapes to the tack and clew, and then disappeared into the jaws of the raving wind.

We had been caught with our pants down and lost our secret weapon. However, providence was on our side and a steady fifteen-knot breeze filled in. We decided to give Antigua a miss and take advantage of reaching on at a tighter angle to the Northwest and make for St. Thomas in the Virgin Islands, some seven hundred and fifty miles away. Three days later *Passage* approached landfall, the trade winds dampened under the darkness of night and we threaded our way through a fleet of small boats moored out from Charlotte Amalie in St. Thomas's main harbour, where the town lights danced over a sea as flat as a carpenter's hat, and the stray sounds of music floated across the water from the shore. Still with no operational engine, we came in under sail, and after making two tight circuits to slow the yacht down, parked all seventy-three feet of *Windward Passage* alongside the dock without suffering a scratch to either her hull or anyone else's, and without further ado hurried to the nearest saloon on swaying sea legs to splice the main brace before the closing time.

The next morning it became horribly obvious the gear box had suffered a major mechanical cardiac arrest. Our attempts at corrective surgery proved futile and we had no time to bugger around wasting time trying to fix it, so minus a functioning iron genoa we took off in haste and got under way in a strong Nor'easter with the main hoisted a third of the way up the mast. Once clear of the marina we spun into the eye of the wind and hauled the rest of the main to full height and *Windward Passage* belted off on a sprint rivalling Jesse Owens' effort in the 1936 Olympics, while a couple of kids on fast Hobi Cats skimmed across the water and raced us out of the harbour.

The old girl ate up the first thousand miles on a roaring reach and flew on north of the Silver Banks, where a wrecked treasure-bearing Spanish galleon sank centuries ago, and travelled on past the Turks and Caicos Islands. Sailing through fields of sargasso weed, which sheltered opalescent-coloured dorado fish under the acres of its gilded tapestry,

Windward Passage
photographer unknown

we glided on by the easterly outcropping island of the fragmented chain of Bahamian Islands, San Salvador, where Columbus first set foot on the voyage to the New World.

Windward Passage gathered two hundred and fifty miles a day and we kept easing her sheets into a broader reach as the wind backed further east and she climbed the backs of aquamarine and kingfisher blue swells, bounding away off the curling crests like a cheetah on the hunt. By noon we swept by Eleuthera and gibed in close to the leeward side of Great Abaco, close enough to see the transparent turquoise kaleidoscope of shallow island waters, and pulled up the mizzen spinnaker known as the Boston Strangler, so named when this kind of sail's lazy sheet has occasionally wrapped itself around an unsuspecting neck in an oscillating breeze and choked a hapless sailor. The wind fluctuated, and adopting a cantankerous attitude the strangler started swooping like a furiously wheeling bird of prey until we canned the bastard before it throttled one of us. The wind whipped up apace and *Passage* careened over the seas like a steaming freight train with spumes of spray blasting out from her proud bow, scattering showers of diamond-bright flying fish in a thousand directions. And as she went she sang, and as any sailor knows, a yacht will have her own symphony of music. The wooden hull hummed like a fine old harmonica, the sound of her timbers busking ballads as she strained at her leash in chorus with the wind whistling through the rigging and down her flanks.

The Trades backed further to the North before running into another weather system, and we dowsed the chute and dragged it down the main hatch before swinging into the last gibe of the trip. The number three headsail carried us over the North end of Berry Island, and half an hour later a sou'westerly shift forced us over to the same point of sail on the other tack – if our luck held we'd be home and dry.

Hauling arse up the North West Providence Channel on our last sixty miles to the Gulf Stream, the old-fashioned but nevertheless effective log which trailed off the stern had been attached to a small metal fish and swivel we'd painted black and soaked in kerosene in the hope of deterring hungry predators as it spun and spiralled in our wake. The cord was attached by another swivel to a brass cone with a glass face like a clock, which enclosed a meter inside and registered the miles *Passage* clocked up. I was down below when Rex let out a yell.

"You motherfucker!"

"What's up, mate?" I asked, sticking my head out of the hatch.

"A shark or a hungry Marlin has just attacked the log and ripped it off," he hollered.

The Loran 'A' swung into action once *Passage* came into range and guided us past the holophotal beams shining out from the Great Isaac lighthouse that rises above the shallow rock-strewn sea bed, and in the distance, at the end of the Channel, lay Grand Bahama where *Windward Passage* had been built half a decade before. Rex had helped construct her with a bunch of Kiwis and a few skilled Bahamian shipwrights, and swinging the wheel to chase a following sea he wandered down memory lane and mused how he wished those guys could see her now in all her glory as she surfed the silver rollers. The big white yacht must have known she was homeward bound and pulled at the reins on a close haul before bolting for the barn door at Spencer's yard in Palm Beach. Once again Rex managed to safely steer the engineless *Passage* up to the dock unscathed, and the next day she was lifted out of the water by a sixty-ton travel lift and carefully moved into a large shed where, after many a mile of sea-trekking adventures, a much needed refit began.

I found Rex the next morning talking to the guys at the yard and pulled him aside.

"I'm low in the freight department mate, I'm going to take off for a while and hitch a ride south and maybe find some work," I explained.

"Ok, Chas old son, but can you get back this way in a few months and help sail the old girl from Florida to California?"

"Sure," I replied, and hoisted my sea-bag over my shoulder knowing I would return before too long.

Sure enough, four months later I bowled on back to Florida to find *Windward Passage* in good shape after her refit. Seven of us saddled up for the five thousand-mile voyage to the land of West Coast dreamers and stoned surfers, and we let loose from the hitching post in a near gale veering into the nor'east. With one reef in the main we sailed out across the watery prairie and into a wild and tempestuous Gulf Stream. The wind and sea hurled themselves at each other in opposing forces, white foaming water and cascades of simmering spray flew over the bow, whipping into our skin with sharp, bitter-edged, flaying lashes.

Our band of gypsies included long-haired Conrad Bagley, a hippy sailor with gaps in his teeth big enough to thread baling twine through and a moustache so thick you could have made a dunny brush out of it. Then there was Kirk Elliot, a strapping, solid-set kid fresh out of college, Billy Sanderson, a gutsy, lusty young fella from Connecticut, who when he smiled flashed a gold-laced fang and sported a nose as kinked as a hose pipe, as well as the original castaways, Jackie, Curtis the Cowboy and Rex, who apart from a few more crow's feet etched into ever-deepening track marks around his grey-blue eyes, looked much the same as when I'd seen him last.

Passage blasted on past the Bahamas on a rollicking reach and the

*The Windward Passage
map by Douglas Hawkins*

following day bolted through the gap between the islands of Great Abaco and Eleuthera before bearing away and starting her charge southwards under a tightly-strapped chicken chute. She lit up like a burning torch and smoked over the following seas, leaving a blazing trail of phosphorous in her wake and setting the ebony-dark and moonless night on fire.

A couple of adrenaline-fuelled gybes down near the Iguana Islands kept the Cowboy's navigating skills on full alert, and as the boat bucked and rolled he mapped a course through the great 'Windward Passage', a fifty-mile wide tongue of water that hangs down between Cuba and the pillars of Haiti, where the trades accelerate in velocity, and bend and twist to the terrain as they funnel through the gateway to the Caribbean. *Passage* was in her element, designed to fly under these conditions, and she roared on through, clocking up twenty-knot bursts of speed. The guys on board were bloody good downwind helmsmen, and soaring along under a one and a half ounce chute we left Jamaica behind us, moving like shit off a shiny silver shovel.

It took us little under a week to reach Panama after a sensational ride and maybe one of the greatest I'd ever had on the trusty steed. Since then, which is nearly forty years ago now, there's been a huge development in boatbuilding materials, and speeds travelled under sail are a whole new ball game. In 2008 I was navigator on a canting-keeled carbon-built Cookson 51' on a run back from Hobart to Sydney, and covered over four hundred miles in twenty four hours, at one point sprinting over eighty-five miles in four hours, which is bloody fast. As for today's big Cats and Tri's, and Volvo 70' boats, well it's mind-boggling what they can do when you think about it.

We pushed on across what was in '73 still an American-controlled Panama Canal with the guidance of a tall, silver-headed ship's pilot who hailed from Florida, and climbed through three lock gates in front of an eight hundred-foot container ship. *Passage* needed four line handlers standing a hundred and twenty-five feet above us, casting down heaving lines with monkey fists which we grabbed a hold of and wrapped around in sheep's bends through the bitter ends of the coils of rope that were fixed to cleats on the deck. The guys above us gathered up the slack and steadied the boat, while the rapidly flooding water swirled in eddies and began to rise up the walls, lifting us higher and higher to each gate. Crossing Lake Gatun we ran with the spinnaker up for five miles or so and then stepped on down into the Pacific via the rest of the canal, accompanied by a powerful tug-boat, which made the going a lot easier and safer.

After clearing out of Balboa at the far end of the canal, we anchored behind a small island in the Gulf, where for as far as the eye could see the water swarmed with sharks thrashing around in a feeding frenzy. No one ventured out for a swim that night. The big, black *Buccaneer* was also California-bound, and in tandem we set a course to the north towards Costa Rica further up the coast. Or at least, I hoped so. I'd heard some of the most beautiful and friendly women in the world lived there.

Sadly it was not to be, and we kept hauling past El Salvador, left Guatemala in our wake and finally reached Acapulco. A wild Mexican night with the *Buccaneer* boys spun into the early hours and the Mescal sent us crazy chasing women at the strip joints up on the hill. I found *Buccaneer's* skipper, the dapper little moustached shipwright John

McCormack early the next morning, sitting on the dock playing his ukulele, still in his gear from the night before. He had a fondness for wearing cravats, and with his hung-over blood-shot eyes, which by this time were the colour of red currants, he resembled a white-throated bush rat. We left to the sound of *Buccaneer's* navigator, old bald-headed, retired boiler-maker Kiwi Bill McKinley warbling ballads from the seven seas to John's strumming, and cast off *Windward Passage's* dock lines to the strains of an old sea shanty.

Blow, boys, blow, for Californ-eye-O!
There's plenty o' grass, to wipe yer moustache,
On the banks of the Sacramento,
Roll her, boys, bowl her boys, blow for Californ-eye-o,
Drag the anchor off the mud, an' let the bastard rip.

In varying yet favourable winds we sailed on northwards along the Mexican coast, and during the day were near cooked alive by a fiery sun until we turned the colour of rich, dark coffee beans. The welcome cool of the evening breeze would bring some respite when it swept out from the land across the water, and under the moonlight school after school of flying fish flashed past our running lights on the bow, turning their reflections red and green, and fleeting shadows flickered across the headsail until dawn chased the night back into day.

By this time Billy and I had become totally absorbed in furthering our study of celestial navigation. We pulled the sextant out of its fine mahogany box, set our watches to the chiming chronometer which sat above the navigation table, and practised shooting the sun and stars. At every available opportunity we studiously calculated our observations using the sight reduction tables, and then in increasing flusters of excited activity, set-squares, parallel rules and dividers, transcribing the results of our efforts onto the plotting sheets. With dogged determination we stuck to our guns through the frustrating tribulations and slowly began to reap the rewards of success when our corresponding fixes eventually started to correlate and read within half a mile of each other.

One morning, nearly half-way across the mouth of the vast gulf that leads up into the Sea of Cortez, Billy and I set about catching lunch and reeled in a fifteen-kilo Mahi Mahi, when Conrad shouted out from the helm and pointed out to the West.

"What in God's name is that?"

Billy looked up from the fish we were filleting and squinted into the distance.

"Shit, we've got a wall of white water heading straight for us. Maybe it's the dreaded Tehuantepec north wind blowing its arse off."

Raised from an afternoon nap, The Cowboy shoved the hatch back and poked his head out from down below like a Seychelles Island Tortoise, and shielding the glare from his eyes with cupped hands looked towards the horizon and the expanse of white foaming water.

"That ain't no Tehuantepec, an' it sure ain't no tidal wave, which you wouldn't know it had passed you by until it hit the coast. I reckon that's the most massive gathering of the cetacean nation I've ever seen," he drawled in his Santa Barbara rancher's twang.

We all looked at him amazed. What he was proposing as cause of the gathering, simmering sea seemed utterly improbable, yet before we knew it a tsunami of dolphins was upon us. They came in countless multitudes, each one a performing virtuoso whirling dervish of spinning quicksilver, streaking through the ocean like mercurial bullets of brilliant blue and white, layer upon layer deep in the clear cerulean water and swimming with impossible grace and power. Their high-pitched and complicated sonar clicks and tones filled the air until the sound vibrated through every bone in our bodies and left us speechless and witness to one of the greatest shows I have ever seen before or since.

They were Striped Dolphins and identified by distinct blue and white flanks, and one or two midnight-black bands that circle the eye and then run across the back to the flipper. And then one further stripe traces from behind the ear and curves down under the belly. This kind of dolphin more often than not moves in groups of thousands in temperate or tropical off-shore waters from around 40 degrees N to 30 degrees S and dives to depths of up to seven hundred meters. When not hunted by the Japanese, or caught in lethal fishing nets or poisoned by pollution, the Striped Dolphin matures at twelve years old and lives to around fifty-five or sixty. In the worst days of hunting up to twenty-one thousand of these beautiful animals were killed each year, and still to this day up to a thousand are caught. Although the Bottlenose Dolphin can just about stand the confines of human captivity and more or less survive being imprisoned in amusement parks, the Striped Dolphin cannot bear the unnatural prison walls, and dies within two weeks of being put in an aquarium.

We watched the marine extravaganza completely spellbound as so many sleek, glistening dolphins' bodies raced past *Windward Passage* paying us no heed at all. We may as well have been a mere floating cork to them as they swept on towards the Sea of Cortez, moving with phenomenal speed and symmetry.

When we reached Cabo St. Lucas, a thirty-knot northerly began to rev its engines, so we slid *Passage* in behind the headland and anchored off a dazzling white beach. The Californians took the rubber dinghy ashore to look up a yachty mate who'd built a restaurant on the pearly stretch of sand, and Billy and I settled down alongside the aft lazarette behind the mizzen, around which were some conveniently painted non-slip stripes that made a perfect backgammon board. We were well into our game when the sound of hollering drifted across the water. A buttercup-yellow, fourteen-foot long Hobie Cat helmed by a lone sailor clad in racing red screeched across our transom on a broad reach, moving as fast as a wahoo chasing a shoal of flying fish. The fella whooped it up on the thrill of the run way out past the headland, shot out into the Pacific and soon became just a small speck on the horizon. The guy must have had a death wish, but with the dinghy still ashore there was nothing we could do about it. Still hard at the backgammon contest and late into the afternoon, a large off-shore fishing boat arrived in the anchorage carrying the Hobie Cat minus its mast but with the bloke still aboard, intact; the luckiest man on the coast that day for sure.

With old friends visited, a few backgammon games won and lost and the anchor chain hauled up from the soft sand below, we hoisted the sails, turned once more to the north and sailed straight into a 'dead muzzler'. The wind lashed into us bang slap on the nose, and the seas bust into a wild, steep confusion off the Cape. We stood the bucking and rearing *Windward Passage* well off the craggy rocks, when all of a sudden a hell of an ominous bang ricocheted across the boat as she plunged into a brute of a sea and thumped into a following wave. The impact parted the baby stay and the mast inverted. Rex spun her around and we cracked off the sheets, and with speed to burn, hurtled back to the anchorage at twenty knots. Safe in the shelter of the bay we repaired the damage with galvanised shackles and some spare anchor chain before pushing away again after dark, and sailing on into the night.

The last leg of the voyage was a bitch. With a deep-reefed mainsail and under a number four headsail we punched into breaking seas, tacking half a dozen times a day. The harsh mist-laden wind cut through our soaked oilskins with the dull thud of a cold knife, and we sailed on past the ragged headlands overlooked by distant Sierra Nevada mountains, keeping *Windward Passage* just outside the roaring white lines of surf and raging bomboras, whose orchestral boom echoed down the shores of the vast empty beaches.

The weather blew itself out eventually and died a death south of the border about fifty miles from our San Diego destination, where we pitched up at Driscoll's yard feeling weary as fuck. We cleared the boat in and shot off to find a bar to resolve a hell of a thirst. It wasn't much of a bar, mind you; we ended up in the shittiest joint on the West coast called The Bole Weevil. Man, it was a dive, but a beer tastes real sweet to a tired, salt-worn sailor. I was just about broke by this time and as poor as a poor boy can be, so leaving *Windward Passage* with empty pockets I trekked out onto the highway and hitched a ride up to New-port Beach where I found refuge under a dinghy on a stretch of sand for a couple of nights and started hunting for work.

In the end I got a job setting up a new warehouse for Volvo, and moved into a rundown motel, paying for a week up front so I couldn't blow the dough. The hobo's hovel was a shabby, worn place, the carpet heavily tattooed with cigarette burns and beer stains, and the bed felt like the mattress had been stuffed with a pile of gravel, but it was better than nothing. By the end of the week I'd found a place to stay with some other yachtsmen, and after throwing my possessions into a worn sea bag went to the front desk to find the guy who had checked me in, only to discover he had disappeared and in his place stood a pint-sized old lady who owned the crumbling joint. Handing in the key I told her I was on the move.

'Okay son, that'll be a hundred and twenty dollars."

"I already paid the doorman when I arrived," I explained.

It didn't take her long to work out the shifty son of a bitch had been moonlighting rooms and skimming the cream off the top of cash flow. Luckily she believed me, and I left her dialling the cops as I headed on down the road.

The Trans-Pacific race was about to get under way, which if I'd found a boat needing crew I would have done, but *Passage* already had a bunch of West coast heavies lined up, and other than that the only decent-sized boat with an available berth was Hughie Long's *Ondine*, which had acquired the name *Blue Pig* for good reason. Bearing this in mind, I decided to keep working for a while and then fly over to England and try my luck at finding a ride on the Fastnet race. In the meantime I moved into an old two-storey house on Balboa Island in Newport and joined a couple of mates I'd raced with on *Sirius II*, one of the most renowned and beautiful wooden classic M class yachts on the West Coast. Thirsty Bertie was a tall angular South African, a likeable good-looking guy who worked as a rigger and never had a problem pulling rich Orange County Porsche-driving chicks. The other bloke, Nelson, a marine metal machinist, came from California and stood out a mile with his bright red hair as curly as an astrakhan fleece which framed his freckled face, half of which was covered by a long ginger beard, and his chaffed, calloused hands bore the scars of a rough working life.

For a couple of weeks I ran around like a blue-arsed fly drumming up various odd jobs, culminating in a terrifying climb up a sixty foot flag-pole a fella hired me to paint. I hauled my arse up to the top with a block and tackle and to my horror found the pin was about to fall out of the pulley. I felt like a doomed coconut about to drop from the highest branch of a tree, and trembling with terror at the thought of the fall managed to bang the pin back into place before I plunged earthwards. I decided mountaineering was not for me, and the next job I got kept me firmly on terra firma, digging up the remnants of a fifty-foot fir tree behind a partially demolished house. It took me and one other guy two days to dig four meters down and get to the bottom of the tap root—still, it was a damn sight safer than aerial acrobatics.

The next bout of employment took me back to the marina to fix the heads on a Columbia 52 which had been sitting idle for a long time. After crawling around on my hands and knees I finally discovered the problem. Both the out and inlet pipes were frozen solid with salt. The outlet had a big loop in it with a metal vent with a siphon break on top. God, it was foul work. The whole bloody lot needed clearing out, along with a mile of atrophied shit. A refrigeration guy was working

84

close by and it wasn't long before we started shooting the breeze.

"Where are you living?" Randy Simkins asked.

"Out on Balboa Island," I replied, "but the landlord just doubled the rent, the bastard!"

"I've got a place just up the road, you can move in with me and my old lady Kendra," he kindly offered.

My luck was about to change, and Randy and I set off for the rubbish tip in search of furniture to equip his tumble-down shack. The Californians and the Japanese have something in common – if something breaks or doesn't work they throw it away. As a result the tip was a potential gold mine of discarded treasure. Our day's pickings included a couple of TV sets, two bicycles, some tables, a ladder, a sofa and a bunch of arm chairs. We loaded the haul onto the back of Randy's rattling truck and once back at the house set about making things more shipshape. The first television had sound but no picture and the second no sound but a reasonable picture, so we stacked them one on top of the other and that was that. Kendra re-upholstered the furniture, and before long we had ourselves a pretty well set up gaff. Needless to say, the tip became a weekly venture, and before long Randy's house became a vagabond's palace. The final crowning glory came when we overhauled the swimming pool and turned it from algae green slime into a turquoise lagoon to swim in during the baking hot Californian summer.

One day I was fiddling around mending the tiles on the roof when a bloke pulled up in red dodge and asked me if I could fix up his place. Before you could say Jumping Jack Flash the business snowballed. I ran a thriving operation with Jackie, a petite blond with lovely knockers, along with a couple of other guys to help handle the load. House after house we renovated and repainted while America was in uproar and turmoil over the Watergate scandal, which raged at full throttle and blared out of our double-decker television.

One lazy Sunday, my long-haired and red-bearded machinist mate Nelson embarked on a little bar-hopping. We went to the popular Rusty Pelican for brunch and a couple of jugs of Bloody Mary before moving on to the Monterey Still, and later hit a couple of bars, Blackie's and The Stag, where the Beach Boys played a gig just outside on a stretch of sand and the place crawled with West Coast babes and dreamers.

Somewhere along the way Nelson told me he had booked a cheap-as-chips airline ticket with a company called Planet Earth in Los Angeles. Shit, I thought, that sounds pretty good; and fun though my land-lubber summer had been, I was feeling the itch to go back to sea, so I took a chance, called the company, booked a ticket to England and posted them the air-fare. At six in the morning a few days later I arrived at what appeared to be an ex-military airport on the outskirts of Los Angeles.

I spotted the ticket tout clad in a crumpled double-breasted blue pin-striped suit, further adorned with a pair of chisel-toed black and white brothel creepers, and perched on his head at a cockeyed angle sat a panama hat with a mauve sash wrapped around it. To add to the mad hatter's outfit, he'd garrotted himself around the neck with a tawdry pink and wisteria-coloured Windsor double-knotted tie.

Honking away like a goose at feeding time he was dishing out tickets to a line of waiting punters. Finally my turn came around and I read the half-capsized label stuck to his polyester suit, which read 'Welcome to Pomair' with his name, Brian Boxworth, underneath. Amongst the jostling, travel-weary crowd Brian looked as out of place as a nun in a rugby scrum. I forked out my I.D and his beady eyes peered down his bulbous strawberry-coloured nose, which gave the impression he had encountered a fist or two during his career, as he scrutinized the document. Shuffling around in a Gladstone bag half full of greenbacks he dug out my ticket, handed it over, and with a slewed grin revealing a bloody great set of false chompers, said in a Geordie twang,

"Have a nice flight to London, Sir!"

I found a bench and sat down, squeezed in amongst an array of various characters, quite a few of whom were hungrily devouring some greasy fried chicken out of plastic containers. After a moment or two the alarm bells started ringing and I asked the fella sitting beside me how long he'd been waiting for the flight.

"Since yesterday. Pomair overbooked the flight and many of us couldn't get on board the plane," he grumbled with exasperation.

"Christ," I thought to myself, "this has all the makings of a diabolical fiasco." I thought I'd better do a bit of Sherlock Holmes-ing and shot back over to the ticket tout.

"What's the story, Mr. Boxworth?" I demanded.

"You've got no problems, Guv'nor," he insisted. "The plane should be here in an hour or so."

I jammed myself back into the tiny space on the bench and waited. Around nine o'clock a pink and purple jet that looked like it had been painted on the back of a bad acid trip, blasted down the landing strip and a heap of disgruntled passengers boarded the garish-coloured kerosene canary, and like an overstuffed can of anchovies we packed on board. I found my seat over the wing, sandwiched between a Chinese nurse and a plump Iranian colonel. Falling back into a horribly uncomfortable seat I sighed and reckoned it could be a long trip. Once airborne, the Colonel dived into a massive sack of Pecan nuts and started chomping until the red dye they'd been plastered with left his teeth looking like he'd used red type-writer ribbon as dental floss, and he mentioned between gulps he was going to Frankfurt in Germany.

"This plane's going to London, mate," I said.

"I've got no intention of going near London," the Colonel replied emphatically, and went back to his nuts.

Turning to the Chinese lass I asked where she was going, and to my amazement she said she expected the plane to land in Manchester in the North of England.

It slowly dawned on me that no one on the fucking plane knew where it was going. To add to the holocaust an announcement came over the intercom informing the unfortunate cargo of hapless travellers that all the heads had broken down and the captain was diverting the plane to bloody Bangor in Maine.

The chattering hum from the passengers turned to an abrupt silence and then, once the realization sank in that it's impossible to take a piss out of the window of a DC8, the reaction turned to a loud and indignant uproar. And there were no in-flight screens or televisions to consult either to find out the plane's location, flight path or estimation of arrival time.

I decided to take a leaf out of the Howard Hugh's method of checking out bearings and leaned over the nurse's shoulder to peer out of the port window. The plane wing was cutting through fields of cloud banks and you could see about as much as looking up a pussy cat's arsehole, but then the acres of cumulus parted and we were out the other side and into the clear blue. Way over to the left the profile of Niagara Falls was just visible, and turning to the Colonel I imparted my assessment of the situation.

"We're passing over Buffalo Bill territory. It shouldn't be too long before the old bus pulls into Bangor."

He stopped chomping on his pecans long enough to think about it for a moment, nodded, and promptly fished out a silver canteen from the inner pocket of his jacket. Filling up a couple of small tumblers with whisky, he passed one to me and sank a toast of 'laissez faire'.

"Fuck the French, mate," I replied and knocked back some bloody superb Scotch.

The purple plane skidded to a halt in Bangor at two in the afternoon in nearly ninety degrees of heat and near a hundred degrees of humidity, and it was hold on to your crank time as a stampeding throng charged for the exit doors. I shot down the ladder with a strangle-hold on the one-eyed trouser snake and bolted towards a fire truck parked on the tarmac for a teeming piss behind the back wheel. When we were all finally herded into the airport terminal, the Pomair representative made another announcement.

"Apologies, ladies and gentlemen, but the spare parts for the plane have to be flown in from Miami and departure will be delayed for a further six hours. As the flight has not left US airspace we will be able to organize buses for you to either visit the local county fair or take a trip downtown."

"Blistering barnacles, that's a hell of a long time to fix the shitter on the plane," I thought to myself, and decided to opt for the excursion into town where I fell into a tavern full of local fishermen, which turned out to be a pretty good way to while away the hours, chatting to the guys and hearing about their latest adventures. Come eight o'clock I stumbled back to the airport, and looking around it became obvious we were all pretty drunk, but blurred vision or not it was obvious the building we were waiting in was not an ordinary passenger terminal.

The vast fabricated sheds served large cargo shipments and we were surrounded by an array of massive glass tanks stacked to the brim with giant bluish-green lobsters. And suspended above the tanks hung a bunch of lights attached to the ceiling by chains. Some idiot, much the worse for the amount of booze he'd consumed, climbed up onto a fork-lift truck and managed to grab a hold of one of the chains and swung out like a baboon over a cluster of his skylarking mates, whereupon one of his intoxicated friends grabbed him around the legs and joined in for the ride. The extra weight was too much for the davit to hold the chain, and with a big bang it tore away from the support beam and the electrical cables leading to the light were left to bear the strain. With a scream and a hell of thunderous thump the two apes pitched head first into one of the lobster tanks. The electrical wires, now stripped bare at the end of the cord, hit the metal on a nearby pillar, and amidst a firework display of sparks and smoke, short-circuited the entire system and the whole place plunged into darkness. Airport security and firemen rushed in aghast at the turmoil, and carted the two trapeze flying fellas out of the building, much to the bemusement of the by now utterly confused passengers.

About this time another flock of disgruntled Pomair customers turned up on the scene, having just arrived on a flight from Europe. The captain of their plane had fucked them around too, and instead of delivering his two-legged cargo to the originally intended destination of New York had decided to dump them in Bangor instead.

At this point the circus took on a whole new level of bullshit when the Pomair loudspeaker crackled into life to deliver another announcement.

"Ladies and gentlemen, due to the unavoidable delay of your plane, we are going to hold a ballot amongst you all to choose which airport in Europe the majority of you would like to travel to."

Bedlam duly ensued. London and Manchester got a good vote, but Frankfurt had plenty of support too, although Brussels ended up with only a mere sixteen in its favour.

"Your requests have been noted," the voice on the intercom blurted once more. "However, we will not be able to inform you of where the plane will land until we are halfway over the Atlantic."

Our dishevelled mob made its way reluctantly up the ladders and back onto the purple flying nightmare, this time accompanied by a team of orange-robed and loudly chanting Hare Krishna devotees. As we shot down the runway, a Dixie jazz band sitting at the back of the plane grabbed a hold of their various instruments and started playing When the Saints Come Marching In.

It was absolute pandemonium until we reached Iceland, where the captain delivered the worst news yet.

"Ladies and gentlemen, this plane will be landing in Belgium."

A unison of groans emanated from every one of us, bar the few that had voted for it back in Maine. I gazed out of the window to see the

English coast left behind as we flew on to bloody Brussels, although by this time I reckoned there was every chance we'd end up in Moscow. Still, the captain stuck to his plan for the first time since we'd boarded the flying calamity, and sure enough an exhausted bunch of passengers disembarked the flying sardine can in Belgium.

The Colonel was loaded to the gunnels with luggage, and although slaughtered before getting on the plane, had on top of this consumed an entire bottle of whisky during the trip and could barely stand up, let alone walk, so I hoisted his oversized, heavy leather satchel over my shoulder.

"What the hell have you got in here, mate," I asked, "a dead prisoner?"

"Twelve bottles of Chivas Regal," he slurred in reply.

"Shit mate, that's great Scotch," I said, giving him a hand and hauling him to his feet.

The nurse and I ended up sticking together and caught a coach to Ostend, took a fucking ferry to Gravesend, a British Rail rattler to Clapham Junction where the nurse pissed off to Manchester, and I tossed my sea bags onto another train leaving for Southampton, then took a Red Funnel ferry to the Isle of Wight. Finally, a long day and night later, I arrived in Cowes absolutely shitfaced with exhaustion and ready to start another adventure that would be shrouded in sorcery.

3

A Sorceror's Lobscouse

The chance for mistakes is about equal to the number of crew squared

Ted Turner

I STAGGERED UP COWES HIGH STREET in a state of total exhaustion, weaving my way through a heaving throng of sailors and spectators who had gathered for the longest running regatta in the world. Knackered after the horrendous Pomair debacle I dropped into the Crown and Anchor for a much-needed pint or three, where I spotted a couple of lads from Spencer's Rigging I knew from early *Crusade* days.

"Hey, Chas old son, what the fook are you doin' in this neck of the woods?" called out Curly from his perch at the end of the bar in a broad Hampshire accent.

91

I ambled over to join him and his mate Gerald and ordered a round of good English beer.

"I'm looking for a ride in the Fastnet," I replied, gulping down a pint of the amber nectar.

"Curly and I joost finished splicing soom wire to rope-running gear on *Sorcery* over at Spencer's yard, I reckon those guys could use a good extra hand for the racing this week," Gerald piped up.

I'd done the SORC and the Jamaica Race on the good looking C & C 61' sloop earlier in the year. Her owner, Jim Baldwin, lived up near Edgar Town in Martha's Vineyard, and during his career made a fortune developing turbo blades for Pratt & Whitney jet engines. Now in his seventies, his longish grey hair swept back from his distinguished face and atop a large, sloping roman nose, he wore a pair of horn-rimmed glasses that almost disappeared into a set of shaggy eyebrows. Jim's American drawl had the timbre of a diesel truck rolling over a gravel road, and in tense moments on the boat the rasp would turn to a lion's roar. A couple of bad race-car crashes had left him with the legacy of a crook back and a bad leg, but he still got around in stalwart style with the help of a walking stick.

And then there was his blond wife, the 'Duchess'. Eileen came from an old American family and always appeared immaculately dressed and loaded to the gills with jewels. She was warm and down to earth, referred to the crew as 'her boys', and without fail would always be waiting on the dock at the end of a race with cases of ice-cold beer and champagne at the ready – yep, the Duchess was a doll!

"OK fellas, I'll go find them," I replied, and hightailed it over to the Fountain Hotel hot on the trail of the boys from *Sorcery*.

Conspicuous by their yellow crewshirts, I found sailing master, shipwright, Sydney 18-footer and one design champion Normy Hyatt, Tom the Pom, Tom the Yank, Macca McDonald, Rob 'the Wharf Rat' Stirling, the robust Aussie 'social director for all boat affairs', and a couple of new blokes I hadn't crossed tacks with before.

"I heard along the kelp line you'd be rolling into town," exclaimed the Wharf Rat. "We kept a spot for you, want to come along?"

"Sure," I replied, "count me in!"

"Jesus, Chas, your Sperry's look half spent," Macca remarked, assessing my worn appearance. "Judging by those shoes you must have hoofed it half-way over the Alps to get here! I hope you have a spare pair because you don't want to buy new ones from the rogue who runs the chandlers down the road. They don't call him The Robber for nothing, he charges worse than a wounded buffalo."

"Don't worry, Macca, I'll put Chas on the main traveller and hopefully Old Man Baldwin will notice the state of them', Normy laughed.

We kept a pair of extra-large scuffed and torn deck shoes on board *Sorcery*, with holes in the soles the size of button mushrooms. If you needed a new set of footwear you put these things on and went back aft and found a position in Jim's line of sight next to the traveller on the weather side and hoped he would sooner or later notice the state of your footwear. Of course he knew the form, and if the race had gone well he'd place one of his big bear paws on your shoulder, shove some green backs in your hand and say in his deep gruff voice,

"Those frightful shoes you wore today are a poor sight on my vessel's decks. Get yourself up to the chandlers and buy a new pair of topsiders."

Without further ado we set off the next morning on the big white sloop for the first race, hurtled all the way around the course on a reach and arrived back in Cowes first over the line. However, it was the next racing escapade that etched itself into my mind for a long time to come. Gale-force winds hit during both the cross-channel and the second in-shore race, and during the latter, wild conditions made for a load of problems. Jim Alabaster, a tall lanky middle-aged English sail-maker from Ratsey & Lapthorn, had flogged Baldwin a big blue spinnaker made out of some fancy 2.2 cloth. It had an oily texture to it and Alabaster reckoned it was as strong as all shit. Under a high cut yankee sail and a reef in the main, Baldwin wanted the new spinnaker hoisted when we closed in on the top mark up near the Needles. It was blowing dogs off chains from the south-west, and once the spinnaker was hoisted to the top of the mast Tom the Yank and the lads on the coffee-grinders cranked on the after-brace and trimmed the spinnaker sheet. With a burst of thunder the chute broke open and we started our charge down towards the Squadron.

The ebbing tide streamed out in a ripping current against the strong sou'wester in steep, short waves, and *Sorcery* lay a fair bit lower in the water than normal. As she pushed like a bulldozer into the sea rushing against her, *Apollo* was right on her hammer, and boat for boat the two yachts closed in on the rocky ledge which runs out off the shore.

Apollo caught a gust and scorched ahead about forty meters in front of us. She gybed and lost it, going into an almighty broach, and lay helpless and floundering flat in the water on her side. Normy gripped *Sorcery's* wheel and tore past the wooden boat, trying to avoid crashing into her. Our turn for calamity was upon us. The rocks loomed and we were horribly close to hitting them. With the pole squared back, *Sorcery* hit a rough patch of water and started rolling like a brewery barrel.

The Wharf Rat was on the bow forward of the headstay, and looking aft towards the stern with the lazy brace in his right hand waiting for the pole to glide in so he could snap in the new guy. Unfortunately the lazy spinnaker sheet had wrapped itself in a half-hitch around the parrot beak of the end of the pole and its jaws wouldn't open. Seconds later we went into a monstrous barrel roll, and the pole's outer end refused to release and dived underwater. Something had to break. There was an almighty bang and the snatch-block on the foredeck, which the fore-guy goes through, exploded and the outboard end of the pole reared up out of the water like a rocket launcher. Its jaws broke open and, spinning like a top, it spiralled skywards out of control. The spinnaker was now free of the pole, swinging wildly out to the port side of the boat, and the mainsail swept the deck, almost taking off Alabaster's head as it shot past him.

We were in shit city. Hurtling into a bloody awful broach, the spade rudder and the keel almost came out of the water, and to add to Alabaster's misery Baldwin lost his balance and went flying over the back of Normy, who was clinging onto the wheel, and landed in a crumpled heap of arms and legs on top of the hapless mainsheet man.

The purchase line that hauled the inner end of the pole up and down, attached to the end of a sliding car and a metal pin at the front of the mast, broke free and the heel of the butt jack-knifed and free-wheeled skywards and with the crack of a rifle shot slammed into the safety stopper. Just before this, the topping lift on the pole's outer end had been eased right off because it had been trying to punch bullet-holes in the kite. It was a perilous situation – the pole had arced under the water and belted back to the shrouds, ending up in a vertical position with the lazy sheet trapped behind it.

Big Syd and I already had enough on our plate with the tails of the fore-guy and topping lift. Macca, the chunky breezeblock-built Aussie, scuttled along the toe-rail like a beaver with only his head and hunched shoulders above water, lifting the pole up as he rushed towards the bow. Right on his arse the quick-thinking, gaunt-faced limey O'Grady brought up the rear, and with his long arms up over his head, helped support the heavy weight, until the pair of them managed to swing the pole up over the lifelines and onto the deck and flick the lazy sheet clear, before retreating like greased lightning aft of the mast.

There's nowhere to hide on the decks of a flush racing boat and we weren't out of Dodge yet. Somehow Kiwi 'Bruce the Goose' Kendall, who'd been hanging onto the mast, managed to pull the fore-guy slack up and get it into the spare block next to the one that had blown up. The Rat was clinging onto a headsail filled with a ton of water, and half of it was being dragged in a keel-haul beneath the boat. By now the spinnaker had wrapped itself around the head-stay a couple of times, to all intents and purposes trying to strangle it. Christ, what a holocaust! On top of which, during the spectacular broach the baby stay, which is the inner forestay, had been released for the gybe and the mast inverted a couple of times under the huge pressure of the oscillating kite. And then a yell came from the cockpit.

"Look out, watch your heads!"

The main thrashed across the deck and blasted over to the other side of the boat. It was the days of wire braces, and by this time there was a mass of stuff tangled up and flying around the cockpit in a serious fuck-up. It was damn lucky the spinnaker was made of such slippery material. Slithering off the head-stay like an eel, the stranglehold unwrapped itself and the Rat managed to secure the brace into the pole, which was up at the head-stay by now, and we swung the pole out and managed to make it back onto the other gybe. After long moments of utter chaos we managed to get things more or less back under control. The only man who benefited from the fiasco was Ken Beacon senior, who happened to be near enough to shoot some spectacular photographs and ended up selling a lot of copies to the crew as shit-hitting-the-fan souvenirs. Amazingly, by the time *Sorcery* crossed the finishing line, the big blue spinnaker was still in one piece and miraculously no one was seriously hurt.

To celebrate our survival the Duchess arranged, in her inimitable style, a crew party at the Gloucester Hotel. Sad to say, the fondly-remembered building burnt down a few years later, but it was a great place in its day and the scene of many a prodigious piss-up. Late as usual, but irresistibly delayed by a pretty girl I'd found in the beer tent that led to a happy hour or so in a bunk on *Sorcery*, I collared big Syd Brown and we made our way up the high street to the old hotel. He'd later regret it, but on the way in Syd found a peg to hang his favourite blue Henry Lloyd sailing jacket labeled 'Dinah', a gift from the owner, a former commodore of the New York Yacht Club. The Commodore gave the coat to Syd for his initiative and seamanship while watch captain aboard his S & S Palmer & Johnston 60' yacht when she lost her rudder in a Transatlantic race and under Syd's supervision still managed to complete the course.

We squeezed into the bar through a crowd packed as tight as a rugby scrum and found the crew from *Sorcery*. Tom the Pom and another English guy, Tim O'Grady, who had a couple of high-heeled good-looking women from Fleet Street under his wing, were in conversation with Peter and Lotte Poland, the owners of the Bob Miller designed *Matchless* who were over from Cape Town. After knocking back a couple of beers, Syd announced he needed some loose change.

"What do you need it for?" I asked.

"I've got to make a phone call," he replied with a mischievous look in his eye, and promptly took off in the opposite direction to the call box and disappeared into the head.

While in there he bought a packet of condoms, opened one up and filled it up with a tube of condensed milk he'd stashed in his pocket before leaving the boat. The red herring prepared, he sauntered back to the bar.

"Oh shit, I've dropped some money," he squawked.

As he bent down to pick the coins up he also surreptitiously dropped the sticky, cream goo-filled condom, which looked exactly what it was supposed to look like.

"Well what have we got here?" he shouted as he held the thing aloft for all to see. "Who's is this?"

The whole bar turned around to see him waving an oozing full condom triumphantly over his head.

"Well I'm hungry and I need some vitamins," he whooped, turned the condom upside down and squeezed the liquid down his throat, until it ran in rivers down his face and plastered his shirt.

Lotte was in hysterics, it was a trick she'd seen before, but the two girls from London were absolutely aghast and vamoosed at high speed out of there, leaving O'Grady in their wake and his hopes for the evening high and dry, which further added to Syd's glee.

At the end of a great dinner and a hell of a party Jim stood up and thanked us for the sail that day, and said the knockdown broach notwithstanding, we were one of the best bunch of blokes he'd ever sailed with. And then he called out,

"Syd, I believe you've had your fill of nutrients for the evening, so if you can't eat all your dinner leave some for Chas, he needs some extra to build himself up," and he brought the house down.

Jim and his Duchess were staying in the hotel, and retired to bed while we carried on carousing and drinking ourselves under the table. Suddenly a bunch of uniformed emergency guys belted in amongst the revelling yachties, yelling out that there was an IRA bomb in the building. The bomb squad arrived in full force and turfed all the guests out of the rooms upstairs, including Jim, who appeared with a nightcap on and armed with a walking stick, and the Duchess wrapped up in a dressing-gown but minus her customary war paint. Big Syd lurched past the hotel entrance to retrieve his much-prized coat only to find a note in its place impaled on the peg saying 'Thanks mate for the loan of your coat, I had to ride my motor-bike home'. Syd was incandescent with rage, having formed a close attachment to the coat over the years. He never did find the guy who nicked it, even though he prowled the streets of Cowes looking for him for days. If he'd found him I reckoned he would have killed him and stuffed his bike up his arse. As for the bomb threat, well it turned out the nearby Squadron's gas burners had been turned on and promptly combusted.

The end of Cowes week is always celebrated with a heck of a fire-work display, which lights up the Solent like the Battle of Waterloo, and this year it coincided with my birthday party. The following morning the booming starting cannon fired off the Squadron's ram-parts, reverberated through the crews' monumental hangovers and the Fastnet race kicked off. After a long slow haul out to the shingles bank at the end of the Solent a Sou'wester sprung up and *Sorcery* worked her way through the fleet, passed underneath the chalk white cliffs and the lighthouse overlooking The Needles and then stood out to sea on starboard tack. Baldwin had spoken to Owen Aisher, the owner of a series of bottle-green yachts bearing the name *Yeoman*, and explained he'd won the Fastnet one year under similar weather conditions by standing well out to sea, convincing Baldwin that if we went far enough into the English Channel before tacking over to port he'd clear the Portland tidal race when the tide changed.

The bulk of the fleet worked their way shorewards and by the time they reached Anvil Point had disappeared for a couple hours into the middle of a dense fog bank. We tacked *Sorcery* over in a ten to fifteen-knot breeze and were well off St. Albans Head and Weymouth just before dusk when the wind switched to the northeast. The star-cut was hoisted and that was the last we saw of a three hundred-strong fleet for a while. All of a sudden out of the mist loomed a billowing spinnaker with a big, red crusading St. George's cross on it, heralding John Prentice's lovely mahogany-hulled 44' Swan *Battlecry*. It didn't do much for our morale. *Battlecry* was fast, but all the same a smaller yacht than *Sorcery* and our spirits fell to the lowest point of the entire trip. I tried to cheer everyone up by saying John was a fabulous yachtsman and maybe it was a good sign and that we were in fact in a better position than we thought.

Two or three decades ago, life on board racing yachts was quite different to the way it is now in many respects. For starters we were not fuelled with the monotonous dehydrated food used in more recent times, and in the good old days it was another affair altogether. Baldwin equalled the same passion for things culinary as my old friend Don Mickleborough and arranged terrific sea-going dinners in a dedicated ritual. He'd kick off by disappearing down below when the sun went over the yard arm, to start brewing Bloody Marys the headman at the American Bar in the Savoy Hotel in London would be proud of, and his son Jay, who was the cook for the trip, would lay out the big saloon table with many a bottle of good wine and knock up a three-course dinner.

The next day a weather report came through on the radio saying a frontal trough, which had been skulking around the English Channel, had moved away to the southeast and an anti-cyclone was building up and moving eastwards into the North Sea, dominating the wind directions with winds light and variable at first, before becoming northerly and then veering to easterly force 2 to 4 and predicting fog would blanket the western part of the channel, including the area surrounding the Fastnet Rock. Bad visibility was already a problem and this latest news didn't look like things were going to get any easier. The morning breeze was freshening all the time and we put up a blooper. *Sorcery* shifted up a gear and roared towards The Lizard, pursued by *Safari*, *Charisma*, *Salty Goose*, the big Mexican ketch *Sayula* and the Brazilian *Saga*. Sure enough, the forecast's prophecies materialized and by the time *Sorcery* closed in on the Fastnet Rock a shroud of thick, pea-soup fog descended and left us in a silent isolated world of grey.

The famous rock sticks out of the Atlantic Ocean off Ireland's most southerly point and a tall lonely lighthouse clings precariously to the side of it. The original construction, built in 1853, was so precarious in fact that when the storming Atlantic gales slammed into its side the keeper's crockery would be thrown off the tables and the tower would rattle and shake against the power and fury of the blasting wind and sea. In old Norse the rock was known as Hvasstann-ait meaning 'sharp-toothed', in Celtic as Carraig Aonair for 'solitary rock', and later nine-teenth-century Irish emigrants named it Ireland's Teardrop, for it was the last part of their homeland they would see after embarking on their journey for a new life in America.

Working away with the radio direction finder, Tom the Pom was pretty concerned *Sorcery* would overshoot the mark and reckoned we needed a man at the top of the mast to see if the view through the fog improved from higher up. The next thing I knew, I was hooked into a bosun's chair and clinging to the spar while being hauled skywards to the cross spreaders by Bruce the Goose Kendall and the Fat Rabbit. A further altitude of eighty foot or so made for a considerably better per-spective. I shouted down directions to Normy at the helm and he bore away slightly and aimed the bow straight as an arrow for the mark. The dull thud of a foghorn echoed out over the water and *Sorcery* rounded the rock, managing to set the fastest elapsed time ever made to that date for the first half of the race. It's been broken many times since, but for a while there the record belonged to *Sorcery*.

Tom set a course for the Scillies, and with the anti-cyclone really set-tled in by this time the low-lying islands, said to be the remnants of the mythical land of Lyonesse, appeared on the horizon in brilliant, flaxen-gold sunshine surrounded by a silver shining sea. It felt good to be sailing under a bright, cloudless sky again before the dappled shadows of dusk fell. For the last sixty miles or so, up to the finish line off Ply-mouth, the wind dropped down to just a whispering breeze, so we came in close to the shore and played the fluky shifts and gusts as they danced off the land during the moonless night.

In the light airs *Sorcery* came perilously close to grinding to a halt a couple of times. The big yacht was heavy, unlike the lighter-built modern carbon-made racing machines of today, and had she got stuck in a windless hole might not have escaped its clutches for quite a while. Stealthily as a black-tipped tailed stoat I crept along the leeward rail, past the ghostly silhouetted men concentrating on squeezing every inch of speed out of the boat, and lay down on my back a few feet from the bow under the sinuous curve of the deep-footed sail. From there, with the aid of a powerful narrow-beamed torch, I had a night owl's view of the woollen tuffs that flowed down either side, a foot and a half back from the leading edge of the light number one headsail's luff. We were sailing her fat and fast, the trimmers had the lead blocks a couple of notches further forward than normal, with the sheets slightly cracked off. All night *Sorcery* kept rolling, digging deep into the bays and rock-hopping around the steep, granite Cornish headlands over which the soft breeze carried the scent of warm earth and freshly harvested farmland.

We clung on to the lead and by dawn still had it. The sea sorcerer's spirit was with us, for in truth such light airs could have dealt the winning hand to any one of the fleet. With the tide about to change, a lucky streaming breeze strayed into *Sorcery's* sails and stayed with her for the last half mile of the race until she made it over the finish at eight in the morning, creaming across the line in front of three hundred yachts. *Charisma* just missed the tide and had to anchor until it changed, while the Brazilians on *Saga* managed to sail around the outside of her. On corrected time *Saga* won, followed by *Recluta* from Argentina and *Charisma*, with *Sorcery* coming fourth.

In those days the old Mill Bay docks in Plymouth were still there, and we tied up against the stone wall where hundreds of spectators lined the way to watch the spectacle. When the rest of the boats began to trickle in they rafted up alongside *Sorcery*, pinning her to the inside and rendering her a well-trodden stepping stone for crews clambering across her decks to get ashore. Like a scene from a western, dust and grit whirled and spiralled in clouds off the street above and rained down on our faithful yacht, until she temporarily became known as the sixty-one foot ashtray.

The next morning I was up on deck when Eric Tabarly appeared on board with a couple of his crew and his lovely French girlfriend Frederica in attendance, a stunning apparition in her see-through lace dress and wearing nothing underneath. As she climbed the wall steps, the boys looked up and almost had a heart attack at the sight of her fabulous body above them. Tabarly had just built the new *Pen Duick*, which he'd designed for the next Round the World Race. He'd sailed a tough and arduous Fastnet, starting seven hours late in Cowes and then getting caught in the tide off Portland Bill, although if we'd sailed boat for boat he'd probably have beaten us. On board the big ketch there was a choice of steering, either a wheel or a tiller shaped into an oversized phallic sculpture for which the boat became famous and many a practical joker took a shot at stealing. There was bugger all ventilation down below, and with a couple of French guys cooking in the galley it smelt like a Left Bank cafe at rush hour, laced with the pungent aroma of over-ripe Camembert and piles of unwashed filthy socks. Either way it was damn claustrophobic down there and not unlike being in a submarine, which would have been a familiar environment for most of her crew as most of them were submariners. It was just as well they were used to it, as an entire circling of the globe's oceans in the upcoming race would have to be endured in these conditions.

We took in a few beers up at the Royal Western Yacht Club, which sits up near the spot where Elizabeth's fighting cock, Sir Francis Drake, waited for the impending Spanish fray. According to Stow's Annals of 1600, Drake 'kept revels on the shore, dancing, bowling and making merry... at the instant of the foe's approach' and uttered his famous words 'There is plenty of time to win the game and beat the Spaniards too', before he went out to demolish the Armada. Even to this day he is still patron of The English bowls players known as The Francis Drake Society. Although as a young man he'd got up to no good, with his mentor Hawkins he went on to save England during those few days in the English Channel and decimated the Spanish attempt at invasion.

Before moving to Tasmania my family originally came from Devon near where Drake was born, and I'd grown up listening to stories about the famous explorer and how he'd played in the estuaries there as a child, and in his youth had gone to sea on a little cargo bark which traded from the Medway across the Channel to France. Some of my ancestors had been master carvers of many a great ship's figurehead down in the West Country, and as a child my grandmother used to tell me that the family had been related to Drake by marriage.

I've always been fascinated by maritime history and can while away hours and days in museums, so before rendering myself three sheets to the wind I cruised on over to the Naval Dockyard to take a look at the figureheads and see what else might be stashed away there. West Country folklore had given Drake the status of near-legendary seafaring wizard, and in 1818 Robert Southey told of how it was believed the Plymouth Leat was created by magic as Drake rode his horse over the route and the water followed him. The museum contains a pair of silver coconut cups he acquired on his circumnavigation, shaped like globes and believed to have been given to him as a New Year gift from Elizabeth I. Centuries later his sword, bearing royal arms with which the queen had knighted him in 1597, was used to knight Sir Francis Chichester after his solo journey around the world's oceans in 1967. A few relics from the *Golden Hind* still survive in the form of a chair in the Bodleian Library, and there's a table in the Middle Temple in London made out of her timbers. As for the maverick sailor's bones, they never returned to England but rest at the bottom of the sea off Venezuela, which may in part be the cause of a myth existing to this day that Drake is merely sleeping and will return as hero should his country ever need him.

Before the race to France started I decided to take a ramble down memory lane and asked the boys if they'd like to visit a few of the Devon pubs my family used to own. My grandfather, Colonel Blundell, had owned Southwestern Breweries, based in the pretty town of Kingsbridge near Totnes, and just before the war the outfit consisted of over a hundred West Country pubs. During the war my uncle had been an officer on board the *Prince of Wales* when a German plane crashed into the bridge, killing the entire crew, and so my father became owner of the family business, which eventually in later years sold out to Courage, the well-known beer-makers.

Jumping on a bus owned by a bunch of hippies, who used the dilapidated double-decker to run stoned punters out to India, we set off for Salcombe on the old boneshaker. How times change things! I'd heard the old brewery was now a nightclub called Feathers, but at least the Shipwrights Arms had remained more or less intact. And so too had the Ferry Pub, a classic Devon waterfront building, where we ran into the crew from the long, slender, timber, Bob Miller-designed *Apollo*, which years later was to flounder on Lady Elliot Island on the Great Barrier Reef, fatally speared by razor-sharp coral. Much carousing took place that afternoon at the waterside pub, and armed with gallons of strong, Devon scrumpy for the journey back to Plymouth, we piled onto the bus and wound our way past willow and moss-green fields surrounded by old dry stone walls and on through a gorgeous English countryside while warbling drunken sea shanties. Fellow Tasmanian, the bespectacled, nuggetty and slow-spoken Phil Wardrop, commonly known as the Nudger, laid on a QLD, a 'quiet little drink' later that evening at the Greyhound pub.

Feeling like I'd been mown down by a combine harvester, the next day we started the La Rochelle Race to France and leapt over the starting line just as the then Prime Minister Ted Heath's *Morning Cloud* finished the Fastnet. A rare heatwave still gripped England and France by their throats, and under a hot and shining currant bun *Sorcery* got under way for the race across the channel in a steady fifteen-knot nor'easterly, flying a big broad-shouldered billowing red and yellow one-and-a-half-ounce spinnaker. The big boy staysail pulled her along like a leaping salmon and I reckon she made a splendid sight with all the crew clad in matching ruby and mustard threads, tearing away from the rest of the fleet on a run with the wind slightly aft of the beam. A strong outgoing tide up our arse gave us an added boost, the distant hills of Cornwall's Lizard Point disappeared in a heat haze, and Tom the Pom lay a course five miles to the west of Ushant.

We threaded our way across the busy shipping lanes, passing super-tankers the size of English stately homes, several warships and an endless array of cruise liners. Four miles west of Ushant, around midnight, the decks turned into a disco show as flashing, rotating rays from the lighthouse standing high on the hill swept over us. Brittany has produced some of France's greatest sailors who learned their art in the face of the Atlantic's full might when it hits the depth change, and roaring rollers fetch across the Bay of Biscay. The tides are notoriously fierce on this part of the coast, both in velocity and rise and fall, and we were being lee-bowed while pushing past an angry snake's tongue of rocks at Chaussée de Seine. We hoisted our secret weapon, the Bruce Bank's reaching 2.2 ounce star-cut, and ditched the big kite. To add to our arsenal we also had John Anderson aboard, an Olympian gold medalist who'd just been sailing Bondy's *Apollo* in the Admiral's Cup, and he brought a wealth of knowledge which he applied with considerable skill to get the best out of the sail over the next six hours.

At dawn *Pointe de Penmarch* appeared off our port bow and the wind veered to the Southeast, so we hauled up the medium Number One as the Wharf Rat spiked the tack and we canned the chute down the forward hatch. Baldwin was in his element – this was the sort of shit he loved sailing in, and clutching the wheel he hardened up in the Bay to keep out of the worst of the thrust of the tide and tried to dodge a minefield of protruding rocks while damp blankets of early morning estuary fog enveloped *Sorcery*. Tom the Pom anxiously watched the depth sounder and constantly checked his bearings with the radio direction finder and a hand-held compass so we could shave the tiny island of d'Yeu as close as possible. The fog burned off the higher the sun climbed and a Sou'Wester sea breeze filled the spinnaker, and the big white boat shy-reached home on the starboard gybe, carrying us over the finishing line at the head of the fleet, before pulling into the little harbour on the French west coast. Although we had a mainly Australian crew, *Sorcery* flew a US ensign, which during our stay in France was probably just as well. At the time Australia was boycotting France in protest at their nuclear tests in the Pacific – we wouldn't have been the most popular guys in town if we had flown the Southern Cross flag.

On a smoking hot afternoon a race reception was held in an airless and muggy town hall where the mayor and his cronies droned on with stupor-inducing speeches for bloody two hours. A strange assortment of warm, neon-coloured drinks were produced after the mind-numbing monologue, with not a block of ice or a cold beer to be seen, but we were parched and slammed down the offerings anyway.

The presentation later that night was a completely different affair, organized by Heidsieck and accompanied by a herd of good-looking hostesses who teetered around on high heels balancing trays piled high with bubbling champagne. In various states of dishevelled array, we were woken the next morning to the sound of insistent banging on the hull to find the chauffeur of a fancy Citroen pulled up beside us on the dock. The Citroen's boss was the owner of a cognac empire, and Baldwin had mentioned to him the night before that the *Sorcery* crew might like to check out his establishment the following day. It's an infre-

Sorcery on a wild and windy day in the Solent (A Sorcerer's Lobscouse)
Photograph by Beken of Cowes

quent state of affairs, but no one had the stomach for brandy that morning; however, somebody had to represent us and we dispatched Donald Elliot. Donald smoked dope but didn't drink alcohol and was consequently in a hell of a lot better shape than the rest of us, so he was dispatched to run the gauntlet down cellar aisles filled with brandy caskets, regardless of his personal preference for hash over alcohol – none of us were up for it, that's for sure.

Although *Sorcery* was a fast boat, Jim Baldwin reckoned he needed a new yacht that rated better under the I.O.R. and would therefore be more competitive. With a buyer waiting in the wings in the States, the time had come to take her back home and hand her over to a new owner. Our captain would be John Bolton, aka Fat Rabbit, who wasn't actually fat, but nevertheless a rounded belly protruded from his stocky frame and earned him the name. He had the gift of the gab that in another life would have made him a good diplomat; he could talk his way out of a wet paper bag, charming his way with ease past the customs and immigration official's bureaucratic bullshit. And should we encounter any other obstacles, he had a masterful aptitude for spinning out fairytales that even a used car salesman would be hard pushed to come up with. I studied his method and it served me well in the years to come; I always reckoned he could have pulled a white rabbit out from under his hat should the need arise.

Tom the Yank wanted to go as far as the Azores to have a look around. Donald Elliot would be the navigator and Aussie Billie – 'Complicated Bill' Edgerton joined us. And Robin, a sparkly, brown-eyed brunette also pitched up for the ride. Now in her late twenties, she was a damn competent helmswoman, brought up on her father's boat, who more recently had studied marine biology at the Woods Hole Maritime Institute in the States. On top of this she cooked like a Parisian chef.

La Rochelle and the hills of Saintonge disappeared over the stern and we set *Sorcery's* big yellow and red cruising chute in a steady 15 to 20 knots of breeze. The sea surfed across from the north west of the Atlantic, remnants of a distant storm that would not bother us. The evening fell and a full, fat-as-butter moon rose high in the sky, beaming her light onto the tops of the swells, turning them into sparkling chards of dancing water. The wind filled the sails aft of the beam and we sailed on the port gybe way out into the Bay of Biscay. It was night-time sailing at its magical best.

North of Cabo Ortegal we gybed and passed the westernmost point of Spain, Cape Finisterre, under the auspices of a strengthening wind. Knocking the chute on the head we pulled it down and spun the old girl into the grinning teeth of the wind, tucked in a reef, heaved up the No. 3 headsail, eased the sheets, poled the headsail out and rolled on down the pipeline towards the Azorean Archipelago. On the fourth day the wind sprang from the South Sou'west and we hardened up on the port tack on a pounding beat, to run down the northern side of Isla Terceira.

The Azores are a group of nine volcanic islands in the North Atlantic and cover an expanse of around four hundred miles between 37 and 39 degrees North latitude, about eight hundred miles from the Portuguese coast and sixteen hundred miles from North America. Settled by the Portuguese in 1427, the Western Isles became the crossroads of the Atlantic, and ships outbound from Europe caught the easterlies south of the islands and those returning hitched a ride on the westerlies to the north of the group. Richly-laden merchant and treasure-carrying ships passing through these waters to and from the Americas and the Orient made the outpost a favourite hunting ground for many a buccaneering pirate or privateer. For some the trip ended in a ruination of another kind. Nearly three hundred wrecks rest their skeletons in the deep surrounding waters, some of whose number include a British naval fleet including the *HMS Revenge* under the command of Sir Richard Grenville, which was sunk by a hurricane five days after battling fifty-three Spanish ships for fifteen hours straight.

We made landfall in little under a week, when the first shadows of twilight began to steal down the mountains onto the fertile plains and scatter into the sea. We eased *Sorcery* into the bay where the town of Vitoria and its limestone whitewashed houses and sixteenth century cobbled streets nestle into its shores. The Fat Rabbit pulled *Sorcery* up alongside a bulky vessel manned by Portuguese sailors stationed in the islands to recover space capsules when they parachuted into the Atlantic and it didn't take him long to swing into action and organize a barter or two. In exchange for a case of Cork gin that tasted like diesel, which we'd been awarded for being the first yacht to round the Fastnet Rock, the Captain agreed to fill *Sorcery's* fuel tanks and top up a couple of forty four gallon drums to boot. Before long the word spread a beautiful white sloop flying the stars and stripes had sailed into the harbor and a gathering of curious locals flocked down to the quay to check out the new lady in town. Amongst the crowd a hank of American pilots moseyed across and with little resistance on our part took us to a barbecue supplied with plenty of Jack Daniels and long necked bottles of Budweiser. Robin scored a hit with the good old boys and the next morning her admirers whisked her off the to the store on the base and loaded her up like a pack pony with Louisiana shrimp, Black Angus steaks and a shitload of turkeys. The Fat Rabbit sat back looking at the haul with the contented smile of a pirate in hog heaven. However, our brim full forty-four gallon drums of fuel needed for spare supplies to charge the batteries, or to motor if we were becalmed on the long trip were still sitting on the decks of the naval vessel.

"We've got to find a way to get those monsters onto *Sorcery*," Donald mused.

Pondering the logistics of the situation he peered at the ship through his thick set spectacles.

I paced back and forth waiting for a brainwave that wasn't happening. I lit a cigarette and wandered up the decks.

"Well, what if we shift the life-rafts down below to make some space?" I prompted taking a look at the emergency gear stashed amidships.

He thought about it for a moment.

"You know Chas old son you might be onto something. I've got an idea, it's going to be tricky, but it might work."

"What's the drift mate?"

"Remember that tumble-down wooden joint up on the hill next to the sycamore tree we walked past last night?" he asked.

"Buggered if I know, we'd drunk a fair bit of the local moonshine. Why do you ask?"

"We need a cooper and if my hunch is right we might be in luck. Let's go take a Captain Cook as you Aussies say," he said, hoofing it off the boat.

We walked into town through the main square and bypassing the winding road scrambled up a steep hill, until we reached the tall tree and a battered shed surrounded by casks and piles of timber. Gasping for breath, Donald pushed a creaking door open and peered inside the corrugated wreck.

"Jesus Christ, a treasure trove if ever I saw one," he murmured.

"This place has got more shit in it than a bower bird's nest mate," I exclaimed.

On the walls hung countless hoops, there were dozens of staves stashed on racks, a high hill of cask keys and a mountain of tubs, barrels and buckets stacked at the far end of the sawdust covered floor. In amongst the chaos stood the cooper, a little man shaped like a beach ball with a bald head. Donald could speak a bit of Spanish and with a lot of gesticulating and sketches the beach ball got the drift and bounced into action. In a matter of minutes he shut the shop, loaded a hefty bag of tools and ropes into the back of a decrepit rattletrap and shot off down the road at bone-shaking speed. Grinding to a halt on the dock beside *Sorcery* he jumped on board. With a lot more hand waving and bastardised lingo on our part he announced with a big smile.

"No problema," he said pulling out his tape measure and pointing to his watch to make sure we understood he'd be back in an hour.

Sure enough he reappeared a while later with two cradles he'd made which were racked and tapered to the drum's dimensions and a timber made support with fixed points, around which were secured to a couple of metal hoops. On a roll by now he hooked up par-buckles to the barrels and attached them to the derrick on the Navy boat and one by one we swung the hulking drums from the ship over to *Sorcery*.

We were destined for Horta, the capital of Isla de Faial, the most western island in the Azores about seventy miles away. The islands sit on top of rumbling tectonic plates and the volcanic peaks from the submerged mountain range, when measured from their base at the bottom of the ocean, are some of the highest in the world. Slipping the dock lines at midnight under a waxing moon and not a whisper of wind, we fired up the 65 horsepower Westerbeke and to the sound of pumping pistons headed out to sea, powering through the darkness on a sea as flat as a billiard table.

At dawn the first rays of sunlight touched Pico's and Faial's towering volcanoes and a morning breeze wafted the white smoking plumes out to the east. All of a sudden three boats under fluttering cotton gaffed rigged mainsails and high cut jibs appeared on the horizon, being rowed fast a mile or so ahead of a chugging steamer. Minutes later a huge and majestic sperm whale broke the surface beside *Sorcery*. A powerful whoosh of air cascaded out of his flaring blowhole and then he dived down into the depths and slapped an enormous and graceful tail fluke onto the water, leaving a swirling footprint behind him.

I have crossed tacks and seen many a whale over the years in many an ocean and recently perhaps the most memorable encounter was while sailing south down the east coast of Australia bound for Sydney. Somewhere off Noosa Heads we sailed into a pod of sixty or so stately Humpbacks and their newly born calves on their long migration back to Antarctic waters for the summer. It was a phenomenal sight, made all the more so when a whale whiter than snow leapt high into the air just off the bow of the boat. It was Migaloo, the pure albino young male and every inch a prince, who for some years now has been making the long trek north from the Antarctic to the mating and breeding grounds in the Pacific and back to the cold southern waters, an incredible journey of ten thousand miles or more. The indigenous peoples say a white whale portends much, for them such a being is sacred and greatly revered. To see him that day was an unforgettable sight as he careered with impossible agility into the blue to sing the haunting songs this species of the sovereign cetacean nation are so famous for. It is almost unthinkable these great animals are still being hunted.

In the eighteen hundreds whaling was a way of life in the Azores, as indeed it was in many parts of the world. Some of the meat would be eaten, but in commercial whaling for the most part the carcasses of these majestic beings are discarded and only their oil used for superficial purposes by those who view the whale merely as a disposable resource. In the Azores the Yankee whaling ships from New England arrived and recruited local fishermen who were attracted by the money and unfortunately we were about to witness a murderous bloodbath.

A 'canoa' is the name used for traditional whaling vessels. Eleven meters long, slender and lightweight timber carvel-constructed craft, they were capable of swift and silent speeds under sail, or muffled oars. Manned by seven men in each boat, the leading helmsman steered straight for the surfacing whale and the man on the bow took aim and fired his harpoon. The unforgiving weapon slammed into the whale just behind its blowhole and attached two thousand feet of line to the innocent and unsuspecting leviathan.

The following events we witnessed still burn in my mind. I'd read about the whaling days and Melville's Moby Dick when younger and seen the oil paintings depicting these scenes in Hobart's maritime museum. But nothing prepared me for the stark reality of what came next and the slaughtering of a gentle giant. The whalers set their sights and harpooned the whale in the shallow water separating the two islands, the lack of depth vastly impeding any chance the whale might have had to escape. The barbs on the shaft of the spear were firmly entrenched a meter or so behind his blow hole. These sentient animals die long and painful deaths and his whole life depended on not letting his attackers get any closer.

The wounded whale dived fast as the crew threw water over what was by now a smoking bollard which the line wrapped around. With the rope straining at near breaking point the vessel took off, towed at an incredible speed with the bow going down further and further as more and more line was paid out until the boat fell back two hundred meters behind the whale. The mighty animal surfaced again, the men hauled in the slack and pulled themselves a hundred meters closer to the poor beast. He dived again and this time kept going down until they nearly went with him. The terrible chase continued for a painfully long time, until finally the agonized whale tired and the three canoes drew close enough to thrust long, sharp-speared lances into his lungs and heart. Slowly the thrashing whale succumbed to his death and the sea ran red with blood.

The steel steamer attached the body of the dead baleia by the base of its tail and crawled along spewing out clouds of black smoke from its stacks and headed for the port of Horta before us. After a couple of hours motoring in the late afternoon we made our way through the basalt walls of the moles into the harbor. The trawler dragged the whale over to the whaling station, a scarred old stone building with an elongated ramp and greased railway tracks which sheared off into the water from a pebbled beach strewn with countless bleached white whale bones, scattered with ribs resembling scuttled ships and skulls that stood out like boulders alongside the jawbones stripped of their teeth. The workers swarmed like ants over the whale. The once streamline dancing fluke was attached to heavy duty cables and the loose end fed onto a large rotating spindled drum, driven by an archaic engine, grinding round with slow revolutions to drag it up the ramp to be butchered.

Two of the whalers at either end of a long-bowed, razor sharp saw severed the tail and made the fifteen foot flukes into a makeshift chopping board. Next the flensers moved in, bare footed, stripped to the waste, their blades cut between the neck and the fins. The sound of the droning motor started again and, using the block's hook, stripped off long lengths of blubber, chopping them into the size of foam beds, before carting them over to the huge cast-iron pots for rendering.

The thought of the scene was too much for Robin. She broke down and wept, vanishing like a wisp of wind off the boat and running up a hillside track to the clifftops. There she sat gazing out to sea, looking for solace to the distant volcanic peaks that rose up from the depths.

In stark contrast to the brutalities of the whaling station the town of Horta is surrounded by a mosaic of sweeping green hills, each pasture separated by winding borders of purple hydrangeas which cascade over dry stone stacked walls. It's been a welcome sight for many sailors over time. 'Horta' originally meant 'Land Ho' cried out by crews when they spotted land. The harbour wall is a seafaring art gallery covered in paintings. For years passing sailing artists have painted illustrations of their yachts on the sun-bleached stone, leaving record of their journey for all who would follow them.

And lo and behold the wonderful *Crusade* sat in dry dock, abandoned by her new owners and land-bound, a pale shadow of her former glory. I climbed the rickety ladder leaning against her side and found the cockpit full of algae-green water, paint blistering off her hull and a mess of corroded winches and halyards, so I spent a while cleaning up as best I could, fondly remembering the old warrior at her best. Fortunately, a few years later, Donald Parr bought the boat and carried out a complete overhaul, painting her dark green, converting the single-handed steering wheel to a double one and changing her name to *Quailo*.

Weather from the Atlantic held us prisoners while a wild westerly gale lashed the island. The October wind tore autumn leaves from the trees sending them tumbling and fluttering to the ground where they danced across the cobbled paths in flashes of burnt sienna and titian red laced with copper. Island-bound and waiting for the weather we took refuge in Peter's Café Sport. The bright blue two-storey stone building has taken a battering from the strong winds and over the years become a famous gathering place for seafaring vagabonds to tell yarns of brine-filled wanderings and gypsy argosy.

It could have been a scene from a lifetime three hundred years ago. The fire kept us warm spitting tortoise shell sparks from the once salt-soaked wood. The flames cast out dancing fingers of gold-licked shadows on the time-scarred timbers and calcimine plastered walls, while the ancient doors and windows shook and rattled with each shaking fist of the irate wind as it pounded the outside of the building and whistled and whirled down the empty streets. Above the mantelpiece and along the rough walls hung faded photographs of great sailing ships and steamers of yore, while lining the shelves glass cases kept carved bone ornaments, engraved with lamp oil black scrimshaw by sailors long gone. Over on a couple of shelves sat a collection of intricately crafted wooden models of square riggers and schooners, captured inside dust-laden green and blue bottles.

On our last night we set off for dinner in a local house and family run restaurant, entering under an impressive basalt and limestone portal. The old boy running the show was a tall, silver-headed aristocrat with an aquiline nose called Eduardo. He guided us to a hefty oak table surrounded by matching solid hand-carved chairs and we sat down to order a few carafes of the rugged local wine. Donald struck up a conversation with the soft-spoken fella and he told us that the furniture had once sat in the boardroom of a Porto wine merchant's establishment overlooking the banks of the River Duro. His grandfather-in-law had bought them and, when his daughter married in the old capital Angra do Heroismo in 1922, given them to her as a wedding present.

"The table was a hundred years old by the time my wife's grandfather bought it, which makes it older than the house and has been in this family for four generations. My wife's family is originally from Flanders and dates back to the fifteenth century when they had been in the service of Prince Henry the Navigator whose sister, the Duchess of Burgundy, recruited two thousand Flemish farmers, fishermen and merchants to settle in the Azores."

While he was talking his wife stooped over a hewed coal-burning oven in the kitchen stirring her pots and pans and the aroma of braised cock in a crock began to fill the house and before too long the table was laden with a feast served in traditional terracotta steep sided bowls. The old patron rattled on while we hoed into the meal,

"And this is my granddaughter," he said nodding towards the door as a long haired beauty emerged from the kitchen.

Complicated Bill looked up mesmerized at the sight of her svelte figure, and gulped back a spoon of burning hot soup, badly searing the roof of his mouth. Donald asked the old man if he had any of the local fado music born along the waterfront in alleys and taverns that the Portuguese seafarers used to sing of life and the sea. Eduardo dug out an old vinyl record and put it on the gramophone sitting on a small antique table in the corner. The rasping music filled the room with a haunting ballad.

"This is the story of a young woman singing of her lover, a fisherman lost at sea while sailing a schooner to Lisbon," Eduardo explained with a faraway look in his eyes.

Late into the evening we made our way down the winding streets back to *Sorcery*, the cold north wind cutting through our layers of clothes. You could almost hear the ghostly wails of phantom widows singing from the clifftops and calling to the sea spirits to return their husbands from their watery graves.

We left Horta in a roistering nor'wester. In no time the island's mountains faded from view and I pointed *Sorcery's* bow towards Bermuda, eighteen hundred miles away. At two in the morning on the graveyard watch we were steering straight into a twenty-five knot wind. A range of lofty cumulous clouds swallowed up the gibbous moon, but every now and then silver beams escaped and broke through the veil, casting wolf-grey and pewter shadows across the dark oyster-gilded water. Leaving his navigational charts Donald hopped up through the hatch and made his way across the cockpit and over to the stern. Shivering in only a T-shirt and a pair of shorts he clutched on to the backstay to take a leak and yelled out.

"Hey Chas, have you got a problem with the steering?"

"No, it seems alright," I called back.

"Well there's a line back here trying to cut my ankle off," he yelped.

"Hold on, there's a hell of a wave coming," I shouted over the howling wind.

We rose up over the face of roller and blasted down the other side, landing in a deep trough with a crashing thud. Billy gathered his wits and hollered down my ear.

"That must be the bloody fishing line he's got tied up in – maybe there's something on it. Christ, I hope it hasn't wrapped itself around the keel."

Donald clambered back into the cockpit squawking a tirade of insults.

"Son of a bitch, I'm fucking drenched, freezing cold and I've pissed all over my pants."

To add to his misery torrential rain began to spill out of the thickening cloud bank.

The line was a makeshift bit of paraphernalia we'd made to catch fish to eat on these longer journeys. The bulk of it consisted of fifty meters of braided white cord, similar to the stuff used on old fashioned washing lines, then a swiveling snatch block, which we used on the spinnaker sheets, and this hooked onto a shackle on the toerail. So there'd be some give if we got a strike we threaded bicycle tyre inner tubing onto the first fathom of line. Finally at the end of all this clobber was a swivel with twenty meters of monofilament to which another swivel and short wire trace connected the 'purple and pink peril', a garish colored squid shaped bait, resembling something a cat had

114

puked up. I feathered *Sorcery* up as high as she would go and spilled the wind out of the sails until we were almost stationery. Without speed creating such a drag the boys managed to put a couple of turns around the free winch and start pulling in the line. A burly wind shift sheared across the cloud's precipice and *Sorcery* fell into irons before she canted over with a lurch. The jib backed and we left it there, let the traveler down and hove to facing north. By this time the guys had pulled the fish almost two thirds of the way in when the Fat Rabbit pulled the hatch cover back and eased his head and shoulders out into the night air.

"What the hell's going on up here, have we busted something?" he thundered over the din.

"We've got a bloody big fish on the line," Billy yelled.

"Well hold your course for another five minutes while I put the kettle on. If it turns out you've caught some prehistoric kraken cut the fucker loose before it wants a cup of char,' he said and slamming the hatch shut pissed off back to the stove.

When the fish got closer to the surface the line started sweeping wildly back and forth and finally by the time it reached the transom Complicated Bill leaned over the side to take a look. Normally unflappable in the face of the worst screw up, he flinched and reared backwards.

"Bloody hell, it's a mammoth sized marlin" he cried falling back on top of me

The great fish's tail was still in the water, but its powerful spiked sword started beating against the backstay with an incredible force, coming perilously close to snapping off the single sideband radio whip antennae.

"Cut it loose for Christ's sake," I yelled.

Bill grabbed a nearby knife and slashed the line and the colossal fish disappeared into the depths of his watery domain in a flash.

The barometer began to fall, a wall of heavy sky loomed on the horizon to the southwest and within an hour a line of white horses some three miles away started charging towards *Sorcery* at a foaming gallop. With all hands on deck we stirred our stumps and hurriedly put two more reefs in the main and with only a couple of minutes to spare doused the headsail and set the number four just as the snarling wind gods reached us. The boat heeled over, her hull creamed through the surging swell and pointed towards Nova Scotia for about an hour until the wind veered to the West. We tacked over till the bow swung in the direction of the Caribbean in a hellishly churning ocean, which belted across the decks until you couldn't tell the difference between us and a bunch of bedraggled sodden sea-rats. The barometer edged up a little and a nor'wester swung in just before sunset and threw thirty-five knots of ball-chilling cold at us, but at least we were back on course and aiming straight at Bermuda.

I anxiously kept an eye on the forty-four gallon fuel drums in case they broke loose, but the Beach Ball back in the Azores had done a crack job and they remained as well secured as peas in a pod and much to our relief held firm while *Sorcery* crashed through the rough weather. The glass reached its peak and like the wind held steady until the following daybreak when we were hit by a secondary front and for another night endured a wicked battering. *Sorcery* burned through the shit like an Amazon and picked up speed, dauntless in her pursuit of warmer climes. Finally late the next day we spotted enough blue sky to make a Dutchman a fair-sized pair of breeches.

Just as we'd gnawed our way onto the back of the Azorean high a shifting wind headed us and knocked us off our course. The ever fickle weather condition finally blew itself out into an exhausted calm, so we fired up the iron genoa and droned away for the next couple of days at around twenty-three hundred RPM's. Gradually we reached the lower side of the high pressure system and found the prevailing easterlies, the satin-smooth sea rippled into life and we hoisted the big jib top and flew on down the line. Afoot again under the reacher and a full main *Sorcery* let rip and gave us forty-eight hours of sensational sailing.

The night skies began to hum with the sound of airplane engines and against the ebony sky you could see just how many there were, all pointed in the direction of the Azores. Little did we know that the Yom Kippur war had just broken out and the U.S airforce was busy with an airlift mission to Israel and landing at Lajes on Teceira to re-fuel C-5 Galaxy aircraft.

The sea is as seductive and unpredictable as any woman, you never know which way the dice are going to roll. Its capricious ways never gives one a chance to rest on your laurels, which is what makes it great in many ways. Just when you think you've got it made, guaranteed

116

something will happen and demand attention. Donald left his sprawling charts on the navigating table and came up on deck to shoot the stars armed with his sextant, only to be thwarted in his attempt, faced with a gunmetal grey sky and a shrouded Big Dipper, which left him with a snowball's chance in hell of taking any sights. I had an uneasy feeling something was brewing and watched the swells beginning to stir in the distance with a growing sense of apprehension. By twilight the heaving waves had doubled in size. The Fat Rabbit asked me what I thought was going on.

"A tropical storm, maybe somewhere off the Bahamas," I pondered.

"Well check out the pilot books and charts with Donald and see what you reckon," he suggested.

Around midnight a short wave radio frequency from Vail, Colorado issued a warning that a storm south of Cape Hatteras had curved around and was stalking northeastwards in our direction. I remember reading about a German tall ship which had sunk somewhere out here a decade before and the sole survivor, the ship's cook, by some lucky chance got fished out of the water by a passing freighter after a week of floating helplessly and alone in the tempestuous sea. For us, cat and mouse was the name of the game. The groans of roaring wind echoed and the rain beat down relentlessly, but thankfully the storm slowed its pace a couple of hundred miles away and the lucky break bought enough time for a high pressure system to develop and block what had looked like an inevitable onslaught when it tracked east nor'east and bust across our stern a day later. Picking up a magic twenty knot nor'easterly *Sorcery* eased unscathed into Hamilton in front of the Royal Bermuda Yacht Club within spitting distance of the pastel pink painted Princess Hotel.

Warren Brown was in town and working on his latest acquisition. He'd bought Ted Turner's twelve metre *American Eagle* and busied himself changing her color from ruby red to robin's egg blue and inscribing the new name *War Baby* on her good looking arse. Warren is probably Bermuda's best known yachtsman and he started his adventures at sea at a very young age. At just three months old he and his mother were travelling on the *Fort Victoria* from New York back to their home island when the ship was rammed on the high seas by the *Alonquin* on a cold December day in thick fog. The captain ordered all two hundred and sixty-nine passengers to abandon the sinking vessel, Warren was grabbed from his mother's arms and tossed over the side, lucky to be caught by a member of the crew in a lifeboat below.

He still has the original *War Baby*, a fine Bermuda dinghy designed by Sir Eldon Trimingham and launched during World War I. He's gone on to own many well known ocean racers of the same name since. People ask him why he does what he does.

"Because I like to go where people don't go, I'm an explorer. Our boat's covered a few miles up in the Arctic and the Antarctic, South America and the South Seas."

He won the Blue Water Medal in 1956 after a 20,000 mile voyage on a fifty-year-old Bristol Pilot cutter and in 1990 he and his crew were awarded the Arthur Hanson Rescue Medal for pulling off a courageous midnight rescue when a man went overboard in rough seas during the Newport to Bermuda Race.

We spent the night at Warren's house, a classic Bermudian stone mansion set on a rise overlooking the ocean. The famous old seadog went over the weather forecasts and encouraged us to haul anchor before a bone-chilling cold front carrying a shit load of wild weather bowled down the line.

"I'd make all speed if I were you boys and try and make it across the Gulf Stream before it strikes," he warned.

On Sunday morning we scurried out through Bermuda's surrounding reefs and by noon were New York bound, but the bitching blow beat us to it. Bang slap in the middle of the Gulf Stream one hell of a storm exploded and an arsenal of blinding lightening and rain broke loose. With zero visibility we were sailing blind. It felt as if we were careening down glaciers when *Sorcery* slalomed mountainous waves on a reach, which left little choice but to bear off. The fury lasted for two days and two nights. Down to two reefs and a Number Four headsail the boat was proving difficult to sail, not dissimilar to riding a unicycle on ice blindfolded. Every few seconds the sky lit up in an electrifying blaze and did strange things to our eyes, dazzling us with piercing white light for long seconds after each strike sheeted across the water. The booming thunder sounded as if Beethoven himself was busting out blood-stirring riffs in the heavens above. Billy and I were on the graveyard watch and I'd just handed him the wheel when a loud shot cracked the air and kept cracking worse than a stockman's whip.

"Shivering rattlesnakes, what the fuck is that?" I yelled.

The number four jib sheet had broken under the strain and a few shredded remnants were all that was left attached to the clue. The sheet had parted at the turning block next to the primary winch, somehow spun into a tight knot the size of a monkey's fist and slammed into the throat of the Lewmar snatch block, jamming the sheets. The sails flogged themselves into a death spin and the block had joined in and was trying to hammer a hole into the deck.

Billy and I didn't have to cry out for help, the noise was enough to wake the dead. The rest of the crew leaped out of their scratchers, bolted out through the hatch and into the chaos. The Fat Rabbit grabbed the wheel, but couldn't tack because the lazy sheet on the weather side had done a loop the loop and ended up with two bites the size of a hangman's noose. By this time the boiling seas were lifting off the top of the waves. The northwest veering gale raged at fifty knots while torrential rain hammered down and drove into our faces, making it impossible to see a fucking thing.

Someone had to get to the bow. My safety harness was saddled over my White Line Seven smock, and hanging off the four-foot leather dangled a mountaineering wish-lock safety clip. I snapped it onto the security of the long strop fixed to the pad-eyes at both ends of the boat and made a dash, half-scampering, half-sliding like an Arctic otter over the deck towards *Sorcery's* semi-submerged bow. The hangman's noose flayed back and forth over my head while the boat yawed her way downwind and the other sheet snapped at my heels. Grabbing the double-grooved headstay I held on. The leach line that runs down the trailing edge of the sail chose to shit itself at this moment and the sail instantly let go into a violent shaking spasm as simultaneously we slewed down the face of another monstrous motherfucking wave. The sail flogged its guts out, slashing to and fro across the foredeck, sweeping perilously close to my ducked head. A couple of inches further and it would have ripped my neck off my shoulders in one easy strike.

The jib filled for the last time with a resounding thud. Crouching in the cockpit Robin readied to lower it, but too late. The seam running across the guts of the sail ripped, the leach gave up the battle and tore all the way up.

Christ knows how we got it down, but somehow we managed, drag-

119

ging the destroyed dacron jib aft into the cockpit before jettisoning it through the hatch onto the galley floor below. Hauling the orange storm jib up was no easy task either. I scrabbled back along the deck, but the lazy sheet reared like a black viper and lashed into me and stove in two of my ribs. The searing pain felt as if I'd been scorched by a red-hot iron, but the mainsail had to come down and finally we secured it with the broken jib sheet and bent the storm trysail on. When all was done I crawled down the companionway for a heavy hit of rum and passed out while *Sorcery* pounded on through the shit and fury.

Once we kicked clear of the Gulf Stream the wind backed, the sea turned a dull green and grey and a freezing northerly was upon us. Bucking the tide and pushing on through the chill rain, *Sorcery* passed through Hell's Gate at the top of the East River and we tied up at Minneford's on City Island in the pitch dark after a bitching and arduous slog. Dog tired we hit the hay and fell into an exhausted sleep until woken early by a cacophony emitted from one the busiest alloy boat building yards in the States, the grating noise of high decibel saws and drills sounded as bad as my ribs felt. Customs and Immigration showed up and once 'welcome to America' papers had been obtained we set about stripping *Sorcery* out and lugging the weatherbeaten sails into storage.

My odyssey on *Sorcery* had run its course. The time had come for the Fall Series in Chesapeake Bay, Annapolis. I jumped on board *Yankee Girl*, an S&S 56 footer and renowned American racing yacht, and started the migration south, which in several months time would take me to Fort Lauderdale. Unknown to me this would lead to calamitous circumstances.

4

Red Herrings and Celtic Calamities

Harken, thou craggy ocean pyramid!
Give answer thy voice, the sea fowls' screams!
When were thy shoulders mantled in huge streams?

John Keats 'To Ailsa Rock'

IT TOOK A WHILE TO GET TO SCOTLAND, and the adventures that unfurled before I got there were not exactly plain sailing; they led to a calamitous episode in the old Celtic country. But first things first.

Late in the year of 1973, a slick green-hulled 48' Cuthbertson and Cassian, a C & C, arrived on the back of an eighteen-wheeler Mack truck at Bob Derecktor's boatyard – or Bob Destructor's as it used to be called in Fort Lauderdale, otherwise known as Liquordale. The truck's thumping diesel engine gave a final roar when the lorry driver shut down the rig and a towering fifty-ton travel lift rolled over to hoist the yacht off the flatbed and place her on a hard stand. Custom built by Bruckmann's yard in Ontario, Canada, new and straight out of the mould, the boat still reeked of the resin used in her balsa core fibreglass construction. Peering up at her under-body, I felt a tap on my shoulder and turned around to find my old shipmate Tom Curnow, a robust nugget from Michigan. Tom was the Captain for the boat's owner, Dr 'The Doc' Keith Wold, an eye surgeon who'd married into the Johnson and Johnson dynasty. I'd sailed with the Doc before on his previous *Miss Elaineous*, a Charlie Morgan 42, in the Isla Mujeres race down near the Yucatan peninsula and got along fine with him.

"Good to see you Chas, what do you think of the Doc's new *Miss Elaineous*?" Tom asked in his gruff motor city voice.

"Let's hope it's not a dog," I quipped, not knowing at the time that's exactly what she'd turn out to be.

Nevertheless, at this point Tom was highly optimistic about her. Small boats had done well in the last SORC and the buzz from both sides of the Atlantic was all about the new Dick Carter and Doug Peterson One-Tonners that had just been launched.

Tom knew I had sailed thousands of miles both racing and delivering an assortment of C & C's and wanted me to go with him on the upcoming SORC. I'd just sailed over from England on *Sorcery*, the C & C 61' with which we'd finished first in the Fastnet Race, and I was at a loose end and low in the freight department. It didn't take him long to twist my arm, so I took a punt and tossed my hat into the ring.

Miss Elaineous differed somewhat from other C & C's and Derecktor's had been contracted to fit out her interior and build a mast taller than the original specifications, and play around with the ballast in her keel. It was a time of rapid development in hulls, rigs and sails, the new breed of One-Tonners from the design boards of Ted Hood and Dick Carter, along with Doug Peterson, the new kid on the scene, were skilfully able to work the International Offshore Rules (I.O.R.) to their advantage, advancing a transformation that would have a major impact over the next decade.

On *Miss Elaineous*, however, we had a miserable time, and it didn't take long to realize the Doc had been flogged a turkey. Our crew work was okay and the Doc's navigation pretty much spot on, but no matter how well we sailed or how much rag we flew, the slow, heavy boat's lack of speed screwed us every time, on top of which we'd been saddled with a ludicrous rating that placed the boat at the top of Class C. The PJ 44's in our class sailed rings round us, and worse still, in light airs a 39' Ted Hood Canada's cupper *Dynamite* left us trailing when she streaked ahead and disappeared over the horizon. The long offshore race from St. Pete to Lauderdale ended in utter humiliation and we were thrashed by the rest of the class. The pair of Peterson *Ganbare* clones, *Magic Twanger* and *Country Woman* crewed by the Barton brothers and their family band must have thought it was Thanksgiving Day when they finished a mere couple of feather spans behind us.

By the time we hit the docks the crew were at odds. The regular crew and the 'strap hangers' who flew in each weekend had quite different ideas of how to make the boat sail fast. At his wit's end the Doc finally axed the 'straps', which meant we lost most of the afterguard, and told Tom to find some replacements. Amongst the new recruits were Kiwi Phil Holland and Gustav, a long-haired Swede, who'd recently been hooked up with Paul Elvstrom's 12 meter campaign. And for the Lipton Cup the Doc also brought along his nephew Woody and Mark, a young bloke from Palm Beach, whose father owned Soverel Marine. At the time I didn't know Soverel from a bar of soap, but it soon became apparent the tall, brash, dynamic guy was a shit-hot sailor.

Pumped up to the gills the Doc took the helm for the start and worked the wheel in a lather of white knuckle tension, before handing things over to Mark. On the short course from Miami to just north of Fort Lauderdale and back Gustav played the main like a man possessed. Hillary, the flame-headed Burnham-on-Crouch bowman was on fire and Phil Holland had his hands full pulling strings and calling trim, while Woody ground his guts out on the winches. It didn't make any difference. Once again we were hammered by the opposition.

"What do you think we can do to make the boat go faster?" the Doc pressed Mark while we motored back to the marina with our tail between our legs.

Mark thought about it for a moment and then dropped a bombshell.

"Compared to the new designs she's already out-dated, perhaps you could convert her into a comfortable cruiser. I'm putting together something slightly heavier than a One-Tonner and I reckon it'll be pretty competitive, maybe you'd like that," he suggested.

"Not really," the Doc replied, "I'm not interested in getting cold and wet in one of those soap-boxes."

As it turned out Mark wasn't bullshitting. His first I.O.R. design, the 36' Moody Blue, similar to a Peterson, but slightly more powerful and stiffer, finished tenth in fleet during the series the following year.

Over in Nassau the following week at the awards night, Appleton's Rum came out with a new liqueur and sponsored an inaugural race to promote it. Because of the distance none of the One-Tonners entered the competition, so the Doc figured we stood a better chance of getting amongst the silverware if we signed up. We'd been using the Loran A navigation equipment, which doesn't cover more than two hundred miles out to sea. The Doc, however, remained unperturbed as he'd just installed an Omega set in which he had considerable faith, and was itching to give it a go. Although the US navy had been operating Omega for some time it had only recently become available for civil use.

The system was a global chain of long-range radio stations that transmitted low frequency signals to the timing of an atomic clock that could be picked up by a ship's receiver. At the start of a voyage it was essential to enter location co-ordinates into the set's memory and from there on it began tracking position, which we then measured on special Omega charts. Unfortunately it could not upgrade itself, so it was imperative for the navigator to keep up with his dead reckoning. Chances of errors inevitably increased over time and distance, particularly by lack of power to the receiver and changes in propagation near local sunrise and sunset. Fortunately Phil Holland had recruited Billy Sanderson as a downwind helmsman, who he'd sailed with on *New World* in the Transpac, and he could help me with celestial navigation if the Omega bombed out.

Apart from the start, and the beat out through the 'Hole in the Wall' above Eleuthera, we'd been close-hauled under a number two genoa in a steady twenty-five knot easterly wind. Fuelled with gallons of coffee the Doc remained firmly glued to the nav station playing with his new toy. Halfway through the race on the third day we passed ten miles to the west of Great Inagua and its radio beacon confirmed our position, enabling us to sail a freer course and change to a jib top and staysail. As we headed towards the Windward Passage that separates

Cuba from Haiti, our path converged with a 44' ketch *Jemel*, designed by Britain Chance and built by Tom Dreyfus in New Orleans. It was a radical machine with a swing keel and a mizzen mast with retractable spreaders. The mizzen was damn near as tall as the mast and the two were linked together at the top by a triadic tubular stay. *Jemel* had a dubious track record, although on a reach she went like a shower of shit.

By late in the day *Jemel* had pulled away several miles ahead of us. By the time we were abeam of Cabo Maisi, Cuba's most easterly point, we were flying a flat flanker, chocked down and reasonably under control. The duel of the dogs changed somewhat and we chased *Jemel* down. We both set spinnakers for the long sleigh-ride to Jamaica, but *Jemel* got into a heap of trouble with a couple of spectacular wipe-outs. It was a hair-raising sight. Her helmsman steered from a centre cockpit, the boom was so low it skimmed over the waves and the boat skidded into a series of killer death rolls. Dusk soon swallowed us up and we never saw them again, but later heard they'd Chinese gibed and were dismasted not far from Guantanamo Bay, where they got assistance from the US naval base.

During the night we gibed over to port and the following morning briefly caught sight of Haiti's mountains away to the east before a thick haze blanketed visibility. The batteries needed a boost and Tom fired up the motor for about ten minutes.

"We've got a fuel injection pump problem," he announced, "but I should be able to fix it."

The Doc finally emerged from down below looking like he'd been on a three-day bender and wearing a three-day shadow cast over his pale face.

"We're thirty miles west of Haiti, near Navassa Island," he claimed.

'Hmm, I'm not so sure," muttered Billy.

He pulled out his trusty sextant and took some sights and came up with findings quite different to the Doc's erratic caffeine-fuelled plots on the Omega chart. The Doc remained defiant, convinced his newly-installed navigation system was the electronic equivalent of Einstein and refused to entertain the idea its calculations were anything less than bang on accurate.

"Your results could easily be wrong, Billy, the land might be creating a false horizon," he insisted.

"I don't think so, Doc," Billy retorted, but his protests fell on deaf ears.

The debate was cut short by a thunderstorm and a change of wind direction, so we gibed onto a faster course in what we figured was the general direction of Jamaica. Tom sorted out the engine so the batteries could be re-charged, but the Omega had surely suffered further ambiguity while they'd been out of action.

Around midnight we sighted the loom of the land and the Doc plotted a course for what should have been Kingston. At dawn we found ourselves at the mouth of a bay where the hills ran down to a ramshackle fishing village surrounded by a clump of tattered coconut trees and the sound of a cock crowing echoing over the water.

"This doesn't look like fucking Kingston," Phil muttered in mutinous tones.

The Doc scoured the desolate scene and remained uncharacteristically quiet.

"Well, that's screwed any chances of getting over the finish line in the money," I muttered.

And indeed it had. In the light air it took most of the morning to cover the last miles to the end of the race. The Jamaican capital had been under siege from recent rioting, it wasn't the most stable of places at the time. The Royal Yacht club was safe as a church, but outside of that we needed a couple of big wagons armed with security guards to escort us back and forth from the hotel.

After the presentation party we took off to the Holiday Inn for a hell of a night, an evening that rapidly disintegrated into a Red Stripe beer, rum and strong Jamaican ganga-fuelled frenzy. We partied on in one of the few spots not affected by the currently imposed curfew and a local band boomed out reggae and calypso, and by midnight the place was honking and crawling with golden-skinned women. On one of the many nearby tables close to the action sat *Sorcery's* victorious crew, amongst them three colourful Californians, the goatee'd owner Jake Wood, his plump flush-cheeked captain Bob Dixon, and devious deckie Phil Strauss, who often travelled under the alias of Dr. Bernard Swartz.

A game of limbo got under way, people dancing with their upper torsos arched back underneath a fire hose, until Strauss, an L.A county fireman in real life, pissed to the eyeballs, slunk behind the crowd and cranked up the fire cock full tilt. Furniture, a bunch of models from a fashion show and most of the boat crews ended up in the pool, and drunken sailors took to the hotel corridors, wrenched more of the fire hoses off their hooks, which coiled up like King Cobras, then unleashed, they sprayed out hundreds of gallons of water until the place was flooded. And all the while the band played, in true Titanic spirit, as the hotel drowned.

The next morning the Doc appeared and surveyed the wreckage.

"Pack your bags," he grimaced, black as thunder. "The boat's leaving in half an hour."

He sure was anxious to hightail it out of town. It may have been the bill for the damages, or perhaps the fact that Kingston was a pretty dangerous place at the time, but either way the decision put a spanner in the works and scuppered a plan to sail up to Montego Bay for some r & r, or indeed to stop off in the Caymans before heading back to the States.

The trip over was a sombre affair. Downhearted the boat hadn't lived up to expectations, we were relieved to step ashore. In the aftermath the Doc put *Miss Elaineous* into mothballs for a spell before donating her to the U.S naval academy in Annapolis, Maryland, where she was employed as a training vessel for the next eight years. Only recently, under another name, she came up for sale in the Virgin Islands for fifty grand. The ad read: 'would make a wonderful cruising boat to sail around the world'. It occurred to me that Mark Soverel had been right in his predictions after all.

Mark went on to design some very quick boats. Twice he finished second in fleet in the SORC with two fractionally rigged Locuras and represented America in the Admiral's Cup in England. The Doc as far as I know never raced again, but became heavily involved with horse-racing and breeding in Florida, before passing away at the ripe old age of eighty. Billy Sanderson became a hugely successful yacht broker, selling mega boats for Camper and Nicholson. And as for that young bloke Woody, the Doc's nephew that ground his guts out on the winches while I trimmed that day, he ended up buying the New York Jets for six hundred and fifty million dollars some years later.

With *Miss Elaineous* out of the picture Phil Holland suggested the remnants of the crew go with him on *Williwaw*, an Ericson 46', and race up to Charleston. We tore down the Gulf Stream's highway, the wind blowing hard in a big seaway as the boat flexed and groaned with each wave she climbed. We charged on down the faces of the following seas and sailed the sky-blue sloop on into the dusk till darkness finally engulfed her.

"We're getting three-and-a-half knots assistance from the Gulf Stream and hauling arse," Billy called out from the creaking, yawling cabin.

By now we'd hoisted a blooper – a stabilising sail which helps stop the boat rolling around so much when the spinnaker is up. This one was a multi-coloured affair we used to call 'The Polack Sausage', or at least it was until we went rushing down a wave and it scooped up a ton of water and burst into a thousand pieces which scattered like confetti over the horizon. Moving fast and without our blooper *Williwaw* began to live up to her alter ego, *Heehaw*, and behaved like a jackass, swaggering and lurching from gunwale to gunwale in the tumbling seas.

Don Pritchard, an African American who hailed from 'Frisco way, had sailed with the likes of infamous West Coast Sailors George Kisscaden and Skip Allen. Clad in bright orange surfing jams with a pea-green T-shirt that had 'New World' in big, gold writing across his back, his hands were full in the wild weather as the boat strained at her leash. His long, lean frame leaned into the wind while he stroked the spokes of the wheel back and forth, weaving us down unseen corridors between the breaking seas like a blind man using a cane with just his senses and intuition.

We were in a world of our own with a low canopy of thunderous cloud weighing down on us, and in the depths of the night it was so dark our helmsman disappeared completely but for lightning flashes that illuminated him into a ghostly silhouetted phantom, made all the more eerie as the glowing amber of the compass lit up his ivory teeth and the rolling whites of his eyes. Out behind us, like whirling embers from a campside fire, a great fluorescent rooster tail trailed in our wake and glittering bolts of light escaped into the night resembling shooting stars. It was all hands on deck, great gusts of wind had us grabbing at sheets and winch handles, and with the shredded stabilizing blooper out of commission the big shouldered 'chute oscillated frantically and had to be choked down to humour the rock and roll. We peeled to a smaller 'chute, and to Phil's utter dismay the big kite blew out and ripped to ribbons in the sail change.

Phil whipped and drove the beast and we scudded on through the storm serenaded by the Beach Boys hollering out 'Surf City' on the stereo. Hard at work, we tuned the orchestra of strings that composed and shaped the main and headsail during the last forty miles of the journey, until the yacht slid out of the Gulf Stream under a rime-cold dawn sky. In the early light, just to windward of us, came the lovely old warhorse *Weatherly*, successful defender of the America's Cup who had defeated the Australian challenger *Gretel*. Soaked to the bone, her long sleek 12 meter hull sliced through the shivering green water and a bedraggled wet crew hung out over the side to help keep her upright. The yacht had been wounded on the trip and was flying too big a jib, with three reefs in the main and a broken leech line caused the trailing edge of the sail to flail and crack like the sound of breaking ice echoing across the wind.

With the inhospitable front upon us we hardened up into a close reach and crossed the finishing line, and a brisk New England breeze blew us up the river to Charleston. Spring was coming in the Carolina's, and thoughts of southern beauties played on our minds until all thoughts of Scarlet O'Hara were abruptly cut short when Billy got his ankle caught in the life-boat trip lines and the raft inflated in seconds, exploding into action like a hot air balloon. The hapless man went down, a flailing octopus of arms and legs until he was jammed fast against the steering wheel. Phil Holland looked on aghast and murmured in his Kiwi drawl,

"Bloody navigators – never let them loose in the cockpit."

Along with all the shredded sails and a destroyed spinnaker pole, this final destruction ruined any chances he had of profiteering on this trip, so to cheer him up we crewed the boat for free up to New York where I parted company with *Williwaw* and hitched a ride on a rattling old train, bound for Connecticut and the little town of Essex, to re-commission some boats which had been stored safely out of winter wind's harm during the cold months.

The next time I heard from Phil was on a long-distance, crackling telephone call and he was sounding a lot more cheerful.

"Chas, I'm working on a boat called *Billy Can*. She has a sister ship that needs putting together, can you come over?"

"Ok Mate, where are you?" I asked.

"Scotland," he replied and hung up.

A few days later Phil's boss, Bill Mackay, picked me up at Glasgow airport. In his mid-thirties, a short, balding bloke with a dry sense of humour, he arrived in a beat-up maroon Ford Escort Mexico rally car and drove like the bloody clappers.

"I used to race motor cars before I fooked oop my arm in an accident at Le Mans," he explained in a solid Scottish accent and waving his free forearm, which resembled a corkscrew, to emphasize the point. "That's how I got into half-ton yacht racing – I can use my good arm to steer with a tiller ok. My boat *Billy Can* is almost ready, but *Off We Go* is still in Ireland – there've been a few hiccups."

I hung on to the edge of my seat as he belted down the road and hoped he wasn't about to crash into another car and either kill me or fuck up his other arm.

He screeched to a halt at the Kingston boat works and I clambered out of the car feeling like I'd just taken part in a Grand Prix and surveyed the scene.

"Shit, this place has seen better days," I mumbled.

"Och aye, there's noo denying that," Bill replied cheerfully.

Situated amongst decaying warehouses, derelict wharfs and dark dead water it looked bleak as hell. For Bill, however, besieged by money and women woes, he found refuge in a tin-roofed work shed that had half its wire-netted window panes stoved in by brick-throwing hooligans and which was for him, strangely enough, a paradise. The rent was cheap as chips, and in the office he'd made out of a converted shipping container, the eau de cologne never stopped ringing.

Pulling my jacket up around my neck in an attempt to stave off the cold northern winds howling through the broken windows, I began to wonder what Bill had meant when he'd said there'd been a problem with *Off We Go*.

"So what's the story with the boat, mate?"

"Aye, well like I said, there's been a wee delay and she'll be arrivin' late."

"Why's that?" I asked tentatively.

"Och, well you know there's trouble wi' the IRA in Ireland now, there's been a lot of violence. *Off We Go* is bein' built by some furniture-makers..."

"Furniture-makers!" I exclaimed, cutting him off mid-sentence.

"Aye, y' know, cabinet-makers."

"Jesus," I stuttered," I've never heard of furniture-makers building a boat before!"

"They're doon sooth," he breezed on. "An' the truck driver has to go through Belfast to get there. The fella was a bit nervous about being shot by the IRA on the way, so he needed a bit of persuadin' to do the trip."

I looked around for the nearest chair, and finding an old crate to sit down on I lit a cigarette, wondering what the bloody hell I'd got myself into.

"So where is he now?"

"Well, he said he'd only go if he could paint the lorry in Scottish colours and put two big red lions on both the doors so the IRA wouldna mistake him for being English."

"No one would mistake him for a Pom in that rig," I interjected, relighting my cigarette and thinking a beer might be good right about now. "Did he make it?"

"Aye, the decoy worked and we heard he'd arrived safe and sound in Cork, but there's been another wee problem wi' the boat yard and it could take a few days to sort things out."

The wind was spilling out of my sails by the minute and I was running out of cigarettes.

"You're stayin' over in the West End of Glasgow, Chas, we'll let you know when the boat arrives," he said picking up the phone, and left me to it.

"Let's hope the boat arrives before I freeze to death," I sighed and set off to find my digs.

Long before the subway was modernised the trains were pretty rough; painted in a hideous marmalade colour they used to travel round in one big circle and so came to be known as 'The Clockwork Orange'. For the locals the system provided a handy travelling watering hole. The world soccer cup was coming on, and over the ensuing weeks I'd often see the old footy jocks carefully tending to paper bags stuffed with booze, while they sat on the trains going round and round the track, shoogled with whisky and listening to the football matches on rasping transistor radios. Undisturbed in their pursuit they'd avoid being thrown out of the pubs come ten o'clock closing time. I ended up using the antiquated transport system quite a bit and nearly froze my arse off walking to and from the station on icy Jack Frost mornings, largely because you could never call for a bloody left jab as most of the telephones had been ripped out of the old red boxes.

Finally the truck carrying *Off We Go* arrived from Ireland and Bill rushed over to take a look at her.

"By Christ, she's fukken ruff!" he proclaimed. "What the fukken hell am ah gonna tell her owner?"

He didn't have too long to think about it. *Off We Go's* owner Barry Filer drove in a few minutes later in a Citroen that resembled a large Praying Mantis. Barry was shaped like a tall, gangly Scottish stoat, spoke faster than a bookie and was as cunning as a Coyote. He'd had a chequered career which involved researching a grass seed in Africa hardy enough to survive conditions in Scotland. It was the first grass to grow in the bloody awful Glasgow climate in fifty years. That stuff took off like a forest to about four or five feet high. It was so tough it was impossible to mow the shit, so he invented blades as sharp as shark's teeth to cut through it. He made a fortune out of both those endeavours, enough to get into racing cars, although he was a terrible driver and came in last every time. He got laid out with the Spanish flu for a couple of weeks and sent his diminutive Scottish mechanic out to race in his place. The little guy won hands down and his name was Jackie Stewart, later to become the great Formula One world champion. Barry's latest dream was to build a yacht swift enough to win for Scotland. It was an optimistic ambition – there was no such thing as a Scottish yacht racing team and it was unlikely there ever would be.

While Barry climbed out of his car, I took a stroll around his boat. It was blindingly apparent *Off We Go* was nowhere ready to go. Looking over the shambles it occurred to me that the Irish cabinet-makers should have stuck to making furniture. She was still bare wood without any bloody paint, there wasn't even a hole in the deck for the mast, and the rudder lay abandoned and unfitted on the floorboards.

"Shit, this is a holocaust," I muttered to myself.

Meanwhile Bill had been trying to stall Barry.

"Oh Barry, aboot the..."

But Barry wasn't listening and began striding over to his prize in excited anticipation. When he reached the boat he froze to the spot in horror. It took him a couple of minutes to take in the catastrophic state of affairs, and then suddenly, as if struck by a lightning bolt, he collapsed on the ground, shaking like a King Rattler. He point blank refused any help and nearly unhinged completely at the thought of an ambulance being called to his rescue, so we hoisted him into his car, and with the crack of doom upon him he wove precariously down the road in a traumatised state like a madman. The next day his wife called to say he was in Glasgow Hospital and intensive care, still distraught at the chaos his boat was in.

He managed to pull himself together, well relatively anyway, drafted some plans and relayed them to me from the hospital telephone while out of his mind on drugs the doctors had given him in an attempt to calm him down.

"I've decided to paint the hull canary yellow and the decks jet black," he slurred.

Three sheets to the wind, he reasoned that this would make it easier to see the miles of rope at night, which was a ludicrous notion – all the halyards were red, green and blue and against a dark-coloured deck would be barely visible. The winches were black as well, so there'd be no chance of seeing those bloody things either. The only thing decks that colour could possibly be good for would be to warm your arse in the rare moments the sun shone in that part of the world.

"The other thing I want you to do," he added, "is to buy a fire axe."

"What the fuck do we need that for?" I asked, thinking the doctor really needed to re-evaluate the pills they'd prescribed.

"To chop the sheets and wires loose at night when there's a foul up. You'd better have that on board the boat."

God knows what he was on, he was so stoned.

I hopped into the cab beside the truck driver to take *Off We Go* half way down the River Clyde to McGruers Boat Yard to try and salvage the situation and do some work on her; not without further mishap. The driver ploughed straight through some low-strung power lines, which thudded down on the boat with an almighty crash, but as I was later to find out, this would be just the beginning of what the disaster-prone driver was capable of. How he'd managed to bring the boat back from Ireland without completely destroying the truck or the boat is an absolute mystery.

It took a week to paint the yacht, or a Scottish week, which is at least two weeks, so I took off to Glasgow with some free time on my hands and met a character who undoubtedly rivalled Barry Filer in eccentricity. Ronnie Mackay came rolling into the boat yard, a big, burly bald-headed man with fists the size of coconuts. His normal attire more often than not consisted of a well-worn leather jacket over his colourful tartan shirts, faded baggy jeans and short, shiny cow-hide riding-boots. He ran a business supplying massive metal pipes from Aberdeen to the oil fields out in the North Sea – Ronnie was Scotland's version of a Texan oilman.

He also had a passion for sailing and had come by the boat yard to ferret around and reel off a yarn or two, and after we'd shot the shit for a while he asked me over for dinner. We got into his shiny new blue BMW and set off towards the family homestead. About halfway there he decided he needed a beer and pulled up to the Doublet Tavern, his favourite watering hole. It turned out to be a lively gathering place and I spotted a lissom lass, a model who came from the Orkneys and the little town of St. Mary's overlooking Scapa Flow, who found modelling a lot more lucrative than studying at university. I launched into some stories of the time I had spent in the Inner Hebrides on the Isle of Muck and we got on like a crofter's hut on fire, ending up in a passionate debate on the merits of the two finest potatoes in the world, both from Scotland: Orkney Blues and Golden Wonders. Scotland scored a big goal in the football and the place went ballistic. Ronnie by this time had shifted up a gear from the beer and was near legless on strong black Scottish rum and way beyond standing, let alone driving home to his by now furious wife. Providence was on my side and Maggie May took me back to her eyrie and looked after me, happily not for the last time, like a laird.

Ronnie caused havoc in the pub, which resulted in him being barred from the Doublet Tavern forever, and I found myself taking pity on his plight when he called me the next day, remorseful of his shenanigans the night before. I decided to take his mind off his current kettle of fish and go sailing with him.

The following Friday evening he drove me down to a waterside pub in Rothesay, where his reputation was still intact, and a fleet of small yachts lay at anchor in the harbour waiting for the start of the race. We dived into a dinner of spit-head pheasant and some of the famous golden wonder potatoes covered in dollops of cream sauce, and washed it down with pints of McEwan's Pale Ale and Old Grouse whisky chasers. Alongside us sat a couple of wide-eyed, excited young crew, Vic and Mick. Ronnie's oldest son Vic was a tall, polite and likeable young chap, and his best mate Mick 'Ginger' Foster was a mischievous freckle-faced redhead. Both of them were keen as mustard, although they'd been almost press-ganged into recruitment. In those days crew were often hard to come by, so the skipper owners had to make sure they had a back-up supply of young guns to pull out of their hat. Sons, daughters and apprentices were usually the first in the line of fire. The kids got gated, or their pocket money was stopped until they stepped aboard ready to crew; the apprentices either drew straws or were put on a roster. If they didn't show up they got sacked from their main job, it was as simple as that.

After the sun had sunk down over the rolling green hills of the Western Clyde, a lilac heather haze slowly dimmed as twilight stalked the oncoming night and the pub bell for last drinks started clanging near on ten o'clock, heralding closing time. The race was about to begin. A hurricane of chaos ensued in the pub. Yachties frantically rushed to the door in a fast flowing ebb tide on their way to the boats, while plenty of desperate drinkers scurried to the bar for final 'silver links', and everyone was caught in irons, like wind against tide, as sailors ran in one direction and land-lubbers in the other. The mass exodus of yachtsmen ended at the harbour wall where dour old Scottish coxswains waited on the ramp to ferry us out to our various vessels in the local launches. We tumbled in over the bulwarks, and a few minutes later scrambled up over the life-lines onto Ronnie's pride and glory, *Fionna*, a Peter Norlin-designed 34' sloop. With only minutes to hoist the sails and cast off we barely made the start. The starting cannon fired up and boomed across the night and the fleet was under way, cracked off on the outgoing tide.

It was time to set a course and I groped around in the dark below decks with a small torch looking for the navigational charts.

"Where the hell are the charts?" I called to Ronnie on the tiller.

There was a deathly silence above, broken by a few whispers, followed by a further hush. After a long lapse young Vic poked his head down the hatch and in his broad Glaswegian accent announced,

"I'm sorry, Chas, Dad's forgotten them – they're still in the boot of the BMW."

I was aghast.

"Shit, I've never sailed in the Clyde before. That means I've only got the compass and a depth-sounder to navigate with."

It suddenly dawned on me that not all was lost. Staring me in the face was my salvation. I was mopping the sweat from my brow with a napkin, one of a stack I had grabbed from a table on the way out of the pub in case there wasn't any shit paper on the boat. Lo and behold, I saw the napkin was decorated with a map of the Clyde. I pounced on an exercise book lying nearby and hastily enlarged the sketch until I had a five-fold larger replica. Then at five-minute intervals I got the boys to report any hazards lurking on the horizon; and where the bloody hell was Ailsa Craig, the rock that was the first mark on the course.

Taking over on the helm, I asked the skipper to mark out in red crayon where we were supposed to be going, because I sure as hell didn't have a clue.

"How far is it from Rothesay to Glasgow, Ronnie?" I asked.

He knew more or less, and with this I could construct a rough scale down to a mile on the makeshift chart. It was crude but better than nothing. It was 'don't go where danger lurks and keep an eye on the depth sounder'. There was no follow-my-leader to help us either; god knows how, but we were leading the fleet of water-rat jocks.

The coast was clear as a bell as we sailed through the night under a moon bright enough for Artemis herself to hunt by and a sky littered with distant stars. Scotland's latitude lies in the mid 50s, where dawn comes early, and rising out of the sea mist of a new day stood the hoary Ailsa Craig. We were high of the craggy rock and hoisted Ronnie's prized spinnaker, a brand new Bruce Banks star-cut, and reached down towards the mark. The orange bag the sail had come out of had not been attached to the deck, going unnoticed as it slipped overboard. For some reason Ronnie looked over his shoulder and spotted what was by now a tangerine-coloured speck in the distance astern. It didn't take him long to put two and two together and he roared like a bull at the lads. The bag had cost him twenty quid. If this stirred him up, he would howl like a hyena with what was to come.

Rounding the Isle of Arran in the afternoon a fresh breeze got up, and reaching and running we made our way along the coast. Nearing the finish the wind started to strengthen, funnelling through a narrow cutting in the foreshore on our starboard side, and dark bullets of wind hurtled around us in wildly wavering gusts.

"Can you see the big breakwater wall up beyond the finishing line, Ronnie?" I called out.

"Aye, we'll be in the pub shortly," he sang back quite happily.

All of a sudden pandemonium broke loose. A crazed blast of wind headed us, and the spinnaker went into a frenzy, collapsed, then twisted around and around the top of the mast until all the halyards deadlocked. We were up shit creek without a paddle. We couldn't get the kite down and we couldn't get the headsail up. By this time we'd crossed the line and were headed straight for the breakwater wall and imminent disaster.

"What the fuck do you want me to do?" Ronnie yelped.

I'd never been involved in such a calamitous catastrophe before, and touch wood I never will be again.

"Fire up the engine and let the pole forward!" I whooped, and jumped back to take the tiller.

By now only fifty meters of swirling water separated us from the bloody great wall of stone – I swung the boat head to wind. The precious star-cut had turned itself inside out and swept back on us like a big blanket, sprawling against the mast, rigging and two sets of spreaders. We had the throttle at full steam ahead, but the sail was in rebellion and prevented any movement forward as we fell further backwards clutching at straws in the face of doom.

In a moment of desperation I decided there was only one way out of sure disaster.

"Grab the bloody flare gun and we'll burn the bastard down!"

Back then most yachts carried flare guns, and Ronnie had a Varig on board, which has a chamber the same size as a single barrel shotgun. The flare's cartridges resemble those of a Winchester or Remington. To load it you breach, slide the cartridge in, snap it shut, cock the hammer and pull the trigger.

"Fire it at the fucking sail!" I yelled.

Ronnie got the drift and raised the relic of a shooting iron, aimed and let loose the shrapnel in the first of three volleys straight at his much prized sail. It took him a few seconds to reload, but we ended up with three scorched, burning holes in the spinnaker.

In Scotland the local sailors often get hold of sheep-shearing clippers and cut them into two separate blades. Then a big piece of fire hose is pushed over the stock for a handle to make a sharp and lethal weapon.

A winning bolt from the blue struck when we found one tucked away in the cockpit.

"Lash the sheep shearing blade to the boat hook!" I called to the boys.

The distance between us and the wall was diminishing by the second, and we were down to twenty meters. Victor stood on the bow with Ginger on his shoulders, trying to dodge being burned by the smoking sail; and tenacious as a fox terrier he hacked and slashed at the spinnaker, brandishing the cutlass like young Jim Hawkins in Long John Silver's adventures. Before long the sail was in tatters, streaming out from the mast and ripped to ribbons, but just in time *Fiona* started making headway, managing slowly to crawl away from likely shipwreck, and we limped across the harbour to the relative safety of a mooring.

Near on dark, we staggered onto a launch and headed for dry land. Ronnie's wife was waiting for him, and with tears in his eyes he told her of his beloved *Fiona's* misfortune. He retold the story over and over on the journey home until his lovely wife could no more bear the thought of further expenses being wasted on disasters incurred on her husband's boat as her aspirations for a new car dwindled by the moment. Utterly infuriated, she pushed a Janis Joplin tape into the stereo and hit the play button.

'Oh Lord, won't you buy me a Mercedes Benz, My friends all have Porsches, I must make amends' warbled out into the night.

A couple of days later I was up on the deck of *Off We Go* fitting some winches, and a more jovial Ronnie appeared whistling 'Fly Me to the Moon'. He asked if I would like to go sailing again the coming Wednesday night. As far as I was concerned once was enough.

"I'm sorry, Ronnie, I'm all tied up here. But how come you you're so happy?"

He looked up at me smiling.

"The insurance company said they'd pay for a new spinnaker."

I had survived a historic if somewhat unhinged initiation into sailing in Scotland – the story of setting *Fiona's* sail on fire is still told on the Clyde to this day. If we were to have *Off We Go* remotely seaworthy there was much to do, so I tracked down a few guys to help out. Among the band was Angus, a huge bear of a man with a heart of gold and an absolute passion for bees. He had a collection of hives full of his treasured friends that made manna from heaven in the form of ambrosial honey, and he would bring jars of it down to the boat. There was no interior below decks whatsoever, and Angus worked as enthusiastically as his bees on the carpentry to finish it, although I used to stand well back when he hauled the mighty ballast of his body up the ladder onto the boat. The rungs could have broken any moment under the sheer tonnage. My brother Richard is an architect and also built wooden masts for Finn dinghies, and he came up from London to lend a hand, along with Tony Castro who was studying naval engineering at Glasgow University. Between them they worked out where to put the hole for the mast, and we fitted the rudder. However, we still had no rigging.

Tear Drop ribbon rigging, designed by Ted Hood, had been ordered and supposedly shipped over from Marblehead, Massachusetts, via Boston to Glasgow. Finally after a long wait, a package the size of a hippopotamus arrived. We opened it to find about the furthest thing you can imagine needed to rig a boat. Inside was a king-size bale of heavy duty barbed wire and rolls and rolls of electric fencing. Two weeks later a farmer, three hundred miles away in Inverness, telephoned to say he couldn't understand why he had received a considerable quantity of technically advanced boat rigging to build a pen for his pigs.

To top it all, Phil Holland relayed the disastrous news that the British Yachting Federation would not allow a Scottish team to compete in the One Ton Cup. Thankfully he came up with a brainwave as to how to get round this latest calamity. Chris Bouzaid, twice winner of the series for New Zealand with *Rainbow II* and *Wai-ainwa* in 1972, had a boat called *Haiti IV*, and along with two other owners from the Land of the Long White Cloud they wanted to form a team and charter *Billy Can* and *Off We Go* to represent them. The still wheelchair-bound Barry Filer had no option but to agree to the plan.

"We need to give the boats Kiwi colours," Phil announced. "I've got an idea."

He'd recently got a letter from New Zealand and asked a sign-writer from a nearby crew to make a stencil out of the picture of the kiwi bird adorning the stamp, and in a couple of days we had a daisy chain of kiwi's stencilled down both sides of the yachts. We were now officially racing for New Zealand, which is about as far from Scotland as it's possible to get.

139

The unusual, flightless bird that now decorated *Off We Go* associated us with a foreign crew and had the added benefit of extracting us from the problems we were about to incur with the long arm of the law during the next few hundred miles of our journey. We were ready to roll and move the show down to Moody's boat yard on the south coast of England.

The same truck driver that had delivered the boat from Ireland turned up, which I should have known from his track record promised a high probability of further problems; and the more I saw him in action the more I realised we were in trouble. We got out of the shed all right and drove a mile or so to cross a bridge that, up until this point, had lasted perfectly well since the Romans built it. Perfectly well, that is, until my truck driver came along. Halfway across the bridge one of the truck wheels went straight through the middle of it. The entire thing nearly collapsed, while the boat precariously teetered on the edge of disaster and hung off the edge of the ancient structure. Miles of busy Glasgow traffic bound for the docks ground to a furious halt, their schedules sabotaged for most of the day, while a bloody great crane was called in to the rescue and stood a hundred feet out from the bridge in case both lorry and boat tumbled into the river below.

Several hours later we managed to extract ourselves from the fiasco and got back on the road, leaving what was left of the bridge worse for wear, and headed on down to Southampton. Somewhere in the Midlands we came across another bridge, this time one we had to pass under not over. Once bitten twice shy, the driver ground to a halt.

"This looks dodgy," mused the accident-prone truckie, getting out of the cab to measure its height, thankfully before ploughing through it. I was just thinking it was unfortunate he hadn't made the necessary calculations on the first bridge that nearly killed us, but before I knew it he leapt into action and let all the tyres down dead flat. We squeezed on through with inches to spare. Then it took fucking hours to reinflate the tyres once we'd reached the other side.

Twenty miles out of Southampton we climbed a steep hill and into a quaint English village, and it was about to become clear that the relentless capacity Jock the Scot had for causing chaos knew no bounds. Half way through the high street we met a double-decker bus coming the other way, and both truck and bus got jammed on a sharp, narrow corner. With both vehicles in check-mate the law turned up,

140

accompanied by a fleet of local rescue services to pull us out before we knocked the Post Office and a couple of houses down, while a stunned crowd gathered to watch the possibility of their high street being demolished as the hapless driver tried to untangle his umpteenth fuck-up. For the third time in two days, miles of traffic from both sides of town came to a grinding halt.

Hours later we rumbled away from the balls-up and finally, absolutely exhausted, made it into Moody's Yard. The boat was unloaded; but I couldn't understand why the halyards jammed in the mast and wouldn't pull through. By this time I had got to know the truck driver all too well and the alarm bells were ringing.

"Hey mate, do you know why we've got a problem with the halyards?" I asked, suspecting the worst.

"Oh," he mumbled, shuffling around and staring awkwardly at the ground, "I picked that mast up from down this way to take up to the boat in Scotland and unfortunately it broke in half when I reversed into a tree."

Apparently the mast had been re-sleeved in a bad repair job that now rendered it completely useless. I told the truck driver to stick around while we lifted *Off We Go* into the water, in case she started to sink. Sure enough, by the time I stepped on board, to my horror the floor-boards were awash and *Off We Go* was going down fast. We lifted her back out in scrambled haste and I looked over towards the truck driver accusingly for what could only be a further holocaust of an explanation.

"Well, I didn't want to mention it, but when I went to Ireland to pick up the boat the cabinet-makers told me I couldn't leave until they had pulled the keel off."

"What do you mean, pulled the fucking keel off?" I yelped.

On further inspection it turned out the keel bolts had not been properly sealed when the keel was moved, and consequently left the boat about as seaworthy as a sieve. All we could do was drill dozens of holes around the bottom of the hull and pour litre after litre of sealant in around the bolts in an attempt to make her watertight.

After a long, hard day it was time to step the mast in, only to be faced with another almighty cock-up. The Tear Drop rigging that had been retrieved from the pig farmer, which by now felt like long years ago, turned out to be the wrong length because the mast was bent.

Because of the material used, the Tear Drop system could only be short-ened, not lengthened. It was obviously out of the question to make the mast smaller, so Kemp's yard had to revert to a conventional wire rig-ging and straighten out the spar.

The first crew to turn up were Billy Sanderson, our navigator, and Phil Stegall from the States. Stegall was originally to sail on *Robin Too II* with Ted Hood and Robbie Doyle. However, an early east coast hur-ricane had wreaked havoc on the New England coast, resulting in the cancellation of their shipping arrangements, so he now joined us as bowman and trimmer. Not long after, Ian Gibbs, the kiwi who char-tered the boat, and his guys Stuart Palmer, Russel Green and Kevin Lidgard arrived from the land of the long white cloud.

Gibbs owned a Bruce Farr half-tonner, *Tohe Candu*, that was being shipped to France for the following month's World Series. Decked out in their dark national 'silver fern' pocketed blazers, white strides and dock-siders they certainly stood out as imposing figures, but soon came down to earth with a resounding crash when they learnt of the current disastrous situation.

Gibbs was under the misapprehension that they would just step onto the boat and go sailing. Although a hard-bitten bloke, to say he swal-lowed the not so good news like a bitter pill would be an understate-ment.

After two ball-busting days of final preparation we tentatively got under way, motoring in the direction of the Isle of Wight on a yacht about as seaworthy as a colander. We passed Cowes, and with the ebb tide up our chuff soon swept through inside the turbulent Shingles making sail as we pressed on beyond the Needles, an array of high sentry rocks that guard the Solent's entrance. Darkness enveloped us and it quickly became apparent a steady stream of water was flowing up through the keel bolts and flooding the shallow bilges. We kept the life-raft at the ready, meanwhile pumping and bailing like mad men, none more so than Phil Stegall who couldn't swim. Finally, dog-tired and demoralized, we hobbled into the ancient fishing port of Brixham some eight miles west of Torquay in Devon. That night the rest of the crew roosted in the guest house next to the Crown and Anchor pub. I stayed aboard, but down below it was wet as an otter's couch, and to sleep safely without drowning I draped an arm over the side of a sat-urated lower bunk. Whenever the water crept past my watch and got as far as my elbow I'd wake up with a lurch, and bleary-eyed pump the whale gusher, otherwise *Off We Go* would have become *Down We Go* and sunk at the dock.

At first light a bunch of brawny shipwrights hauled us up the slipway and began hammering strings of oakum into the keel join before adding a steady stream of sticky white druid's sealant. It was a desperate last fix, and on a wing and a prayer we were back on the water by noon with less than two days to get our act together. We sailed out into the bay to practise shuffling the cards for the upcoming game.

Rapid changes were taking place in rigging. One of the developments was the Tim Sterns patented Twinstay, that originated in America and provided a groove down both the stays front and back, swivelling around so you could do inside-out peels, which enabled going from one sail to another without ending up bald-headed or minus a sail for the minutes it took to hoist another like it did with a single-grooved headstay or the traditional piston hank method.

The Kiwis, having never used this system, were highly apprehensive at first. However, after several hours practice Gibbs drummed up a squall of dissention when he suggested piston hanks be sewed on to the headsail luffs. The Kiwis were also used to end for end gybing on their Farr seven eighth's fractional rigged half-tonner. Two pole gybing was completely out of the question, so we put a lot of time into perfecting single-pole gybes.

We were far from a united party. The gallimaufry of character differences had created an inevitable cross current of friction between the various factions. The disgruntled Gibbs could become agitated after a few gin and tonics and I gave him a wide berth ashore, but to his credit, once we went racing all differences were left behind.

Ready or not it was time to start thinking about the race. The One Ton Cup was a hulking great thing cast out of several kilos of silver, dating back to 1899 and the French 'Le Coupe International du Circle de la Voile de Paris'. In 1971, regulations were changed under the International Offshore Rule. A new rating limit of 27.5' was introduced with most of the yachts being 35' to 37' in length. By 1974 it had become one of the most prestigious trophies to win in the world. The series consisted of three 27-mile Olympic courses and two offshore races of one hundred and sixty, and three hundred nautical miles.

Amongst the really hot competition was *Terrorist*, an extreme radical design by American Bruce King. A bilge boarder boasting two asymmetrical foils, the owner Al Cassel had built her out of aluminium in his spacecraft workshop in California. Her fat and metallic-coloured hull gave her a pot-bellied appearance, but upwind she simply flew like shit off a shiny shovel and could claw herself to weather. My old mate Rex Banks was bowman on board, and whenever we came in shouting distance while jostling around at the starts he'd yell across,

"Have you guy's got your fishing rods on board?" or "Have you caught any fish yet?" in reference to the river that bubbled up through our keel bolts.

Then there was *Gumboots*, a Peterson design built at Lymington by Jeremy Rodgers and Bill Green of GRP Construction. Extremely stiff and powerful upwind in a breeze, she was the prototype for the Contessa 35. Also fast downwind, fin-keeled and spade-ruddered was *High Tension*, designed by Dutchman Jac de Ridder, built and sailed by George Stead. The peach of the fleet, however, was Golden Apple, built by George Bushe. Lovely to look at, she had a varnished mahogany, cold-moulded hull with teak decks and carried a Lars Bergstrom swept-back rig of a very small mast section with severe shroud loads. I have to say, the difference between her and the two Scottish boats was about as far apart as a Stradivarius violin and a Tennessee Horner fiddle. Harold Cudmore drove the boat and Killian Bushe, only nineteen at the time, was bowman. Killian is now one of the most highly regarded carbon fibre specialists and built the last four winning boats in the Volvo Round the World Race.

Most of the fleet, including the many S & S and Carter boats, were around 35' to 37' in length, although there were a few exceptions like Michel Joubert, a crazy hippie Frenchman who'd gained notice the previous year with *Revolution*, a radical Admiral's Cupper. He came out with the 32' lightweight flush-decked with low free-boards *Subversion*, that with its transom-hung rudder and massive sail area, became known as the 'Submarine' because it was so wet. And *Ceil III*, a Bob Miller 40' was long and skinny, resembling a tapered medium-weight cigar, and had two trenches inserted either side on her flush deck for sail trimmers to sit. She'd won the Sydney to Hobart race the year before and just smoked downwind, even though she must have taken a hammering in the sail area to compete.

We actually didn't do too badly in the first race. The wind was light and fluky and a few monstrous shifts turned positions on the last leg upside down. The most memorable episode in the middle distance off-shore race was when a motor launch ignited into a ball of flames and exploded. A batch of racing boats, including *Gumboots*, gathered nearby in case needed for a rescue operation, and time allowances for the diversion were calculated into the final results in the Committee room. *Terrorist* looked like a serious contender for a while but broke her mast which put her out of the running.

The final race loomed, a long-distance course of around three hundred miles to France and back. On the return leg from the French coast, a heavy upwind bash, we almost met our Waterloo. With the backstay well-wound up *Off We Go* and her garish yellow paint job, that Barry Filer had chosen in his chemically altered state, began bending like a banana. The modulation caused even more cold English Channel water to flood in, and passing under the lee of St. Katherine's on the Isle of Wight, we prised up the floor-boards to take a look a closer look at things. It didn't look good. A torrent flooded in through a frightening split from the mast step right along the keel. Even with two guys going hell for leather below decks, pumping and bailing with anything that came to hand from buckets to saucepans, it was touch and go.

There's one of two choices to make as you approach the dark grey rocks of Portland Bill when facing an adverse tide in the perilous stretch of water known as the Portland Race. Either you give this hazardous stretch of volatile water a wide three-mile berth, or come in real close to skim the majestic sea-sculptured stones.

Sir Francis knew tidal tactics all too well, saving England when he scuppered the Spanish Armada when they were trapped in irons near the notorious landmark, with a two-pronged attack on a fair tide.

We decided on the inshore option, where the current doesn't run at such a force, and had the added benefit that if we hit a rock we could almost step ashore if we sank. After safely clearing the shallows on the eastern side of the Shambles Bank, we ran into a fierce southerly set, sweeping us sideways towards Portland Race. It wasn't until we crossed to its inner side that we dared ease the sheets and found ourselves in the path of another yacht taking a bold line and almost kissing the rocks.

By the time we were almost abeam of the stone obelisk marking a dangerous rocky ledge, the loom of the lighthouse towered above us.

The other yacht revealed its identity, *Windsprite of Hamble*, sister ship to *Ydra*, the previous cup winner. On board were well-known sail-maker Bruce Banks and former Fireball world champion Pete Bateman. It gave us a reassuring feeling, for it was doubtful if any other competitor knew the waters around Weymouth better than these wily old foxes on their local turf.

Both boats almost ground to a standstill when to leeward a wall of roaring white waves from the southern avalanche of water flowing down both sides of the Bill collided head on into the incoming flood tide. We teetered precariously close to its grasp and on the brink of another fiasco, until another a powerful back eddy intervened, thrusting us out of harm's way towards Lyme Bay. When all was said and done it was pretty remarkable considering the circumstances. We finished mid-fleet.

Doug Peterson had three of his designs placed in the top five, including overall winner *Gumboots*. When we arrived in Torquay, wheelchair-bound Barry Filer sat waiting on the dock. The old sod was still heavily sedated on the Doctor Feelgood pills, which had done little to allay his fury with the Irish furniture-makers who had built fucking *Off We Go*, and he let off a tirade of near unintelligible language threatening to sue the shit out of them for causing the monumental cock-up.

Damn near broke, I interrupted Filer's rant just long enough for him to pay me some of the money he owed, muttering he'd fix me up with the rest if he won his court case or managed to sell his disastrous boat. There wasn't much sense in hanging around. *Off We Go* got carted back to the Hamble and Billy Sanderson and I set sail on the president of Volvo's boat, *Victoria of Sweden* in search of another adventure.

Years later, quite by chance, I stumbled across *Off We Go's* carcass at Moody's boat yard in Burseldon on the Hamble River. Stripped of her hardware, her yellow hull plastered in dust and dirt she sat propped up in a derelict shed, separated from the keel and rudder. Rumour had it some sort of settlement was made out of court between Filer and the furniture-makers, but one thing was for sure: on a simple handshake I'd bought myself a holocaust of misadventure – and certainly none the richer for it either.

5

Renegados in Brazil

A life on the ocean wave,
A home on the rolling deep;
Where the scattered waters rave,
And the winds their revels keep.

Life on the Ocean Wave – Epes Sargent
(1813 – 1881)

WHAT A BASTARD IT HAPPENED IN THE EARLY HOURS of the morning! Art arrived from New York on the red-eye, stumbled onto his boat, and for some inexplicable reason defied his own rule: 'The owner does not trespass forward of the mast'.

"Fucking son of a bitch…!" came a yelp and one hell of a thump as

147

the sound of the bloke who paid for the beer and the fun tickets crashed headlong down *Myth's* forward hatch. After an urgent phone call a bunch of paramedics armed with a meat wagon showed up and carted poor old Art off to hospital. A few hours later our skipper Tux reappeared with the damage report.

"Ok fellas, here's the good news," he boomed in his strong New England accent. "They operated on the boss's busted femur, nailed in some pins and a metal rod – the airport buzzers will go crazy when he flies home – and the bad news is that where his old lady disliked boats before this screw-up she bloody hates them now. She's pulled the plug on Art's racing and the show's over."

He paused to open a can of cold Heineken, and wiping the sweat off his brow, turned to me.

"Cheer up, Chas, and get your arse up on deck, there's a good-looking piece of jail-bait waiting on the dock to see you."

"Sounds promising, mate," I said, clambering up the hatchway to check out the action, and pulled on my shades to shield my eyes from the harsh Miami sunlight.

"Hey, I'm over here!" a girl's voice sang out.

It was Annie Greenberg, her long dark hair swinging over her shoulders as she sauntered towards me wearing a pair of tight white shorts. Tux was right, she looked quite a sight. She flashed a dazzling smile rivalled only by her shining deep brown kitten-shaped eyes over which perched a North Sails sun visor that read 'Only Ocean Sailors Get Blown Off-Shore'.

"Hi Chas, we heard about the drama this morning and figured you might be looking for a ride. My Dad and I would like you to race with us on the SORC Miami to Nassau race."

Annie's pa Jack was a leading heart surgeon and I reckoned she'd keep him pretty active over the next few years with all the tickers she would bust. I followed her shapely arse up the pontoon to meet her father, and before I knew it was under way, heading out to sea on *Jack Knife*, the Doc's powder blue Charlie Morgan 42' ketch.

A late winter storm had lashed its way over the Carolinas, a strong Nor'Easterly whipped up the Gulf Stream and the rag-tag crew made up of college kids and medical interns found their initial enthusiasm wilting in the worsening conditions. By dusk we'd sailed well into the axis of the stream amongst big sets of rampaging white rollers, and were hard pressed under a fully reefed mainsail and a piston hanked hybrid jib, a sail a bit bigger than a number three – a strange beast of a thing known as a 'mule'. Fatigue and sea sickness had their way with both the crew and the good doctor, who in all probability had been tinkering around with some half-carked patient's heart twenty-four hours before. In dribs and drabs the boys slowly disappeared down below to lay low in their scratchers, and I figured I'd better make sure the last two colts left on deck were well tethered to the cockpit so they didn't get washed overboard. Fortunately the boys came from tough stock somewhere up north of Maine and were as tall and strong as a couple of bulrush clumps.

Isaac's lighthouse appeared on the horizon off our starboard bow, rising above an isolated rock, and I kept the boat high of the course, while the wind slowly backed eastwards. *Jack Knife* bucked and lurched into the heavy seas and the Doc poked his head out of the main hatch, looking as sickly green as a gherkin, made all the worse an apparition when the glow of the instrument lights caught the contours of his haggard face. Barely audible over the blasting squalls, he squawked,

"We're taking in gallons of seawater between the leeward genoa track and the chain plates on the starboard side – the floor-boards are awash and it looks like the electric pump has burned out."

"Fuck, that's all we need," I muttered under my breath, and yelled out to the Doc,

"Can you get the guys to hand-pump the heavy-duty whale gusher before we sink?"

More or less holding our own, *Jack Knife* gained a degree or two of protection as she slowly clawed her way under the lee of Grand Bahama.

"Chas!" the Doc hollered out again as he forced the hatch cover back. "The *Mary E* is putting out a Mayday. She's seven miles northeast of the Hen and Chickens lighthouse and the poor bastards on board are preparing to abandon ship."

"Where the hell is she?" I shouted back.

"Pretty close," he bellowed over the roaring wind, "less than a mile away, about fifty degrees to starboard."

"There she is!" cried out the two Maine boys in unison as a red parachute flare rocketed into the filthy night sky and exploded. I bore off

149

towards the stricken vessel while *Jack Knife's* gusher pump hit the skids and water poured in through the leak, swilling over the floor-boards down below.

"Grab the buckets and saucepans and bail your bloody guts out, or we'll wind up as fish food!" I gasped, grappling with the helm.

The Doc eased his way up into the cockpit, and crouching down on his knees, managed to unzip his oil skins and take a leak over the stern.

"Christ, it's a hell of a night, we can barely stem the deluge down below!" he gasped. "The battery's low and the goddam motor won't start – it's a gasoline atomic four, Chas. Do you know anything about the damn things?"

Down below was a chaotic scene, far worse than I had imagined, and a ton of salty brine sloshed around on top of the bilge boards while mayday messages from the *Mary E* crackled out over the radio at full tilt. I lay down on top of the frames surrounding the main bilge and groped around with spread-eagled fingers, my face barely clear of the filthy water, before finally locating and breaking free the suction end of the gusher hose.

"Shit!" I swore to no one in particular and pulled out the cause of the blockage – a tea towel, a woollen beanie and the remnants of a supper we'd never got around to eating, a splendid Scottish smoked salmon and boiled egg kedgeree.

"I don't think the lads will be too interested in last night's dinner," I said, handing Annie a bucket full of the slop, "but tell them to start pumping their guts out again unless they want to swim the rest of the race."

Suddenly a familiar voice cannoned out of the VHF radio. It was my old mate Captain Tits announcing that the *Mary E* had floundered, but all the crew had been rescued and accounted for, including the cook Juliette, who he intended to keep warm in his bunk for the rest of the trip.

"Is that the wild chick with the scar on her cheek?" Annie asked.

"Yeah, that's her. She used to be a cocktail waitress at the Miami marina tavern until some crazy woman glassed her face," I grunted.

"Hey Chas!" someone shouted from up on deck. "I think we can see first light!"

Sure enough, dawn was breaking. *Jack Knife* cleared the Berry Islands and we started hauling arse on the final leg to Nassau, crossed the finishing line and, because of the broken motor, ended up getting a tow in before safely tying up in a berth at the Pilothouse marina.

Parched as smoked kipper, dog-tired, and the saturated yacht in a total shambles after the gruelling forty-eight hour race, I set about repairing the bilge pump. This involved straddling across the top of the fuel and water tanks with my arse up in the air, hanging from my toe nails, armed with a screwdriver. I very nearly didn't make it to the bar, an uncommon occurrence admittedly. During the storm a couple of cases of Tuborg beer, stored either side of the chain plates, had been punctured and gallons of the golden ambrosia had run out of the cans into the bilges. While I lay on top of the stainless steel tanks with my hands on a beer-soaked pump, some arsehole decided to hook us up to shore power. 110 volts of electrical current shot through my body and bounced me up in the air like a squash ball. A situation made a hell of a lot worse when the plug was shoved into the socket three times.

"Stop, for Christ's sake take the fucking plug out!" I yelped.

Nearly fried to a crisp, I was still alive, but my left leg was shaking like a rattle snake.

"Shit, I'm sorry Chas! Maybe you could come up to Miami and I'll run some tests on your ticker," suggested the Doc, casting an eye over my near toasted body before throwing in an extra offer of watching some open heart surgery as part of the excursion.

As fate would have it, while I was recuperating on deck, a forty-foot Sparkman and Stephens sloop flying a Brazilian flag and called *Peanut Brittle* pulled up alongside.

Peanut Brittle's owner, Jose Laporte, was small in stature and big in charisma. He wore Woody Allen glasses, had eyebrows as thick as badger brushes, sported a shock of grizzled hair and had a huge torpedo-shaped Cuban cigar hanging out of the corner of his mouth.

"You must be Chas from Tas," he said, eyeing up my frazzled state, "my crew speak highly of you. They say you've done a fair bit of sailing, have an unusual way of recounting your crazy adventures, and the captain Tom Rinda compares you to a Tasmanian devil, a hardy beast they couldn't root, shoot or electrocute – I guess he was right on the latter point. Have you ever done the Buenos Aires to Rio race?"

"No, I haven't," I stammered, trying to get a grip on my still shaking leg "but I'd like to."

151

"Well, I'm planning to do the next one. They only hold them every three years, so there's enough time to forget how bad the previous one was," he grinned. "Let's go and talk about it over lunch."

Right from the onset Laporte and I got along pretty well. At the jam-packed Pilothouse he conjured up a table out of nowhere and a waiter appeared quick as a flash with a couple of ice cold Beck's beers, some large bowls of conch salad and the right fighting tools to tackle it with an unusual turn of speed I'd not experienced on previous visits to the joint. But I didn't know Laporte then, not like I did later when it became clear he was the unofficial Chargé d'Affaires for Brazil and spoke half-a-dozen languages. In short, he was a serious operator who did things in great style and had a hell of a lot of fun while he was doing it.

Shooting the breeze, we gnawed our way through a chargrilled grouper and polished off a bottle of Chardonnay as Laporte began to lay out *Peanut Brittle's* upcoming schedule.

"This is going to be a good trip. First we go north to New York before the Bermuda race and then ship the boat south for the Rio Circuit," he explained.

Visions of beautiful Brazilian women flickered through my mind. I thought it sounded like a pretty good plan.

"So, amigo," he enquired "are you on for the campaign?"

"You bet!" I agreed. "Once I've finished tomorrow's Harbour Race with the good doctor I'll jump aboard *Peanut Brittle*."

"Fantastico, this is good news. We leave for Fort Lauderdale in a couple of days. You can call me Joe," he said, shaking my hand.

And that was it – my destiny for the time being was sealed. *Jack Knife* tore through the next day's race and came in second, a result which the Doc was over the moon about, and although he offered me work looking after a new Ron Holland two-tonner he would build the following year, I declined. I was South America bound and flying high with the promise of adventure in uncharted territory.

A couple of mornings later the first rays of sunshine rose above the harbour and Joe, his captain Tom Rinda and Frisko, a college kid from Ohio and I stole north towards open sea on *Peanut Brittle*. Around the middle of the day it became apparent that the second lunch Joe and I had together would not be quite as successful as the first. Joe's cooking, which along with navigating was an absolute passion of his, was of the combustible kind.

"This should keep the wolf from the door," the flamboyant Brazilian hollered up from the galley as he knocked up a Portuguese stew, throwing in a shit-load of gear he'd loaded up with at the local market.

Tom and I were breathing in the spicy aromas wafting through the hatchway when all of a sudden a thunderous explosion erupted down below.

"What the fuck...!" I yelled to Tom.

"Christ, the galley is on fire!" he spluttered, sticking his head through the smoke pouring out of the hatch.

"The fuel pipe connected to the stove is leaking!" Joe cried out.

"Jesus, it looks like an Aussie bush fire down there!" I shouted back. "Someone put the damn thing out before we lose the boat."

On the whole, salt water is the best way to deal with a metho ignited fire; however Frisco, unfamiliar with fire-fighting techniques, grabbed a chemical fire extinguisher, that although it had the desired effect of preventing *Peanut Brittle* from burning to a cinder, plastered everything with a heavy white dust and left the inside of the boat looking like a Columbian snow storm had hit. And worse, it all got wet when he tried to clean up the carnage, and turned into a mass of bubbling foam.

Apart from several cases of pretty good Beaujolais all other provisions were destroyed and the stove completely fucked; however, salvation lay just a few hours' sailing away. As we rounded the headland of Chub Quay on the edge of the Bahamas, another racer, the heritage one-tonner *Ghost*, lay at anchor and none other than my old friend, Tito Techosky appeared in the cockpit.

"Hey you, Tassie devil, you're welcome to raft up here! We've been conch-diving and are loaded to the gills for tonight's dinner," he called out in a southern drawl as coarse as a flugelhorn.

The barrel-chested weather-battered Tito cut a formidable figure, and before too long he and Laporte were chewing the fat as if they'd known each other for years. Tito wasn't bullshitting about the conch either. *Ghost's* tender was full to the brim with helmet-sized shells, and his crew armed themselves with razor-sharp knives and hammers to cut and tenderise the tough flesh.

"This is a damn good piece of kit, Chas old son," he said, producing an old-fashioned hand-operated metal meat-grinder. "It's made by your Limey mates, Captain Kangaroo gave it to me. Poor bastard, it wasn't long afterwards that he went overboard somewhere off Cape Hatteras."

Tito's crew ground up the conch and cooked up a storming meal which we devoured like hungry gannets.

"So Joe, what's the story with *Peanut Brittle*, how did you give her the name?" Tito asked, settling back for the evening.

"Well, amigo," said Joe, lighting one of his favourite fat cigars and puffing a plume of smoke into the night air, "I asked Olin Stephens to design her for the One Ton Cup in Newport. She started life with the name *Mach II* after another yacht I have in Brazil. However, the import duties are pretty heavy there so we decided instead to register her under the Bermudian flag. My lawyer said we couldn't use the name *Mach II* again and I had to think of a new one as quickly as possible. Do either of you know John Marshall from North Sails?"

"Sure!" Tito and I nodded simultaneously. John was a well-known sailor and highly regarded sail-maker master.

"Well, although he never let it slow him down in any way, John suffered from seasickness. Before the race he mentioned he felt a lot worse with alcohol or heavy foods, and so he decided instead to try a new candy bar called Peanut Brittle to keep him going. The race turned into a long, rough ride, and when he came down below to check on my navigation the smell of dinner cooking affected him so badly he vomited the sticky candy bar down the back of my neck. The incident stuck in my mind, and hard-pressed for time to think of anything else I went with the name *Peanut Brittle* for the new boat."

"What are your plans for her now," Tito asked, laughing at the story.

"I'm leaving for Houston tomorrow for a meeting with Bunker Hunt and to check out some oil platforms before going up to New York for some racing," he replied.

"I'll be damned!" Tito replied, running his calloused fingers through his beard. "I spent some time in the early '70s working in the Gulf, south of New Orleans, out on the Marchland fields offshore when Shell had that terrible fire. They let it burn for over a month until Red Adair came in to handle the disaster. I knew a guy down there that worked on the power boats Adair used to race in his spare time, who said the ace fire-fighter reckoned he'd made a pact with the devil that if he ever ended up in hell they'd install air-conditioning for him so he wouldn't put the fire out! What about you, Chas old son? What points of the compass are you headed for next?"

"I'm sailing *Peanut Brittle* up to Long Island for the Onion Patch series, then headed for South America, mate," I replied.

"Shit, that sounds like an adventure in the making – Chas from Tas in Brazil," Tito ruminated. "Well, let me know how it goes in Rio, you Taswegian bastard, and watch out for the women down there, they're spectacular!"

When we got to Rhode Island, instead of renting a simple bed and breakfast for the crew to roost in, Joe commandeered a massive Newport mansion called Salve Regina, which for most of the year operated as a ladies' college and was consequently known as Saliva Vagina in America's Cup folklore. We pulled to a grinding halt at the gates and surveyed the imposing 19th century manor, surrounded by lawns big enough to graze a herd of buffalo.

"Perhaps I've overdone it, Chas," he said with considerable understatement.

The baronial-sized front door swung open and Joe's wife Nellie, clad in high leather boots, tight blue jeans and a low-cut leather jacket, swept out onto the driveway.

"Hi Joe," she said embracing her husband, and then turned to me.

"You must be Chas from Tas," she murmured, taking in my raggedy appearance. "Your reputation precedes you," she continued in perfect English adorned with a slight South American accent. "You might like to stay in the room in the attic known as the Captain's Den."

Following Nellie's well-sculpted Brazilian bunda, I trekked upstairs to the top floor, found the den and chucked my clobber inside. I liked my new quarters, it had terrific sea views and you could see all the way across to the front gates and check out who was coming and going.

Quite a few people came to stay during our time there. Bald-headed fellow watch captain Alan, who was strong as a Brahma bull and known as 'The Turtle', had taken time off from captaining American politician Bill Buckley's cruising yacht to join us. He'd run into Penny Whiting, from the famous Kiwi yachting dynasty, and her cousin Maria, who'd both made a pit-stop in Newport while sailing around the world on the beautiful yacht *Tequila*. The girls had been at sea for a few months, and it didn't take much arm-twisting from The Turtle to persuade them to come and hang out at the mansion for a while. The long-legged Maria was happily hi-jacked by a burly bloke named

'Nut' Bennet. Nut had worked for many years up in the mid-West at Sturgeon Bay for Palmer Johnston's, the biggest private yacht-building yard in the States, but had been put out to pasture after injuring himself. A favourite amongst Australian sailing crews, he had at one time worked as a linesman on telephones and taught the boys a special dialling technique which, for a dime, would connect them Down Under using Nut's special code. With an enormous grin one night over dinner before the race started, he looked up from his plate while grappling with a lobster pincer, to answer a mate of Joe's question as to how he got his name.

"Funny thing that, I guess it's a family tradition," he replied in a slow mid-Western drawl. "My father was called Old Nut and I was known as just Nut. My eldest son is called Half Nut and his younger brother Quarter Nut. And then of course there's my daughter – she's known as No Nuts.

Over the next few days we prepared and provisioned *Peanut Brittle* for the race to Bermuda. Our single-sided radio developed a tuning problem, which only a specialist technician could fix. Nut mentioned to Joe there was a Spaniard around who repaired off-shore trawler fleet's radios. We tracked him down working on Hughie Long's maxi *Ondine*, commonly known as the *Blue Pig*, and skippered by my old mate Tom the Pom from *Sorcery* days. There was bad blood between Long and Joe, but this didn't stop the Brazilian from shooting over to the *Blue Pig* to look for the Spaniard. Suddenly, a portly little fella sprang out onto deck like jack-in-a-box in a furious frenzy after being told Mr Long wouldn't be showing up to see him until the next day. Joe seized his moment, quickly engaging in a rapid-fire Spanish conversation with the little tornado, the general gist of which included a mutual exchange of their dislike for Long. Before we knew it, the Basque and the Brazilian took off in the direction of the Black Pearl, a legendary yachtsman's watering hole. An hour or so later they emerged from the bar tanked up on New England chowder and chardonnay.

"Amigo," the pint-sized sparky announced to Tom the Pom, "I have no hard feelings towards you, but Señor Long can shove his radio and his *Blue Pig* up his arse. Señor Laporte is now my primo concern."

And with that he worked for the next hour, squeezed like a ferret up a rabbit-hole deep inside the smallest space you can imagine at *Peanut Brittle's* rear end repairing the problem.

Meanwhile, back at the Saliva Vagina, I ambled into the kitchen looking for a beer and got into a rap with Nellie while she put together a hamper of Joe's favourite food for him to take on the race. Nellie didn't have the slightest interest in *Peanut Brittle*. She tolerated her husband's passion largely so he would do the same for her various pastimes. I lent her a hand in the kitchen, aware it would be best to find a topic of conversation which avoided anything to do with boats.

Chatting about her Argentine rancher father, we got onto the subject of horses.

"Si Chas, I like horses a lot. Not so long ago I went to visit a big stud farm called Blue Grass in Lexington, Kentucky, which owns hundreds of race horses."

"Shit, that sounds sensational," I said wanting to know more, my interest pricking up in case she knew of a fast horse I could take a punt on.

"It certainly was," she affirmed, placing a leather valise of Joe's beside the hamper before standing up and brushing specks of imaginary dust off her shirt. "The year before last the Blue Grass owners did very well during the English flat racing season, and just two weeks ago their French-trained horse Empery won the Epsom Derby with Lester Piggott in the saddle."

"Who owned the stud?" I asked.

"It belonged to Bunker Hunt. Joe does business with them."

Bunker Hunt discovered LOT 65, a Libyan oil field worth sixteen billion dollars, and in 1973 was temporarily declared the richest man in America, before getting screwed over by General Gaddafi. After failing to gain control of the silver market in the States, Hunt declared bankruptcy in the mid-eighties.

"They had a fabulous Peruvian stallion down there who sired the Argentine mare Pamplona II, who then produced a foal, the famous Empery," Nellie explained. "In fact, Winston Churchill owned the great horse Vienna, Empery's grandsire."

Nellie knew her oats when it came to horses, and I was thinking it would have been pretty good if I'd had this conversation with her two weeks ago before the Epsom Derby kicked off, and put a bet on Empery who ended up winning.

"I remember Churchill's daughter Sarah telling me of one of her father's favourite sayings," I said, memories of *Carlina* drifting through my mind.

"What was that?" Nellie asked, filling a couple of cups with strong black coffee.

"Oh, he would say, 'There's something about the outside of a horse that's good for the inside of a man'."

"That's probably true," she laughed. "I've always wanted to own one; but you know Joe, he's crazy about yachts," she added ruefully.

Finally the day of the race dawned and a huge flotilla bound for Bermuda got under way. A large high pressure system sat off the Eastern sea board and in fickle, light winds we pushed *Peanut Brittle* across the powerful Gulf Stream and headed southeast towards Bermuda. Conditions tested crew's temperaments to the limit and it took every ounce of concentration to squeeze the breeze like a concertina. We brought the true wind forward and sailed under apparent angles, chasing zephyrs and distant clouds which hung over the deep blue ocean. The sea lay smooth as alabaster, alive with flashing vapour trails, as some underwater predator chased shoals of fleeing prey.

The fleet sailed one of the slowest races in history. We were down to bread crumbs and rationed drinking water by the time we finally arrived in Bermuda and crossed the finishing line. I reckon the most memorable incident of this racing classic was the self-inflicted 'cry over your shoulder' tale of *Bumblebee III*, owned by John Kahlbetzer. His pronunciation of 'R' came across as 'W', much to the delight of the guffawing larrikins sitting on the weather rail who would hear him yell out to his captain and tactician, hard-arsed Tasmanian 'Frizzle' Freeman,

"What's the course, 'Fwizzle'?" at high volume.

It would be a mistake, however, to underestimate the crew assembled on the well-known boat – they were extremely competent and feared by the Americans. Ocean racing is all about yacht design, technology, skill and experience. *Bumblebee* had it all, and amongst her crew at the time was a fantastic navigator, none other than the world's best joke teller, David 'Fang' Kilponen; also the nugget from Metung on Victoria's southeast coast Steve Bull, known as the Calf; and Dave Birchenough, a tall, curly-headed and unassuming yank who'd sailed with Teddy Hicks on *Noryema* when she won in '72 under wild conditions.

For *Bumblebee* this year's effort was another story altogether, and after the race Lenny Bourke, a rugged Aussie known as 'Have a Chat Bezerk' due to his incessant talking, told me the tale of what transpired.

Ahead of them on the track they could see the unmistakable colours of the American S & S warhorse *Running Tide*, a bigger yacht with a higher rating. All they had to do was press on, make no mistakes, and the race was in the bag. However, by some misfortune *Bumblebee* crew missed the rounding mark off Kitchen Shoals and took some time to realize their mistake. By the time she crossed the finishing line the crew had torn four spinnakers and suffered a misadventure which cost twenty-nine minutes. *Running Tide* stole the show and roared in as overall winner, fourteen minutes ahead on corrected time. At the presentations, while the opposition celebrated, a heap of bridesmaids from Down Under were inconsolable and last seen drowning their sorrows in Dark and Stormies down on the water front in Hamilton.

Joe decided to cut loose while he was in Bermuda, so after the presentations he took me, his daughter Patricia and a mate called Pontuel from Rio, to a good Portuguese restaurant. I'd met Patricia briefly before and thought her a shy, retiring kind of girl – which just shows how wrong a guy can be. She showed up for the evening dressed to kill and with a glint in her eye that spelled trouble. After Joe left late that night Patricia dragged me on to the dance floor, and not long after insisted I take her home saying she didn't trust the local taxi drivers. I arrived at her house more or less in one piece and got towed up the garden path, through the front door and into a dimly lit hallway. A chorus of loud snoring bellowed out of her father's open bedroom door. Terrified he'd wake up to find me shagging his daughter, I teetered in the corridor about to make my escape. But hell-bent on having her way with me, Patricia stuck her tongue down my ear, grabbed my arse and in a flash yanked me through the door of her lair.

"Ssshhh, don't wake Papa!" she whispered, ripping off my clothes.

My abductor had a voracious appetite and was as supple as an ocelot. I felt like I'd spent the night being keel-hauled by the time we set sail for New York the next morning.

After a rough passage *Peanut Brittle* made her way by the Ambrose Lightship towards the East River on July 4th. Celebrations were in full swing and the sky alive with fireworks blasting into the night sky above the World Trade Centre's Twin Towers and the United Nations building. We sailed on up through Hell's Gates to City Island amongst a fleet of magnificent tall ships gathered for the bicentennial, it was a magical sight, reminiscent of a bygone age. Pulling into Minneford's boatyard tired and thirsty, I figured I'd have a couple of beers and catch up on some sleep. Tom Rinda wandered over while I wrestled with the hose and washed the boat clean from her salt-worn miles, but any ideas I had for some rest were about to veer off into another direction entirely.

"Get your best gear on and take a shower. The boss's daughter is out there and wants to see you," he grinned.

I looked up to see a big black stretch limo waiting, a chauffeur in the front and Patricia in the back.

"Christ, I've only just recovered from the last time I saw her," I muttered.

Rambling up the dock wondering what my immediate fate might be I stuck my head through the window of the limo.

"Hi Chas, I was in the neighbourhood and thought we might go out for the evening," she stated in a tone that wasn't about to take no for an answer.

I told her I didn't have much money, whereupon she opened her bag and produced a bunch of hundred dollar bills as thick as a cheese-cake.

"Cash isn't a problem, Chas, let's go," she said, pulling me into the back seat, and with that the driver sped us off into the city.

We found my old friend Doc Greenaway, a mountain of a man who had spent a lot of time working in New York hospitals. He'd originally come over to the States from Australia with Sir Frank Packer's America's Cup challenger *Dame Pattie* and stayed on afterwards. The Doc knew the Big Apple like the back of his hand, from the finest bars to the lowest dives. In times past he'd taken me everywhere – the Bronx, Harlem and Madison Square Gardens to watch the fights and eat oysters and cherry-stone clams. This particular night he took us to my old mate Fran Schneider's studio to watch one of the latest of the Kung Fu movies. Fran was knocking out at the time 'Phantom of the New York Subway System'. The film had been an instant success. It was so popular with the guys from the ghetto in Kingston, Jamaica, that after five viewings the local movie proprietor had to close the cinema down – the damages caused by the excited audience cost him a lot more than he made from the full house that packed in each night.

Fran's movie was sensational and it wasn't hard to see why the fans had half torn the theatre down in Kingston. It had the added effect of revving Patricia up into top gear, and without further ado she shanghaied me back to the famous ballet dancer Margot Fonteyn's house near Central Park in a drunken state. Margot was a good friend of Nellie's and the family would stay at her place while in town.

"Margot used to give me a few ballet lessons," she stated as we lurched into the sizeable sitting-room.

I don't know if much ballet came into it, but for sure Patricia was about to give me a future taste of South America. She had me over a barrel, dragged me down on to a large Persian carpet and pounced on me like a mahout astride a howdah on an elephant's back. If ever a woman was keen, she was that night.

Hobbling back onto *Peanut Brittle* the next morning and limping along like a cowboy after a night's cattle-rustling, Tom looked me up and down.

"Jesus, what happened? You look like you've been through a corn-shredding machine."

"Bloody nearly, mate, I could use a beer!" I gasped.

We set off to re-fuel at the Jonathon Livingstone Seagull Restaurant and downed a few cold Heinekens in an attempt to clear the fog of a fourteen carat hangover. Falling into a chair I stretched out my legs, only to discover a briefcase under the table.

"Hey, someone's left their briefcase here," I said.

"Well, it's sure not mine," Tom remarked.

I pulled out the bag and opened it.

"Jesus Christ!" I gasped. "These are the blue-prints for the latest American 12-meter *Enterprise* and a bunch of modification plans for *Courageous*."

The plans in the case had been drawn up at New York naval architects Sparkman and Stephens, by Webb Institute graduate Dave Pedrick under the old master Olin Stephens, and the briefcase belonged to Chuck Sadler who was in charge of the building project over at Minnefords.

"Son of a bitch, if Bondy and the Australians got a hold of these the next America Cup challenge would be brought to a standstill," I said, stating the obvious. "Where's Sadler at the moment, Tom? He's gotta be shitting himself about losing this little lot!"

"I reckon!" Tom agreed. "Last I heard he'd gone rock-climbing."

I admired and liked Chuck, the guy had a streak of steel running through him as tough as the pitons he drove into the rock walls or the frozen faces of waterfalls he scaled in winter time. He'd also sailed with Joe in the same race in which John Marshall unwittingly inspired *Peanut Brittle's* name.

"Do you remember that story of Joe's about Chuck?" I asked Tom, while knocking back another quick beer before hoofing it over to his office. "At the end of a race *Peanut Brittle* ran into fog and ploughed into a rock which punched a hole in her bow. Sadler was perched on the shitter taking a dump when it happened, and without missing a beat ripped off his long-legged thermals, picked up the emergency wooden plug for the heads outlet pipe and hammered both the plug and his pants into the gaping crack with a crank handle from the nearby two-cylinder Volvo engine before going back to wiping his arse."

I found Chuck sitting at his desk, with a look of forlorn misery on his face and the dog and bone in hand, making desperate phone calls.

"My God, Chas – thank Christ for that!" he exclaimed with relief, as I handed over the million-dollar bag.

12 meters at the time were being built out of alloy, *Courageous* being the first defender built out of this material. Alloy is fairly easy to operate on, to cut and weld the sections together, much the same way a 'nips and tucks' man uses scalpels and needles in cosmetic surgery procedures. Sadler had a lot of expertise in aluminium, having worked at Derecktors before moving to Minnefords. The two yachts were built on the basis that *Enterprise* would be the defender and *Courageous* her trial horse. However, with Ted Turner, the legendary 'mouth from the south' at the helm displaying all his flamboyant bravado, and with a yacht's name to match, she went from underdog to victor and stole the crown for America once again.

Interestingly it turned out *Courageous* had just been re-measured to comply with the 12 meter class rule, and it must have been a quite a shock to those involved when they discovered that she was lighter than the weight originally declared on her racing certificate when the boat competed against Bond's challenge with Southern Cross in '74. Had this fact been revealed whilst the series took place, the Australians would have protested, and in all probability she would have been disqualified. But the fact never came to light and the bird had flown, so the oldest sporting trophy was once more safely bolted to the floor of the New York Yacht Club. Having said that, with high-tech yachts such as these, less weight means a faster performance in lighter winds and, conversely, slower speeds in heavier weather. Considering the manner in which *Courageous* flogged Southern Cross, even with adjustments to her sail area, the water-line length, or fixing other attributes in line with the stipulation, she would still have ruled the waves.

The time had come to ship *Peanut Brittle* over to Brazil and it was a hell of an undertaking. Back then Brazil inflicted an incredible 300 per cent duty on all imported items, but because the boat was Bermuda registered, this meant she would escape the exorbitant tax fees. Joe made a mile-long list of gear he wanted over there and we loaded the old girl with enough marine hardware to fill a chandler's shop. It took days of arduously packing and stowing our extensive cargo into every available nook and cranny before shoving a mountain of sails on top of the booty. And just as we heaved a sigh of relief thinking the job done, a van arrived at the yard laden with half a dozen bloody hang-gliders for *Saga's* crew to play with. After loading those damn things on board, *Peanut Brittle* resembled an over-stuffed aircraft-carrier.

Tom and I flew out of Miami and arrived in Rio on a sultry, steaming hot day, and by the time we reached the yacht club our shirts clung to our backs like wet leaves. We jumped onto a launch and headed for Guanabara Bay and the naval dockyards, where a Lloyd Braziliero transport ship carrying *Peanut Brittle* lay at anchor. We found Joe standing beside the ship's German captain and a dour-faced mulatto fella with an attitude to match, dressed to the hilt in a customs uniform and sporting a heap of gold jewellery. Joe bided his time while the usual bureaucratic bullshit ran its course and the customs guy pored over the manifest, eyeing up the bulky pile of hang-gliders with increasing suspicion. In those days no one really knew what they were, the sport was in its infancy, so Joe set about convincing his officious opponent they were a standard part of *Peanut Brittles'* ocean racing equipment.

"That may be, Señor, but I wish to inspect your cargo or I will be forced to impound your yacht," the customs official pressed on.

Joe was ready for him and signalled to his shipping agent, who promptly stepped in and took the customs man aside.

"You should know that Señor Laporte has a close standing with the President, General Geisel, and that a report will be filed on the handling of this situation," he said with a steely look of intent in his eye.

The customs guy made a sharp intake of breath and rapidly started back-peddling as it dawned on him that he was straying into dangerously deep water.

Joe seized his moment and pounced.

"Do you like Scotch?" he asked the official.

"Si, muy bien," he replied.

"I have an important meeting to attend in half an hour, and if you can clear my yacht immediately I have a case of Chivas Regal as a token of my appreciation for your efficient handling of this business," Joe said, handing the fucker a lifeline.

And with that the papers were signed pronto, hands shaken, and a floating crane lifted *Peanut Brittle* clear of the container ship and lowered her into the water.

Rio captivated me right from the moment I laid eyes on the place. Never has a city won my heart as quickly. It had it all, from magical Sugarloaf Mountain, a coastline laced with white-hot beaches, and a beautiful harbour at the heart of it all, which rivals Sydney for sure. The first couple of weeks flashed by, we were so busy. The crew we'd picked up down there were operating on South American time and proving unreliable, so we fired most of them, and shortly afterwards Tom announced he was quitting.

"You've got to be kidding, we've only just got here!" I exclaimed.

"I met this fabulous chick in City Island. She's gonna buy a truck and we'll take the scenic route back up to the States," he explained somewhat sheepishly.

"Shit, that's like taking coal to Newcastle, mate, this place is crawling with wild women," I said in disbelief.

"Yeah, well that should keep you busy for a while, Chas old son, but this one's different. I wanna marry her and this trip will be a honeymoon," he replied, his mind made up.

And so it was. Within a week he bade farewell and I took over running *Peanut Brittle*.

Not long afterwards Eric Schmidt, a wonderful Brazilian of Danish descent, stepped aboard with a wealth of experience under his belt, and from then on it wasn't just plain sailing but more a case of 'watch your step Johnny Walker and don't look back'. And he brought with him a bunch of young guys from the Niteroi Yacht Club, all keen as mustard.

The boys were junior members of the tiny yacht club, often referred to as the English Club, a grassroots establishment that breeds champions and boasts more Olympic medals than any other sports institute in the entire country. Eric and his twin brother Axel were great sailors, and under their father's guidance grew up sailing Snipe dinghies. They both became not only national but three-time world champions before graduating into the Star class, where they finished fifth and sixth in the '68 and '72 Olympic Games. It was quite a sailing dynasty; their nephews Lars and Torben Grael later went on to become Olympic and world champions several times over, before hitting the Volvo '70 Round the World scene.

Off-loading Peanut Brittle in Buenos Aries, nearly a fatal exercise

None of the kids had access to the Rio Yacht Club, so I would take *Peanut Brittle* around the corner, past the Sugarloaf and over to Leme Beach, where they would swim like fish out to the boat and clean the bottom of the her until she was slick and slippery as an eel, before jumping on board and coming sailing.

In those days the Rio Circuit was in its infancy and consisted of a series of offshore races that started in the old coffee port of Sao Paulo, to the south of Rio, and ended up with a long distance run off Buzios which lies to the north. Back in the '50s Joe and his mate Doc Sucksdorff discovered Buzios when they went on a fishing expedition to Cabo Frio. While inspecting an early 17th century stone fortress, once used as a stronghold against marauders, they learned of a safe anchorage about fifteen miles to the north. Joe left early one morning

Taking Nach's children out sailing on Peanut Brittle in Buzios, Brazil
Photographer unknown

before the northeast sea breeze picked up momentum and made his way up through a chain of small islands and their roaring surf breaks, rounded the Buzios peninsular and pulled into the protected harbour. Stunned by its beauty he immediately fell in love with the place. Once inhabited by pirates and bands of runaway slaves, the tiny fishing village was named Ossos, or 'bones' after the humpback whale remains found there. Joe ran down to a scalloped sandy beach where he threw out the hook. As he told me one day:

"Chas, I kept thinking about that bloody fortress and decided I'd build my own."

He managed to lay his hands on five acres on top of a hill at the northern end of the beach. With bugger all there and no power, water or telephones, he drilled a bore, installed a generator, planted a botanical garden, and then began to build his Casa Grande. Fifty years ago Buzios was the best kept secret in Rio, but then Brigitte Bardot turned up with her Brazilian boyfriend, and by the time she'd been photographed with her tits hanging out, everything changed. The cat was out of the bag, as Joe put it. Real estate guys swarmed the place like a plague of locusts and snapped up all the available land, until the once unknown paradise became known as the St. Tropez of Brazil. That's

166

when Joe built a bloody great wall around the Casa Grande for a bit of privacy. He also had another idea. Midway along Ossos Beach there still remained a spacious property, on which sat a quaint old chapel. It was here that Joe hoped to build a yacht club. It wasn't an easy proposition, for it would involve obtaining a blessing from the church authorities, convincing the navy to give permission to build as they controlled all the water rights from the shore line out, and also get the nod of approval from the Governor of Rio.

However Joe had a formidable partner in a great man called Lauritz 'Natch' Lachman, who hatched a plan of attack when *Peanut Brittle* won the Lloyd Braziliero Cup, sponsored by the company he worked for. At the end of the race during the evening presentation of a huge silver cup, he coaxed the admiral of the Brazilian navy to join our crew table. By the end of the night Natch looked pretty happy, and with a Cheshire cat grin and blue eyes sparkling, clapped me on the back announcing:

"We've got the admiral in our pocket, Chas, he's coming to Buzios. Joe will go crazy when he hears the news – we'll build that bloody club if it's the last thing we do!"

And it was true. He had one foot firmly in the door of his dream.

Peanut Brittle arrived in Buzios ready and raring to go. The night before the race the committee held a meeting to discuss whether or not the course should be shortened. The suggestion at this point was vetoed. However, at an impromptu gathering on the beach the following morning, the decision was reversed and the course was indeed shortened. Unfortunately this news was totally unbeknownst to me, and for some inexplicable reason no one had mentioned the change in plans to anyone on sailing on *Peanut Brittle* either.

Unaware of this crucial information we set sail for the long version of the race and blasted across the starting line all guns blazing. The navigation was a dead reckoning affair, only aided by a sextant and a radio beacon perched on a cape sixty miles away. The first leg took us on a twenty-five mile beat into the trade winds and along the coastline riddled with submerged rocks, and it became no less intense a moment when we rounded Santana Island, ripping past the lighthouse to the sound of thunderous surf tumbling onto the scarred cliffs.

The next mark lay seventy miles to the east. We hoisted a small star-cut spinnaker, and taking into account a two knot south-westerly set in the current, held a slightly higher course than the other yachts around us and confirmed our rounding of the mark on the VHF at about midnight. When dawn broke a heavy mist descended, but fortunately *Cabo Buzios* was smack on the bow, only half a mile away. We slid between the cape and a sun-seared, bird-shit bleached clump of rocks, and not knowing this was now the revised finishing line, headed back up towards Santana Island, which took us the best part of the rest of the day.

Meanwhile, back on shore, the finishing touches to the presentation festivities were being completed at Joe's mansion. Nellie commanded a fleet of maids, and a flock of gardeners spruced up the spectacular gardens in preparation for the shindig. About this time Joe arrived, and seeing all the other yachts back from the race and safe at anchor, became concerned that *Peanut Brittle* was still absent from her mooring.

"Where's Chas and my boat?" he asked Pelicano, the sailing master from *Saga*. "Did he know the race was shortened?"

"I don't know, Joe, I just assumed someone would have told him," Pelicano replied, scratching his head.

Joe sent his caretaker Jean up to the tallest hill on the peninsular to see if he could spot *Peanut Brittle*. Jean was a reformed alcoholic, but would still scatter igloos full of Antarctica and Brahma beer all over the estate gardens, so wherever I walked there was a cold drink at hand. He scanned the horizon anxiously, and just before a search party was dispatched to find us, he spotted *Peanut Brittle's* sails in the distance.

"Señor, Señor, Chas volta agora!" he cried out.

And indeed we were returning, flying downwind under a wind-filled blooper, a billowing spinnaker decorated with Brazil's national colours of green and yellow, and running into Osso's bay.

Joe met me at the presentation under a big purple-flowering Jacaranda tree.

"Welcome back, amigo, you sailed the full course, didn't you!"

I grinned and nodded back.

"Well, you know what you've got to do, son? Protest to all these bastardos standing around here because they shortened the course and never told you."

We won the protest and were awarded triple points, and *Peanut Brittle* ended up winning the series, a bloody enormous silver teapot and a full-sized cannon as big as a brigantine.

Roberto, the owner of *Wa Wa II*, bounded up to me and shaking my hand vigorously and laughing like a train, announced:

"Chas, you have become a martyr! What's occurred today has been a long time in the making. This is the first foreign boat that's won the Rio Circuit, and the result will revolutionize ocean racing in Brazil. Muito obligado, amigo!"

The party was a fabulous affair; Joe's and Natch's dream came true that night. The various authorities gave permission for the yacht club to be built and 'jeitinho' achieved, which means finding a way to get something done no matter how seemingly impossible it may seem. And if you happen to visit Buzios and walk down the ocean promenade Orla Bardot, you'll come across a statue of the gorgeous Brigitte Bardot, and nearby is the yacht club Joe and Natch founded; and further along next to the Casa Grande there's a road that runs out to the end of the peninsular named Jose Carlos Laporte Rua.

For me, though, further dramas began to brew that night on the back of a wild forty-knot rogue storm blowing in from the east.

"Chas, Chas!" yelled Phil Wade, clambering aboard *Peanut Brittle* in a frenzy. "*Albacore* has disappeared from her mooring!"

"What fucking time is it?" I groaned.

"Christ knows, but near dawn. I fired a crazy marinero today from the crew, maybe the bastard stole it, but you gotta help me find her!"

"Son of a bitch," I sighed, dragging myself out of the scratcher.

Phil and I took off at high speed in the dinghy to look for the yacht, and searched high and low until first light, when we rounded the corner of the headland and found Albacore caught on some rocks in a raging surf. And worse, the big anchor chain had wrapped around a bloody great boulder like an anaconda, the keel crashed on the bottom, and the bow was being pulverised on a low overhanging cliff.

"Shit, it's a holocaust! We've gotta get on board, mate!" I shouted through the wailing wind.

Ploughing through the surf, we managed to pull up alongside the stricken yacht and clamber on board.

"We're going to have to cut through the anchor chain to get her free!" I called out, and dived into the chaos down below decks to look for some tools. I found a hacksaw amongst an upturned load of pickled fish and tried to cut through the chain, but the blade broke in seconds.

Phil pulled some bolt cutters out of the wreckage in the bow and yelled to me to put the engine in hard reverse while he chomped through the heavy metal links until Albacore broke free.

"Spin her round fast, Chas, and let's get the fuck out of here before she's smashed to pieces!" Phil hollered.

With a great victory under her belt, *Peanut Brittle* was shipped down to Argentina on board one of Lloyd Braziliero's freighters, and I flew into Buenos Aires to make sure she was unloaded safely. I was a man on a mission and in a hurry as I headed towards the shipping terminal in the big main port and rushed past the main gates of the navy yard. All of a sudden I heard an ominously loud click of a rifle. Grinding to a halt, I found myself staring straight into the sights of a loaded weapon. In 1977, before the Falklands war, Argentina was run by a full-scale military regime which you didn't want to fuck with.

"Oh shit," I muttered under my breath, raising my arms before pointing to *Peanut Brittle*.

Lesson learned. Don't move like a sky rocket in that neck of the woods unless you're under fire.

I boarded the transport ship and climbed the ladder up to the yacht, where she sat in a cradle astride a huge stack of forty-foot containers, alongside a five hundred-ton floating crane waiting to unload her. The stevedores grabbed the bit from the low end of the crane and hooked the spreader bars onto the lifting straps wrapped around her belly. The way this is done is critical. If you liken a yacht to an egg, when you squeeze it from end to end nothing happens. But held too tight around the guts, you end up with a handful of yolk and broken shell. If you do that with a big boat the results can be devastating – and expensive.

For the second time that day I came horribly close to carking it. Like a hooked trout, the crane raised *Peanut Brittle* up and up until, at around ninety feet above the deck of the freighter, a loud crack and a couple of teeth-shattering clangs rang through the air. To my horror I spotted a large bolt whirling past in a blur and heard the sound of metal hitting metal as it bounced across the containers far below. The Argentinians jabbered in a frenzied panic and the blood almost drained out of me. As the yacht precariously swung out into mid-air, I looked down a hundred and fifty feet into an uninviting filthy brown River Platte, while the crane driver fought to keep control of *Peanut Brittle*, lowering her way too fast towards the water. I felt like I was on one of those creaking vintage elevators, out of control and headed for doom. I've never been sea or air-sick in my life, but this was another space in time. With my arsehole halfway up my oesophagus it was too late to jump, and only Superman could have made the leap if the yacht went into a free dive. Seconds felt like hours as the guy on the crane slowly brought his swaying cargo to a tenuous halt, accompanied by ghastly rattling groans from the ancient contraption's blocks and sheaves. By the time we eventually splashed down in the river, more or less in one piece, I chucked my guts up and into the river.

By the skin of her teeth – and mine for that matter, *Peanut Brittle* was ready to roll for the race up to Rio de Janiero. The evening before we left, a 'parillado' – an Argentinian barbecue, a raucous affair of music and drinking – got laid on for the crew. I remember it vividly because the ravishing Frederica, sometime girlfriend of Ted Turner, showed up looking sensational.

"That's a great dress you're almost wearing," I remarked as she parked her perfect arse nearby.

"Oui, merci Chas, it's fiesta time, non?"

At which point a Brazilian bloke who piloted for Varig airlines called Eduardo made a beeline for Frederica and whispered in her ear.

"Merde, this guy is an arsehole, non?" she indignantly exclaimed, turning to me.

On the barbecue menu were grilled bull's balls the size of ostrich eggs, and Frederica stabbed her fork into a couple of them, eyeing up her offender.

"The problem with you, Eduardo, is that you don't have any bollocks, and even if you did you wouldn't know what to do with them. That's one thing about Ted – he's got balls."

A shamefaced Eduardo slunk off into the crowd, but the defiant Frederica wasn't finished yet and leaned over towards me, her breasts firm and hard as perfect round Cox's Pippin apples.

"That little shit wanted to know if he could get into my knickers later tonight."

"He wouldn't have had much luck, Frederica, you never wear them anyway," I said laughing.

Late into the night when the wood on the fire had burned down to ashes and the band had played a last tango. everyone began to make their way home. I ended up sharing a taxi with Yogi, a bespectacled, pint-sized German who sailed on *Duva*, and our cook Pedino Velino, a wiry, volatile Brazilian who was hard of hearing and completely deaf in one ear. Word had it that a few years ago he'd had an affair with some big gun's mistress in Rio, and when her jealous lover found out, the fella hired a hit man who tracked Pedino down in a crowded café to kill him. Fortunately the assassin was a lousy shot and Pedino only copped two slugs in his shoulder. It looked like our taxi ride might be heading into similar disastrous territory when my fellow passengers decided to kick on to the local red light district. Pedino got into a furious, hot-headed argument with the taxi driver, which escalated into a full-on brawl and brought the cops running. The other two guys hoofed up a side street and I was the only sucker left on the scene to arrest.

In a second I found myself handcuffed and bundled into a military truck and promptly deposited in a garrison, tossed into a dark, filthy cell where the sound of some poor victim having the shit beaten out of him echoed through the dank walls from above. As luck would have it, I found my tattered passport in my sailing pants pocket and showed it to the brute of a commanding officer when he strode into the slammer. Wondering how the hell I might get out of the clutches of this latest predicament, I suddenly remembered Papa Frers had been at the party earlier that evening. Frers was a legendary yachtsman and near deified in Argentina. Thankfully, mention of his name and my connection to the Buenos Aires Yacht Club got me out of the joint before the night was over and I staggered back to the marina with my knees still knocking.

Although Pedino had escaped arrest, he arrived on the dock the next morning looking as if he'd done a few rounds with Mohammed Ali. Hobbling along all busted up, he sported a black eye and a couple of bumps on his skull the size of goose eggs. Natch blew a fuse. Not only was his cook a mess, but also bloody late, and then to top it all the dishevelled little fella announced he wanted to pull out of the race.

"That's enough of your bullshit, Pedino. Get on board and start work pronto!" Natch ordered, between clenched teeth.

The bedraggled Pedino unhappily hauled his arse onto *Peanut Brittle* and disappeared below to stow a heap of perishable supplies in the string nets hanging over the forward bulkhead close to the engine.

The race got under way in lousy, choppy, wet conditions and we punched into a strong twenty-five knot headwind, while the ebb tide ran like a bitch as the boat banged through muddy uninviting water for the remainder of the day and the following night, before escaping the delta and heading north up the Uruguayan coast. Meanwhile, Pedino further added to Natch's fury when he found the luckless cook had stored a battery of eggs in amongst the fruit and vegetables in the forward nets, and during the rough sail they had beaten themselves to a pulverised pulp. The liquid oozed down under the engine, mixed with diesel, and made an evil fermenting cocktail which created an execrable stench. Crawling around doubled up in the small stinking space I almost succumbed to the fumes, and swearing furiously at the hapless Pedino, set about trying to suck up the foul brew with a bilge pump.

And the hits just kept on coming. Our main helmsman Roberto, a world-class Soling sailor, got pitch-poled head first down the main companion way during a sod of a stormy night. He recovered consciousness only to discover he'd lost his eyesight. Several hours later we managed to rendezvous with the Uruguayan coast-guard vessel, whose crew rushed him ashore for medical help. Conditions worsened, and finally, several hundred miles out to sea, a pampero blasted through. A monstrous cigar-shaped cloud chased in from the southwest and hit us with a fifty-knot blast, not dissimilar to a southerly buster in the Bass Strait. It blew like a bastard for a couple of days. Under the chicken chute or storm spinnaker, the blasting wind hurled *Peanut Brittle* into a wild broach, and our navigator Pontuel, a big solid man, demolished his bunk under the strain of the impact, crashed onto the floor and broke three ribs. We'd lost another helmsman and still had seven hundred miles to go. No sooner had the pampero abated into a downwind slide, it was replaced by a solid north-easterly twenty-knot plus trade wind and left us beating into a dead maggot.

Battered and bruised, we eventually crossed the finishing line to the sound of a thousand drums revving up for Rio's carnival, and the scent of suntan lotion drifted across the water, heralding the promise of hoards of hot women. The Rio Yacht Club is famous for holding one of the best carnival balls in town, and this one made sure it lived up to its reputation, providing gallons of Cachaca, a sugarcane rocket fuel which sent the revellers crazy; and to add to the heat a fleet of girls from the previous year's winning samba school were shipped in to shake their tail feathers and set the place alight. One of them was simply unbelievable, dressed like a tigress and her fabulous body plastered in paint. Lachman spotted me in the arms of the beauty and tossed over the keys to a far better hacienda than the one I roosted in, and I waltzed the wild girl over there as the sun rose. By the time she'd had me for breakfast, brunch and lunch, I looked like a Cherokee Indian covered in streaks of war paint. And that night I ended up with a tambourine player, a sequinned, rhinestone-studded princess dancing at a back street barrio 'pagode' party, a style of samba that musicians play on cavaquinhos, while the drummers hammer out smoking rhythms.

By the time I hit the road for Buzios a couple of days later my head was pounding worse than a bateria's drum. A sensation made all the worse by Joe's chauffeur Antonio, who drove like a bat out of hell.

"Ola Chas, I drive like the champion Fittipaldi, non?" he called out over his shoulder.

"Yeah, but this isn't a Formula One race, mate," I groaned.

"Merda," he shouted "that's bad shit!" as the silver Galaxy's front wheels hit the millionth pothole and sent my pounding headache through the roof.

The ridges of the mountains fell away in the city haze behind us, the flat plateau spread out to the east in front as we sped towards Buzios at high speed. And slobbering all over me were Laporte's three drooling Boxer dogs, a boss-eyed bitch, her extremely dim-witted brother, and their father, who unlike his offspring was a magnificent-looking beast called Max. He rode in the sedan as if he were a Roman general in a chariot, standing on his hind legs, his head and front paws hanging out of the window, going insane with excitement as we shot by herd after herd of Brahma steers. The last twenty miles were the worst when he caught the sharp salt scent of the sea, and knowing he was on the last stretch to the Casa Grande he turned up the volume of his ear-splitting bark to an almost unbearable level. We pummelled down an atrocious dirt road in a cloud of dust and finally rose over the peak of a steep hill, and the peninsular with its dazzling white beaches and the deep blue of the South Atlantic exploded into view. Antonio screeched to a halt at the Casa Grande, and faithful Jean the caretaker and the usual multitude of maids rushed to greet us carrying a pile of freshly-cut coconuts, the juice of which I can highly recommend to ease a killing hangover.

After resting up for a couple of days I strolled over to Armacao, a dusty mile or so south of Ossos, to listen to the musicians at the Estrangeiro bar play bossa novas and haunting, ghost-like Portuguese ballads beaten out on rasping double basses, which sounded like the blues played with rusty kitchen knives. It was here I met the wonderful Donna. Around her late thirties and in full bloom, her deep brown eyes said it all – you could have drowned in them. At the end of an electrically charged evening I thought I'd test the waters and offered to take her home. She cut me off at the pass but left a glimmer of hope as she stepped out of the bar.

"Carlos, I'm going to Ossos beach tomorrow, look out for me there," she murmured over her shoulder before disappearing into the night.

I reckoned I had a snowball's chance in hell, but lo and behold, the next afternoon while I busied myself with work on Joe's cruising sloop, I heard the sound of tapping on the hull and a woman calling out in a husky voice,

"Buenos dios, Señor, can I come aboard?"

I belted out through the hatch to find the glistening wet, bikini-clad Donna climbing up the ladder on the far side of the boat, well out of sight of the beach. She didn't linger on deck; not that I minded in the least. We disappeared down below for a sensational afternoon. And so it went for the rest of the week, my lissom siren swimming over to visit and taking me to never-never land.

Come the weekend, Joe rolled into Buzios. I found him at the local cafe, sitting in the cool of the shade under a big Poinciana tree. Leaning back in his chair he paused for a moment sizing me up, a plume of smoke from a Dannenmann charuto, Brazil's finest cigar, spiralling up in the air.

"I hear you had a good sail with a Rio Tinto's head honcho from London recently," he began.

"Sure," I replied, "he was a nice bloke."

"Well, you certainly entertained him with your stories, and he told me he had a lot of fun after the rounds of stressful meetings he'd had with Generals Pinochet and Geisal."

Then he paused, taking a sip of beer before continuing in a more serious tone of voice:

"However, before you get too carried away with yourself, there's another matter I wish to discuss. I have reason to believe you've been recently having an affair. Is that so?"

I stared at him in astonishment. It was impossible to fathom out how the hell he knew about Donna. She'd swum out to the boat inconspicuously each day and no one from the beach could have possibly seen her climb on board from the far side.

"Yeah, I have."

"Ah, si Chas, I thought so. It's a serious matter. The woman you've been throwing your leg over happens to be married to one of the highest-ranked colonels in Brazil's military. He's a ruthless bastard, and if he finds out you've been screwing his wife he'll have you killed."

"Shit, no wonder Donna went to such lengths to keep out of sight!" I gasped, while thinking to myself that she'd sure as hell been worth it, even if the result may be about to give rise to treacherous waters.

"I know about the affair, but luckily for you the Colonel doesn't yet. Fernando Pimental Duarte's new boat *Tigre* needs to be sailed back from Argentina. I'm sending you over to pick it up. At least you'll be out of the country for a couple of weeks, and for god's sake try to keep yourself out of any more trouble," he stated firmly, with a look that made sure I got the message.

"Shit!" I said again, reaching for another beer to calm myself down.

A couple of days later, on a storm-stricken morning, Tom the Pom and I lugged our clobber out of Buenos Aires airport and headed for the marina. The sky was the colour of dark granite, lit up by flashes of stark silver lightning streaking overhead.

"Pampero, Señors!" the taxi driver yelled, glancing nervously overhead at the looming heavy weather, and slammed the cab door shut.

Buffeted around like a ping-pong ball in the gathering wind and barely able to see through the driving rain hammering across the windscreen, Tom shouted over the din,

"It's lucky we're not at sea, mate!"

"Yeah, it's blowing dogs off chains. Look at that!" I answered, pointing at a bunch of uprooted trees blocking the road.

Finally, after an expensive detour, we reached a tributary that runs into the River Platte where the yacht we were to sail to Rio was berthed. *Tigre*, one of Germain Frers latest designs, had been launched just before the race to Rio, but after breaking some gear had been forced to retire. Pepe, German's younger brother, showed us around.

"Hey Pepe, where are the life-rafts?" Tom asked.

176

"Ah, si amigo, this is a bit of a problem..." replied Pepe.

"Bloody hell, we need a six-man life-raft in this weather for sure!" Tom insisted.

"Merda, they have to be imported, non? And it takes two weeks, maybe more. You guys have much experience for sailing in this weather, you will be ok, si?"

Tom leaned back against the guard rail and took a stand.

"Look Pepe, your father is a demigod around these parts, but I bet even he carried a sturdy clinker dinghy in case of emergency – not that I give a shit whether he did or not. However, one thing's for sure: Chas may look like a poor man's Jesus Christ but he can't walk on water, and I doubt your three marineros can either, so one way or the other you're going to have to find us a fucking life-raft or we're not going anywhere."

Pepe got the message, realizing Tom was dead serious.

"Ok, I will call my father and see what can be arranged," he capitulated.

In the meantime we kept busy scurrying around the local chandlers and hardware stores buying the gear needed for the voyage. Loading up the galley hardly cost much in those days; if you spent more than five U.S bucks on a humungous steak and a bottle of wine you'd have been well and truly fleeced. And the five cases of local whisky I stowed, later to be used to bribe the guards at the Rio Yacht Club so I could get girls into the club, didn't cost much either.

Pepe delivered on the life-raft. It showed up courtesy of the Argentine navy. Old Papa Frers could move mountains, and his efforts produced a twelve-man vessel packed inside a large fibreglass cylinder. What vintage it was and whether it was seaworthy remained anyone's guess, but with little time to fuck around further we shoved it on board and hoped for the best.

Both Tom and I were travelling on British passports at a time when the English were not the flavour of the month in Argentina. The military junta were beginning to rumble over the Falkland Islands issue, and feeling the agitation beginning to crank up we were anxious to be on our way. By the second night at sea we reached Punta de Este and pounded along the Uruguayan coast on the starboard tack in a thirty-knot nor'easter.

"We've got to tack or we'll be pulverised!" Tom called out, barely

Tigre *flying downwind before a Pampero off Uruguay on the way to Rio 1977.*
Photo: Tom Richardson (crewmate)

audible over the boom of roaring surf hitting the rocks.

I hurried down the deck to free the leeward runner, and to my horror discovered that the clevis pin, which runs through the bottom tang of the lower rigging to the chain plates holding up the mast, was missing.

"Where the fuck is the screwdriver?" I yelled to Tom.

Only a few meters from the first of a huge set of breakers crashing onto the jagged shore and likely shipwreck, I dashed back to the cockpit, grabbed an old Philips head and rushed back to jam it into the hole where the pin should have been.

"Ok Tom, swing her round, this thing had better bloody hold," I called out.

It did, and miraculously we pulled out of harm's way, and dropping the mainsail, bore away on an easier course.

Danger averted, I began rummaging around in the tool box for spare parts.

"These split pins are made out of damn poor material, they'll sheer off in a minute," I told Tom. "What the hell are we going to do to secure the rigging?"

In the end we used seizing wire, and it was just as well, for as dawn

178

broke a dirty black sky raced in from the south, and on its trail like a hound from hell came another raging pampero. After a shit fight with the blasting wind and days of little sleep, exhaustion set in. Tom managed to get some sextant sights from a couple of stars, plotted our position, and went below to grab a few hours' rest. In case the young lads got into trouble over the next few hours, I lay down for a catnap nearby in the cockpit, wrapped in my oilskins, and fell into a dream. In fact, I was sitting on top of an elephant in Burma and riding out of a forest wading into some long savannah grass, and came across a large log blocking the path. All of a sudden, surrounded by a bunch of fiery-eyed growling tigers, one of them leaped up to grab me. I woke up to the sound of a massive thud.

"What the hell was that?" I shouted.

My tigers had turned into the two Argie crew guys who'd been knocked off their feet with the impact and landed on top of me with an almighty thump. The boat ground to a halt, and Tom flew out of his bunk at the aft end of the boat, landing head first on top of a sack of onions way up forward.

"Christ, we've run aground!" I heard him groan.

"It's a whale, mate, we've hit a fucking whale!" I yelled down the hatch.

"*Tigre's* lead keel must have hit the leviathan like a sledge hammer and slid up the animal's back until she skewered around into the wind, absolutely dead in the water.

The moon cast enough light to be able to see that the whale was a hell of a lot bigger than us and dwarfed the boat. The water surged underneath us and I near froze in terror as the moon suddenly vanished and the whale rose, arched high above us, and his flukes, the size of a Ford flat-back jalopy, blocked out half the sky.

"Bloody hell, it's Moby Dick all over again!" I yelped while trying to hang on to the helm.

We were completely immobilized, the boat caught in irons and the engine's batteries under the chart table disconnected. For the next few seconds our lives lay in the lap of the sea gods. The whale unleashed its final payload of compressed air and its tail walloped into the ocean, missing the boat by a walrus's whisker.

"Hold on, for Christ's sake!" Tom yammered.

A motherfucker of a wave roared over the boat, flooded the cockpit and overflowed in a cascade down the open hatch. I heard a gurgled cry from below as Tom got swept off his feet by the sheer force of water. The mighty whale pulled up stakes and plunged into the dark depths leaving a huge tell-tale phosphorous signature footprint behind him. It reminded me of a song the famous mariner Uffa Fox penned in the Bay of Biscay: 'When they tickled the tail of a great big whale with a half inch nail...'

We were still in dire straits. Down below *Tigre's* decks the impact had caused chaos. The flat section of the boat's under-body in front of the keel had concaved under the floor-boards, and a couple of aluminium frames had twisted and contorted out of place. One of the welds cracked and a torrent of water sprayed into the resulting breach, which left us bucketing it and chucking it like madmen until dawn. By daylight the situation was serious. In order to try and fix the problem we demolished the galley sink and extracted all the salvageable self-tapping stainless screws, sawed up some timber and shored the bow up. Finally, late in the morning after hours of arduous labour, we managed to attach a long strip of rubber mat over the top of the makeshift repair to stem the flood, and stuck a load of sail battens, silicone sealant and the self-tappers to hold it in place.

Thank god *Tigre* had been built out of alloy. If not, we'd have foundered and been forced to take the life-raft for a test drive – which in all probability would have been about as useful as an ashtray on a motorbike, and with a sigh of relief we limped into Rio days later. Tom the Pom and I had sailed a couple of thousand miles together on this trip, but all up between us had accumulated around a quarter of a million miles at sea. The Argentinian lads, in contrast, had just completed their first big venture and probably wouldn't be forgetting the episode for quite a while.

It felt good to be back in Brazil, and a big relief to find out the colonel was none the wiser for my affair with his wife, so thankfully I escaped a grizzly retribution and resolved to try and stay out of trouble. There were some interesting characters floating around Rio at the time and I got to meet a few of them.

Early one hot and hazy morning after a night out on the town in Ipanema, I strolled in through the yacht club gates and my boatboy Dado, a Mulatto lad from Bahia, Salvador, rushed out to greet me with an anxious look on his face. Dado spoke a dialect quite different to the locals in Rio, and over the past six months the two of us had developed our own bas-tardised lingo of Bahian, Taswegian Portuguese that only we could understand, although at times it could be a hit or miss affair. I decoded from this particular morning's scrambled com-munication that a small yacht had arrived and the lone sailor on board had been arrested on an arms charge, and could I help.

It turned out Yuri the Israeli didn't have a gun on board his sparrow-sized boat but did own a bazooka, an anti-tank weapon which he kept to protect himself against killer whales. After a lot of diplomatic assistance, phone calls and telegrams to

Yuri (Gidaliahu Shtirmer), Solo Circum-navigator 1975-1977 UK-UK, on his tiny boat New Penny in the Rio Yacht Club yacht basin, after sailing from Melbourne non-stop around the Horn to Rio.

Brazilia he got out of jail, but his weapon was confiscated and the authorities gave him eight days to sort out his problems and leave.

Yuri was a tall, skinny, bearded fellow, and tattered salt-worn rags dangled loose from his weather-beaten frame as if hanging off a washing line. In fact he was all skin and bones, a torn and frayed seagoing scarecrow blown onto shore. If he had been a horse he'd have been knocked back at the knackers' yard, and his little boat didn't look much better. At just under twenty-two feet long, his vessel *New Penny* was sloop-rigged and twin-keeled with a faded, worn powder-blue hull, which I suspect at one time had been a much deeper blue, and streaks and speckles of rust encrusted her pale grey decks. The Israeli refugee invited me aboard after traipsing back from jail on the low tide. I swung down onto the deck by way of the raggedy rigging which dan-gled off the small mast. On top of the sliding hatch covering the companion way sat a Perspex bubble, and Yuri demonstrated how he could sit on the steps, wedge himself into a cocoon beside a wash-board in the cockpit and brace his feet against the wind vane-steered outboard rudder which hung from a couple of davits, as if he was on a sailing dinghy. Upside down in the bilge lay a rusted engine strapped to the original supports, and the entire coach roof was covered in dark, sooty grease from his cooking.

Beads of sweat rolled down his gaunt, angular face while he boiled the kettle on a small primus and offered me a cup of tea, a commodity as rare as hen's teeth in the land of coffee, and we sat for a while as he began to unwind from the stress of his predicament.

"How does the tea taste?" he asked.

"Not bad," I said, lying through my teeth while sipping the grim-tasting brew out of a near fossilized tin mug.

"I made it with the last of the water I picked up in Aussie," he explained.

"Well Yuri, that's the first water from Down Under I've drunk since leaving in 1969. Cheers mate!"

Now I assumed, quite wrongly but who could blame me, that Yuri and the *New Penny* had sailed from England, down to the Cape Verde's, past the Ivory Coast and Senegal and across to Brazil, but as we drank the pitch-black brew, Yuri told me a little of his journey. After being discharged from the Israeli navy he took off for England and bought *New Penny*, added the bubble and the small self-steering wind vane, and set off to circumnavigate the world via the great capes. Somewhere between the Cape of Good Hope and Australia the little boat's spindly spa broke. He managed to repair it and splice the sections back together by sawing off a piece of his emergency steering oar, and under a jury rig made landfall on the West coast of Australia. He found a bit of work there, and with the few dollars he made in wages was able to replenish supplies and patch up *New Penny* before pushing on to South America.

"I've been at sea for over a hundred and twenty days and I never caught a fish."

"Why's that mate? I asked.

"The fish are my friends," he said, "although I was worried about Killer Whales."

I laughed, but then again it was a bloody small boat.

"Where in the hell do you sleep?" I enquired, looking around the matchbox-sized interior.

He explained he lay across *New Penny* and that way he could spread-eagle himself against the overhead and hang like a gecko when his little cockle shell was either pitch-poled or knocked down in the incredible weather conditions he encountered. To try and keep the boat steady in the Southern Ocean's enormous following seas, he would pave out a hundred metres of half-inch blue polyurethane rope like a great snake. The engine provided some kind of ballast, which was just as well because he was rolled over nine times, but each time *New Penny* somehow managed to right herself, all rigging standing. Apart from the boat – forget about the life-raft, there wasn't one – the clothes he stood in and forty bucks in his pocket was all he possessed in Rio that morning a long way from home. Although I realised over the next days the truth of the matter – *New Penny* was really his home.

Out of the woodwork popped a very pretty young Jewish girl who had learned somehow of Yuri's plight. She came down to the yacht club, rolled up her sleeves, and ignoring his protests got down on her hands and knees and scrubbed and dried his boat from one end to the other until it was clean as a whistle. And Yuri got to work repairing the worn out and ripped mainsail by cutting chunks out of his heavy jib top for the material he needed, and traded the polyurethane rope in exchange for a couple of pots of antifouling. The galvanised shackle supporting his head-stay was almost completely corroded and needed replacing, so I gave him a good stainless steel one and a pin to fix the rudder to the gudgeon. A South African mate of mine cooked up a couple of feasts and Yuri just ate and ate to fill up his hollow legs and top up his empty Ned Kelly. By the time his eight days were up he gathered about four small paper bags of provisions, and early one morning simply slid out of port and was gone.

All sorts of seafaring waifs and strays ended up in Rio, and there was none with a more bizarre and strange story to tell than that of a yacht called *Twilight*. Early one overcast morning a long slender 9/8 rigged yacht slid in past the breakwater wall under the Sugarloaf mountain and into the Rio Yacht Club. *Twilight* had beautiful lines but looked very tired and worn after a long voyage. When the yellow quarantine flag came down, the various officials went on their way after stamping their stamps and pocketing half the entry permit fees. Such was the system in Latin America in those days, corruption was part of life and you rode it, for only a fool would try to buck it. I met *Twilight's* American owner and his German wife later that evening out on the balcony of the yacht club's restaurant which looked across the harbour, and over a cold beer they recounted their adventures.

Mark and Maizie Claphorn were in their early thirties and wanted to do some long distance sailing, so they chucked in their boring nine to five jobs, got hold of a boat and set off across the Pacific and Indian Oceans fetching up in the Red Sea. In Saudi Arabia they were arrested as spies and flung into prison, where they went through quite an ordeal. Unable to get any assistance from the US embassy, things went from bad to worse when one of their crew tried to escape from jail and seriously injured himself. Maizie was eventually released from the slammer, and not long after one of the Saudi princes freed her husband. The boat in the meantime had been hauled out of the water and got pretty damaged in the process. The burning sun had opened up the caulking in the planking of her once good-looking wooden hull. The Claphorns befriended the prince and he offered the couple some expensive Brookes and Gatehouse gear to make up for the government's misunderstanding. They got out of there as fast as possible, shoved off down the East coast of Africa, installed a brand new Caterpillar engine on *Twilight* in Durban, which they didn't pay for, and then rounded the Cape of Good Hope bound for Rio.

"Shit, that's quite a trip!" I exclaimed. "Where do you reckon you're headed next?"

"Well we've pretty much run out of money, so we'll fly up to the States and work for a while, I guess, and pick up the voyage when we get back," replied Mark.

The famous offshore sailor and damn good sail-maker Roberto Pelicano offered to cut a deal with Mark and Maizie saying he would take care of their yacht, which would remain in his stewardship as collateral until they came back, against which he lent them eight thousand bucks for air tickets and travel. The Claphorns agreed they would return as soon as possible, but weeks turned into months, and all the while *Twilight* sat on a mooring, her underbelly becoming host to massive clusters of barnacles, mussels and seaweed. Every day Pelicano's marinero would go out and pump the bilges dry – she leaked like a sieve and would have sunk at the mooring if left unattended.

With no word from the Claphorns, Pelicano started to get anxious about his eight thousand oxford scholars and began to think the couple would never return. Both Natch Lauckman and Eric Schmitt were interested in buying *Twilight*, but the big problem was the 300% duty on purchase of a foreign vessel, and so a plan was hatched to avoid paying the hefty tax. If they could pull the new Caterpillar engine out of *Twilight* and sink her, then salvage the vessel and sell the old engine, Pelicano would retrieve the money he'd lent. It probably would have worked but it was not to be. Mark Claphorn's fated journey was about to take a disastrous turn.

I had become mates with some Aussie blokes, Big Joe, Billy Blitz and Stretch, all three of them divers for Petrobras off-shore rigs and platforms, and when on leave I'd take the guys to an infamous club, the Sunset Bar in Ipanema. It cost a buck to get in the door, and once inside the joint it was wall to wall women. I had a girlfriend there, Luisa, who was part Brazilian and part Japanese, stood about 5'4," and her beautiful satin hair tumbled down her back to about a foot above her knees. One night, just before I took her home from the club, I got set upon by a jealous former lover and a couple of his amigos. Unfortunately for them my Aussie diving mates were close by and quickly jumped in to lend a hand. In a New York second Big Joe had the attackers by the throats and rattled their heads together like sabres. Walking home with my three solid bodyguards we got to talking about *Twilight*, and it turned out Stretch needed a boat to pursue his favourite hobby, which involved regularly taking off on expeditions and disappearing into the ocean's depths to search for sunken treasure. He decided he would try to buy the boat and flew up to New York to get hold of a New York copper he knew in an attempt to track down the Claphorns.

A week later after numerous enquiries, Stretch and the policeman discovered Mark in Syracuse, New York, but by the time they arrived it was too late. The unfortunate fella thought the law was coming after him for another reason, and fearing the worst shot himself, and his body was on its way to the morgue. However, before he topped himself he'd left a note addressed to the Commodore of the Balboa Yacht Club. In the letter he explained that one day in California he had jumped on board a boat he didn't own called *Twilight* and apologized for not bringing her back. As irony would have it, had he waited just another few hours he would have ended up ten thousand dollars richer with the greenbacks Stretch had with him to buy the vessel.

I also spent some time with H.W. Tilman, the famous English explorer, mountaineer and adventurer. Listening to him tell stories of his action-packed life held me spellbound. The old war hero won medals in both wars, and at just eighteen years old was on the Western Front where the average life expectancy for a subaltern was eleven days. He survived to fight again at Dunkirk and commanded a battery at Alamein, and at forty-five years old he volunteered for service and parachute training, which then took him behind enemy lines to fight the partisans in Northern Italy and Albania. Later he prospected for gold in Kenya, bicycled across Africa, travelled through Central Asia by a route rarely attempted since Marco Polo, and made a tough voyage across the Patagonian ice-cap. A deeply private man, he shunned publicity and didn't like the idea of sponsorship or large crewed expeditions, so he pioneered two-man odysseys, even when climbing the Himalayas. The great man won the Founder's Medal, the Royal Geographical Society's highest award, and once, after giving a lecture about his journeys to a bunch of Sandhurst Army cadets, one of the young guys asked him, "Please Sir, how do I get on an expedition?" Tilman promptly answered by saying, "Put your boots on and go."

Although ranked one of the world's outstanding mountaineers by the time he reached his fifties, he considered himself too old to climb much above 20,000 feet and instead he took to the sea, becoming one of the first blue-water cruising sailors to sail to both the Antarctic and the Arctic in a succession of old Bristol pilot cutters. He visited some pretty remote and desolate places, where few men had trekked before, and sailed in the same way he had climbed, for the sheer joy of it. He turned up in Rio on a converted tug-boat with a gaff rig and a bunch of mountain climbers on board. In his eighties by this time, it was remarkable that he spent four or five hours every day in the burning heat working on repairs up at the top of the mast. He left one day to climb Smith Island in the South Atlantic. It was his last voyage. En route to the Falkland Islands his ship disappeared without a trace, and neither he nor his crew were ever seen again.

And I'll never forget Doc Sucksdorff, an old mate of Joe's who had served alongside the Brazilian expeditionary forces in Italy during WWII. The Doc was an unusual, inventive fellow, who among other things came up with the idea for a deadly contraption called the 'Cobra', a spear-gun that had a CO_2 charge in it. His most successful innovation was the technology which detected the gender of unborn children, and this wheeze ended up making him a fair few bucks. Joe would often roll into the yacht club armed with a bottle of Glenlivet whisky to entice Sucksdorff, and show him a heap of plans and prototypes for oil platforms and pick his brains from a wealth of knowledge the fella had stashed in the back of his cranium.

One evening The Doc hurried over to see me at the bar, and cupping his hand, whispered in my ear,

"Do you know where I can get some cheap whisky, Capitano?"

"I believe I may be able to help you out there, Doc. Do you like Black & White, the blended stuff with the two Scottish terriers on the label? I can get you a case for a hundred bucks." I wondered why he was straying off his usual territory of single malts.

Just by chance a couple of days earlier a French ketch from the Ivory Coast had arrived carrying a bunch of bedraggled jazz musicians and a shitload of whisky. I'd bought four cases to deal with the yacht club's restriction of only being able to bring my 'spoussa' past the gate. It hadn't taken the guards long to work out that I appeared to have more than a couple of wives, and their tedious enforcement of the regulations was having a detrimental effect on my love life. The guards were an unsavoury bunch of corrupt fuckers, and the only way to get around the problem and bring my girlfriends in was to bribe them. The whisky worked like a charm.

"I'll take the lot," announced The Doc.

"What do you want it for?"

"It keeps Mrs Sucksdorff happy."

"Shit, she must drink a lot of it!" I exclaimed.

"She doesn't like it much herself but needs it for our little 'beija-flors' or 'flower kisses'."

"What the hell are they?" I enquired, thinking he must have lost his marbles.

"They're tiny iridescent-coloured birds. We grow orchids up at our place in the mountains, and in amongst the pot plants my wife hangs bowls of whisky and honey. The birds have become addicted to the brew and never leave our garden. We've got a lot of butterflies that get into it too."

"And what about bees, do you have them as well?" I asked, half joking.

He leaned back and paused to think about it for a second.

"Bees, bees, hmmm... Not that I've noticed, but did Joe ever tell you about the time we went spear-fishing together up near Cabo Frio and a swarm of African bees landed on the boat?"

"Nope, I haven't heard that one," I replied.

"Well, we had to abandon ship and dive overboard and swim for our lives or they'd have killed us," he said, getting quite steamed up at the memory and gesticulating wildly with his hands.

"Oh shit, we've got so many things that can kill you Down Under, mate! Talking of lethal insects, I discovered a load of sawdust floating down from the big supporting beams at Joe's house the other day, and found a bunch of holes in the timber half an inch in diameter that looked as if they'd been bored with a drill. They wouldn't be those killer bees, would they?" I asked.

"Meu dues, non. That's the dreaded Carpenter Bee. They have saw legs and will go through timber like a toredo marine worm. Those beams will look like a Swiss cheese inside – the house will collapse!" he said, pulling on his jacket. "I've got to go now, but for God's sake tell Joe he must act quickly!" he said before shooting out of the door with his driver in tow, and loaded up to the gills with whisky for his birds.

From time to time I used to share a few jugs of the local brahma chopp beer with Ronnie Biggs, the notorious train robber, a friendly bloke with a great sense of humour. He had a wary old codger ex-pat mate I used to know called Henry Liteman, and when Ronnie first fetched up on Rio's shores he often drank in the club's English bar as his guest under the alias of Ron Cook. Ronnie's drinking days there were numbered, however, after Scotland Yard tracked him down and blew his cover. Barred as an undesirable from the Rio Yacht Club, his favourite watering-hole became a pommy-styled boozer called 'The Lord Jim'.

In 1977 the British navy, represented by a fleet of frigates including *HMS Jupiter*, arrived in Rio. The *Jupiter* was on a goodwill mission, and a bunch of officers on shore-leave showed up at the Lord Jim and got to drinking with Ronnie. Totally unaware of his past or who he was, they invited the likeable guy on board one of Her Majesty's finest ships for a cocktail party. Ronnie had a ball, and after consuming half a dozen good British meat pies and a bucket of lager, got photographed prancing down the gangway half pissed. Reuters published the shots the next day, which flew around the world as fast as shit off a shovel, and resulted in a massive uproar in the House of Commons when the news hit that the Queen's navy had played host to one of Britain's most notorious fugitives.

Indirectly, this fiasco had led to my meeting with Ronnie. My mates Trevor and Banco, who had sailed around the world on *Sirocco*, Errol Flynn's lovely old wooden boat, had been so taken with Rio that they decided to sell the yacht and set up a business running uncut gems from Brazil to California, where they flogged them to wealthy clients in Beverly Hills and Hollywood. Both guys decided to cash in on Ronnie's latest scandal, so through Liteman I arranged to hook them up with the old tea-leaf at his crumbling mansion in Santa Theresa that he was renovating. During the nineteenth century the area had once been a pretty smart part of town, but had now decayed and become a dilapidated shell of its former days. Ronnie didn't give a damn about this, of course, he liked its position on top of a steep hill which gave him a bird's eye view of the city and out over the harbour.

The morning we arrived at the mansion he was in an agitated frame of mind. News had just broken that one of his workers had been murdered in a nearby alley. Still distressed, he pulled out a satchel of grass and rolled a couple of spliffs while the fellas hit him with their idea.

"We're going into the T-shirt business, Ronnie. We think maybe you can help us and we'll cut you in on the deal," Banco explained.

"Sure boys, whatever I can do to help!" he replied.

The next day we met at the foot of Sugarloaf Mountain and took a bunch of photographs of Ronnie adorned in an *HMS Jupiter* sailor's hat, holding a pint of beer in one hand and his thumb up in the other. Trevor and Banco produced hundreds of T-shirts, printed the photograph and added a slogan underneath: 'It's Great To Be Free In Rio' emblazoned across the front; and they added Ronnie's signature underneath for good measure. Striking while the iron was hot with political outcry back in London about Ronnie attending the party on *HMS Jupiter*, the boys flew over to England and flogged the bloody lot to a delighted public, who were fond of the train-robbing rascal, and the boys made a small fortune from the venture.

Ronnie wanted to learn how to sail and managed to contact one of his old inmates from Wandsworth prison, who had since been transferred to the Parkhurst slammer on the Isle of Wight, where they were building Fireball racing dinghies in kit form. He got one these sent out to Rio under the guise of furniture and put it together himself. I offered to take him out on *Peanut Brittle* for a spin but when he discovered we flew under a Bermudian flag he backed out. Once bitten, twice shy; the navy incident had given him a bad scare and he thought he might be arrested by the Poms.

"I've already escaped from an English jail, mate, I don't want to be banged up in another one!" he said with some feeling.

He talked about Australia too.

"Oh I love the Aussies," he said in his strong East London accent "Great place, mate, they always like to help a crook."

And indeed he had been helped out while on the run Down Under, and got tipped off a couple of hours before the cops raided his hideout. He managed to make it out of the country on a Greek cruise ship leaving Melbourne destined for Panama, where he continued his run overland and travelled south to Brazil. One day I asked him about the train robbery.

"I never got involved in beating up the train driver, Chas. After the raid we stashed the loot in a farmhouse, and unfortunately I took off my gloves to eat some baked beans and chucked the tin in a bin. The gang moved on but the blokes from Scotland Yard tracked down the farmhouse and got my fingerprints off the can they found in the bloody garbage."

It had been a small but expensive mistake which kept Ronnie on the run and dodging his way round the world for a while until he found a safe haven in Brazil. I heard a little more of these adventures a few years later when I ran into my old pal Scotty off an American yacht called *Jubilation*.

"I met someone you know from Rio, Chas, a guy called Ronnie Biggs. I skippered a Ted Hood designed big ketch and chartered it to a film crew who apparently wanted to make a documentary about the Amazon. When we arrived in Belen at the mouth of the river the camera crew disappeared into the jungle, and ten days later arrived back at the boat with a large heavy object trussed up in a coconut sack, which took a couple of strong men to load onto the yacht. Whatever had been stashed in the bag was still wriggling and writhing, and when

190

I asked the guys what was inside it they told me it was a giant Amazonian river otter on its way to a zoo for breeding purposes, and did I have a stronger bag to secure it. It seemed a bit strange at the time, but the crew were a bunch of surly bastards and I wasn't about to argue with them."

"What do you reckon was really in there, Scotty?" I asked.

"Yeah, well, good question mate, things weren't quite as they seemed. I sailed those guys about fifty miles out to sea when all of a sudden this old geezer I'd never seen before shows up on deck. I asked him who the

Exploring the Amazon with the African Queen. Photographer unknown

fuck he was and he said, 'My name's Ronnie Biggs and I could use a beer and some grub'."

"Shit, so who were the guys pretending to be a film crew?" I enquired.

"Turned out they were ex-military men turned mercenaries and they'd kidnapped Ronnie in the hope of ransom money from the British government. I'd been chartered to drop these blokes and their prisoner off in Barbados, where Ronnie got turned over to the authorities. In the end the case went to court, and the judge ruled the train robber had been illegally removed from Brazil and the case was chucked out. Ronnie went back to Brazil and received a hero's welcome."

And indeed the guy was a bit of a legendary outlaw in Rio, and although he always said he missed England, he ended up having a pretty good time down there.

Land-lubbering is all very well, but by late June I began to miss the sailing, so I decided to remedy the situation by hauling my arse over to

England to crew on *Tigre* during Admiral's Cup week. I commandeered fifty kilos of finest Brazilian coffee and piled it on board the yacht before sticking her onto a container ship bound for Southampton. The coffee came in handy for the guys at Spencer's Rigging on the Isle of Wight, and fired up on the strong brew they produced more work that winter than ever before. A great regatta kicked off with about thirty countries competing. The Brazilians went crazy in the evenings, dancing, drumming, shaking, rattling and rolling up the high street, and turned the staid old town of Cowes into carnival time, a far cry from its Victorian past.

In the first few races *Tigre* did pretty well and made the top ten or so, until disaster struck halfway through the week when we rounded the Cherbourg mark and the mast fell down with an explosive bang. After pulling into the French port to sort out the fiasco we made it back to the Isle of White, but had blown our chances in the series. One evening shortly before the Fastnet Race kicked off, a phone call came through to the crew house we were shacked up in behind the Royal Corinthian Yacht Club. Lo and behold, it was none other than Yuri the Israeli.

"Hi Chas, I heard you were over here racing."

"How the hell are you, Yuri?" I asked.

"Oh, pretty good. I sailed *New Penny* all the way from Rio and wanted to thank you for the shackle and pin you gave me. Maybe she's got a few more sea miles in her yet," Yuri said hopefully down the crackling line.

"Let's hope so, mate. Good luck wherever the wind blows you!" I said, happy to hear he and his little boat were still in one piece.

I didn't have time to see the wandering hobo, but sure enough, further down the track while I was in old San Juan in Puerto Rico and about to deliver a 40' sloop up to New York, I picked up a couple of crew who knew Yuri and had last seen him sailing his beloved *New Penny* through the Mediterranean.

Admiral's Cup drew to a close, autumn and cold English weather lay right around the corner, and I wanted to leave before it set in. Although before going, I escaped a worse fate than freezing my arse off by the skin of my teeth. An American girlfriend Julie had come over from Chicago to stay with me for a while with marriage on her mind, an institution I've done my best to avoid at all costs.

Tigre in 1977 Admirals Cup. On the run down the Cowes foreshore to the finish off the Squadron caught by a strong gust, flying a blooper, a full sized one-and-a-half ounce spinnaker and still have a full reef in the main. The leading yacht in front is John Prentice's Battle Cry. Photo: Beken of Cowes.

"You've got two choices, Chas: either you come back to the Great Lakes with me and work with my brother in the logging business, or lose me!" she stated with that look women get in their eyes when they close in for the kill.

No contest. I booked a flight for Brazil immediately and hoofed it out of reach up to London. I'd arranged to meet Tom the Pom at the Turk's Head in Knightsbridge and down a few pints before catching the plane out of town. It often goes that way with yachtsmen, you never know if you're going to see your mates again, so greetings and farewells are usually accompanied by the consumption of considerable amounts of alcohol. As the afternoon drifted along my vision blurred somewhat and the small print on my ticket became increasingly difficult to read, but I could have sworn the departure time read 1800 hours. By the time I got to Heathrow airport the bird had flown and my plane was well on its way to Rio. On more sober inspection of the schedule I saw the flight departure time read 1600 hours. To make matters worse, the air traffic controllers went on strike the next day, so I was stuck in London with no money until they made their fucking minds up what to do. And then I lost my passport.

I sought shelter with some friends who lived in a quaint cobbled mews in South Kensington, just opposite where Lionel Bart lived, the guy who wrote the musical Oliver. Bart was quite a character, and his friend Keith Moon, The Who's infamous drummer, used to come by and visit the girls next door and throw rocks through the window when he wanted to go carousing. In fact, over the years the whole street had become well known for raucous parties, so in case things got out of hand I hid my passport somewhere under the wall to wall carpet of the house I was staying in. When the time came to leave I was fucked if I could remember where I'd stashed it. Eventually I tracked it down and got going back to Brazil, but not before Natch Lauchman sent me via bloody Lisbon in Portugal to pick up a shit load of his favourite Cuban cigars where, he insisted, they could be bought at a knock-down price.

I arrived in Rio carrying a sailing bag stuffed to the eyeballs with cheroots for Natch, and found him anxiously waiting for me in the yacht club.

"Thank god you're here, Chas!" he gasped. "I've got a problem. There's an important shipping conference I'm chairing for Lloyd Braziliero, and some of the foreign clients want to go sailing. I've got my captain Renaldo with the gammy leg on standby with my boat *Cosa Nostra*, but he speaks zero English and I need someone who speaks the lingo to look after these guys."

"No worries, Natch, I'll do my best to help you out," I assured him.

"Fanstastico. And I also want you to take a couple of them out on the town – you must know every place of disrepute from here to Ipanema Beach. They're important clients and this is their first trip to Brazil, so you'll have to keep an eye out in case any 'malandro do morros' try to roll them. My driver will be at your disposal and here's some cash in American dollars to pay the bills. Meu deus, I'm running late. Tudo bem?"

"Tudo bem!" I replied giving him the thumbs up and thinking I'd better be alert to the dangers of the malandros, the scoundrels from the hills.

"Obligado amigo. Tchau!" he said over his shoulder and hurried out of the club.

Early the next morning a limo dropped off my two charges at the dock. Both were Scandinavians, but other than this they differed as much as a wombat from a walrus. Karl the Dane was a naval architect, a tall skinny chap with mousey fair hair who wore square gold-framed spectacles that bridged across the top of a pantella-sized hooter, and his mate Eric the Norwegian was a marine engineer and built like a six-foot tall brick shithouse.

I introduced myself, and after having my hand mangled by Eric's bone-crushing handshake, I guided them on board the waiting *Cosa Nostra*, a forty-seven-foot power boat.

"Fellas, would you like a couple of cafezinho?" I asked. "It's Brazilian coffee, known locally as being strong as the devil, hot as hell and sweet as love."

"Yah, captain," Eric the beanpole replied, and glugged back a shot of the strong brew.

Natch's marineiro Renaldo began to champ at the bit and rev up the vessel's big Fiat motors.

"Bom dia, Señors!" he yelled. "Ola tudo bem?"

"Yeah, all's good Renaldo, let's go!" I replied, grabbing a handrail as he jammed the control levers into fast forward and belted out into Guanabara Bay.

"What's that place?" the Skanda fellas shouted out as the Imperial palace and its plaza came into view.

"It's where the emperor's used to roost," I called back over the din of the engines.

"Do you know anything about its history?" Eric hollered back.

"Yep, it's pretty interesting," I said, climbing down from the bridge. Renaldo put the *Cosa Nostra*'s engines into idle and I began swinging the lantern with the two Vikings.

"The royal family, along with fifteen thousand loyal followers, set sail from Lisbon on board a fleet of forty ships bound for Rio with Napoleon hot on their heels, leaving the mad queen mother in Portugal to face the music. When they arrived in Brazil the prince regent, Dom Joao VI, booted the existing governor out of his residence and announced himself the new ruler. About a decade later Wellington flogged Napoleon at Waterloo and the Queen passed on, so Dom Joao declared Rio the capital of the Portuguese empire and made himself King, which meant that Brazil became the only New World colony ever to have a European monarch. He had a son, Dom Pedro I, an imbecile by all accounts who spent most of his time shagging, resulting in a heap of illegitimate children. Some years after taking over from his father he was forced to abdicate, and his only legitimate heir, Dom Pedro III, inherited the title at just five years old."

"When did they declare independence?" Karl enquired.

"Oh, around the early 1800's, two years before George Smith founded his malt whisky distillery at Josie's Well in Scotland. The Scots and Portuguese were well connected in the liquor trade, and whisky became Dom Pedro's favourite tipple," I mentioned tongue in cheek. "Dom Pedro ruled successfully and times were prosperous, apart from the Paraguayan war in 1865, the same year the civil war ended in America. He invited ten thousand Southerners to resettle in Sao Paulo and it became the hub of Brazil's cotton plantations – it's said the Confederados, as they're known to this day, still fly confederate flags from their homesteads and have traces of their original southern accents."

"How do you know this stuff?" Eric asked, looking surprised.

"Bloody good question, mate. Earlier this year a fleet of US navy ships showed up down here and I took some of the Tom Cat and Phantom jet pilots they call ghost-riders from fighter squadron 142 off the *USS America* out sailing a few times. They had all been briefed about the history because President Carter's got distant relatives living in Americana. The ship's newsletter published a quote from the movie 'Gone with the Wind' about a land of cavaliers and cotton fields called the Old South that still survives in Brazil."

"That looks like Disneyland," one of the men called out, pointing to a lime-green gothic palace sitting on Fiscal Island.

"That's where they held the last imperial ball before Don Pedro got booted off the throne, but not before he brought the British in to build a railroad system that connected the coastal ports to the coffee plantations up on the plateaus, and he also managed to achieve his life-long ambition and abolish slavery. Half-a-million freed slaves poured into Rio, much to the coffee baron's fury, and backed by the military they exiled the Imperials to France."

"Ola Chas, vamos!" Renaldo called out. Deciding it was time to get going he hurled the boat around and we thundered our way back across the bay on water as flat as a matador's hat, while the two passengers sucked on long necks of cold Brahma beer.

"You know a bit about the history here, Chas, what do you know about the girls in Rio?" asked Eric with a rapacious look in his eye.

"They're sensational, mate. You'll find plenty of them on the beaches around here dressed in next to nothing. In fact, when a bloke called Janio Quadros became president in 1960, he caused an uproar when he had tea with Che Guevara, and then sealed his demise when he tried to outlaw the dental floss bikinis and got chucked out of office pronto."

I spent the afternoon taking the two guys to Ipanema beach so they could check out the action, although frankly the pair of them had buckley's chance of scoring. Karl, the gangly Dane, pulled on some Speedo swimmers, or 'budgie smugglers' as they're known Down Under, and it looked like he'd stuffed a bloody fully-fledged cockatoo upside down in the front of his swimmers. Eric didn't look much better, stark staring white and lumbering across the sand; I heard the local girls laughing and calling out to the 'juburu and cobra', which in the local lingo means the great white shark and the snake. I left them to it and took off up a cool tree-lined side-street for a much needed silver link in one of the open air bars, wondering how the hell I would entertain the odd couple that night.

"Hey Chas!" a voice called out from over the road. It was Simone, an old fling of mine and friend of my mates Trevor and Banco, who'd first met her on their epic voyage around the world on *Sirocco*. In her mid-thirties and a bloody good-looking woman, Simone had pole-danced her way round various joints to pay her way through university, and now managed a night club where she ran an armada of dancing girls.

"How are you, honey?" I asked, strolling over to give her a kiss, and sat down to order a jug of coconut batidas.

"Si, pretty good, and the fridge is fanstastico, the girls are very happy!"

"That's great," I nodded, remembering how some months ago Stretch the diver and I had hauled a forty-dollar fridge up the outside of a crumbling building to a shabby apartment where Simone and six of her girls lived, dragged it into the small kitchen and plonked a case of Argentinian wine in it for good measure.

I told her about my dilemma with Eric and Karl and she leaped into the breach, laughing like a train when I told her Karl was hung like a donkey.

"I can organize some girls for you, come over to the club this evening and if your Danish friend needs some extra attention there'll be some capable hands to help him out."

And so a pretty good night ensued, and the last I remember of Karl was watching him being drowned in the breasts of an Amazonian-sized woman, a well-known basket- ball player dressed in a skin-tight red dress. I, on the other hand, ended up in a hotel that reminded me of a Moorish castle I'd seen in Spain once, on a heart-shaped double thumper with a contortionist of a girl called Marissa who had me holding on by my toe-nails and bounced me up and down like a squash ball until the early morning, when she announced she had to go to church and make her confessions to the local priest.

Well, that was the end of my duties with the Scandinavians, and I heard no more of them until I ran into Natch after he returned from an unexpected trip to Europe.

"What were you doing over there?" I asked him.

"Well, Chas, you won't believe it, but that crazy guy Eric caused a lot of unexpected problems at the conference and I had to go over to sort things out. He'd eaten some Nero di Seppia, you know one of those squid risottos in ink sauce, and it made him real sick. The next day on the way to an important meeting he got held up in a traffic jam in the Novo tunnel, where the strong car fumes were too much for him. First he threw up out of the window, and then, desperate and unable to get out of the car, he decided to take a shit in his briefcase."

"Jesus Christ!" I grinned. "What happened then?"

"Unfortunately the case was full of important confidential and classified blue prints from the naval architects in Hamburg we were meant to be reviewing. Unfortunately, these documents were now plastered with the remains of the squid risotto and the shit that poured out of his arse," he said, almost exploding himself with laughter.

Although I didn't know it, my time in Brazil was about to come to an abrupt end just two days before Christmas. Haaken Lorentzen showed up down at the launching-ramp of the Rio Yacht Club late one afternoon while I struggled to put *Mach*, Joe's cruising yacht, in the water. If the Frers family were thought of as deities in Argentina, then the Lorentzens were the Brazilian version. Haaken's Norwegian father Erling had served in the underground resistance against German occupation forces in WWII, and after the war worked in his family's shipping business. He later moved out to Brazil, and in the early sixties diversified and established a eucalyptus forest north of Rio on barren land, subdivided by strips of rain forest, and developed what would become the world's largest paper pulp mill. A keen yachtsman, it was through his sailing pursuits that he met King Olav's eldest daughter, married her, and Haaken was their twenty-three-year-old son.

"Hey Chas, I'm afraid I'm the bearer of bad news, we'd better go and have a beer while I tell you what's happened," he suggested.

We found a table at the local bar and sat down.

"What's up, Haaken?" I asked tentatively.

"My father told me to forewarn you that the new Commodore and the cronies on the committee have passed a motion blackballing you from the yacht club."

"What the bloody hell for?" I asked, although I'd known the bloke was an arsehole for some time and so far avoided him like the plague, but sooner or later I had a hunch I'd find myself embroiled in a heap of deep shit.

"It's about bringing so many girls into the club, and not one of them is your wife," he explained.

"But everyone knows I don't have one – and I'm not about to, either!" I replied with some feeling on the matter of marital confinement.

"Yes, well everyone is well aware of that fact, Chas, but nevertheless the commodore is convinced you're a polygamist and claims he saw you coming in through the gates in the early hours the other night draped in women," he said with a wicked grin on his face.

"Son of a bitch!" I muttered, knocking back the rest of the beer and thinking the current commodore more of a prick than I'd imagined.

On Boxing Day Haaken and I sailed *Mach* up to Buzios where I broke the news to Joe and Natch, who although not happy about the situation, were sympathetic to my latest conundrum.

"I'm sorry, Chas, I was away when the commodore held the meeting and there was nothing I could do to keep you out of trouble," said Joe. "But don't worry, I want to take *Peanut Brittle* up to the States and donate her to the King's Point naval academy and then get a big boat to sail around the world and compete in all the great ocean races. I'd like you to come along too as part of the campaign."

"Sure, Joe, that'd be great!" I agreed.

Sadly Joe got sick before he got the ball rolling. He fell foul of the unforgiving tap-dancer and passed on to fiddlers green. I always remember him as a great friend and mentor with whom many adventures had been shared, and I felt his loss deeply.

I didn't hear the news until later, so thinking I would be seeing Joe again in the near future I upped sticks, slowly making my way to Salvador to explore on into the Amazon and take a break from the yachting scene for a while. I arrived in Manaus where the waterfront was the hub of the town. Not far from the formidable floating docks the British had built back in the rubber trade boom, and surrounded by decaying colonial buildings and a jig-saw of jumbled houses on stilts which ran down to the banks of the Rio Negro, was an enormous market, situated amidst the constant coming and going of flotillas of double and triple-decker ferry boats continually motoring back and forth from the planked piers, unloading and loading with passengers and produce.

The fish-market operated out of an 1880's French-styled wrought iron building with a soaring corrugated tin roof and stained glass windows. Rows of roosting vultures perched along the guttering, oblivious to the crowds of milling people and ready to pounce and brawl over the fish remains dumped outside on the muddy ground. I'd arrived at the tail end of monsoon season, and the rain hammered down on the roof until it reverberated like a mammoth steel drum. Inside, dozens of bare light-bulbs dangling on chains lit up the long rows of tabletops smothered in hundreds of strange species of fresh water fish. It was at one of these tables that I bumped into the Bodkes, a recently retired couple from Pennsylvania. I'd been checking out an awesome-looking shovel-headed catfish covered in silvery grey tiger stripes, with white whiskers strong and long enough to string a banjo.

"That's a Sorubim, there's a similar one they catch in the Mekong River in Vietnam," a tall American wearing a pith helmet standing nearby remarked to his pint-sized wife.

The Yank seemed to know what he was talking about, so I joined in the conversation and we hit it off right away. Dave Bodke had served in the army corps of engineers and his missus Jeannie as a field nurse.

"In the Amazon," he went on "there's over three thousand species of fish, and fifty percent of them are catfish. Now see these ones, they're Douradas," he said, stabbing his finger in the direction of half a dozen heavily-bearded yellowish-green varieties. "And those bright yellow ones etched with three black bars are Peacock Bass, and they're two of the finest fresh-water fighting fish in the world."

Some of the specimens seemed like strange prehistoric creatures, with sabre teeth on snake-like heads. Walking back out into the sunlight we passed a bunch of fish flensers, hacking and sawing away at carcasses the size of sheep, the black and red heavily-scaled Pirarucu, a Brazilian cod that grows up to two metres and weighs over a hundred kilos.

It turned out the Bodkes wanted to do a trip up the river, and rather than take a punt on a ferry boat and end up stranded in some shitty backwater creek, I decided to join them, and for the first and probably the last time in my life chartered a boat, a lovely old sixty-footer from the turn of the nineteenth century. Timber-built, sporting fine teak decks, her high proud bow swept down a narrow hull with a sweet shear to a classic counter-stern. She'd once been a steamer, the stack on top of the pilothouse the sole evidence of its conversion to diesel. A tarpaulin canopy extended out from the pilothouse over the aft deck, and the 'veranda', as Jeannie liked to refer to it, was a wonderful place to sit and sip batidas at sundown. The captain Chico, a Mestizos with a face as creased and tanned as the caiman bags they flogged in town, knew the river like the back of his hand. It ended up being quite a big crew – an interpreter, an engineer, two guides, and from Chico, a 'Mama', a heavily-breasted mulatto woman who knocked up the nosh and doled out a constant stream of exotic tropical fruit drinks.

We christened the fine old tub the *African Queen* and took off to explore the great river for a while; caught piranhas with short deep bodies, blunt faces, malignant eyes and lower projecting jaws covered in razor sharp teeth by the dozen, using acai berries for bait; and saw hundreds of Howler monkeys and spider-webs as big as fishing nets. At night we would pull into isolated out-posts and eat barbecued Tambaqui, a gigantic fish turned on a spit and covered in banana leaves.

Dave had brought along a few books, and lying in our hammocks reading one afternoon while we were tied up to a clump of trees, he looked up and said,

"Hey Chas, listen to this. At the height of the rubber boom down here there were twenty-four pubs, an English brewery, a bullring, a racetrack and an opera house. Some guy had a stable of racehorses and when one of them won would give the beast a bucket of champagne to quench his thirst. After the meetings he'd invite a crowd of revellers for a night's drinking and dancing on his Clyde-built riverboat where he kept a tame lion, which used to prowl around the decks as a substitute security guard."

Dave's tales from his history books were pretty interesting, and he'd tell us about how the Americans built the railroads from Bolivia to Manaus; and when the Brits stole the rubber seeds and planted them at Kew Gardens in London before transferring them to Malaya, that was the end of the rubber business in the Amazon; except they left one thing behind – the beloved soccer ball, and try as they might they can't beat Brazil at the game to this day! He also had a copy of President Roosevelt's adventures in the Amazon during 1914, describing how he had encountered Piraibas – fish over three meters long weighing in at over six hundred pounds, and when he bathed he made sure he was in stockaded enclosures for fear of being attacked by them. But it was the next species of fish he knew something of that put the wind up me.

"You have to watch out for the Candiru, Chas. It's a small cat-fish a couple of centimetres long that lives inside other fish's gills and sucks their blood. It can swim up your prick or arsehole and tenaciously hook on in there with sharp spines. A navy surgeon operated on various victims, and in one case had to slice a guy's bladder to remove the fish. This book I've got here by William Burroughs mentions them, and his time in this neck of the woods with ayahuasca, the plant that shamans have used for healing over hundreds of years."

"The local booze trips me out enough, Dave, but holy shit, you won't get me in that water!" I exclaimed, shivering at the thought of a bloody cat-fish swimming up my dick.

It didn't seem to bother Dave, though. I heard Jeannie shout out to her husband one morning,

"Don't forget your tights, honey!"

"I sure as hell won't," he grunted back, and appeared on deck in a pair of boxer shorts under which he had pulled on a pair of his wife's pantyhose.

"What the hell kind of outfit is that?" I asked.

"It's to make sure the Candiru don't attack me."

"Christ, are you going swimming?"

202

"Yep," he replied, and plunged into the swirling, muddy river-water.

After the trip up the Amazon I began to feel the pull of the open sea and being on board a vessel less cumbersome than the *African Queen* – it was time to start making my way up to the States. I headed for Bogota in Columbia. It wasn't the safest place at the time, and the boys from *Sirocco* had given me some good advice from their days up there dealing in emeralds. Kidnapping was a common occurrence, on top of which bandits had a nasty habit of shooting taxi drivers, shoving the bodies in the trunk of their cabs and then taking their place at the wheel to pick up tourists, rob them, bump them off as well, and add the body to the cargo in the boot. After about three runs a day they'd take the car to a steep cliff, torch it and push it over the edge, corpses and all.

I managed to escape this murderous end, but instead found myself victim to a lousy combination of altitude sickness and food poisoning I'd picked up from a foul meal in a local café. Consequently I saw a hell of a lot more of the shitter than I did of Bogota. Finally, a few days later, I made it out to the airport, bound for the States.

I heard later in the year from my old mate Tux of some news that gave me a chuckle. Not so long after I'd left the '77-'78 Whitbread Round the World Race, yachts rounded the horn on the second last leg and arrived in Rio. Tux, along with his crew on *King's Legend*, a Swan 65', attended the presentations, which coincided with the yacht club carnival ball. It turned into a wild party and things got pretty out of hand. A bunch of security guards were called in and got tossed into the pool, at which point the riot police were called in and turned on the tear gas. In the aftermath heads rolled, including that of the commodore who'd played such a hand in ending my days in South America, and the bastard was booted out of office. During Cowes week in '79 I ran into my old skipper Fernando Pimentel Duarte from *Tigre* in the beer tent.

"I'm the new commodore of the Rio Yacht Club now, Chas, and your *persona non grata* status is no longer an issue. You're welcome back any time you're down that way."

"Thanks, amigo, I'll drink to that!" I replied, ordered a couple more beers and handed one to Fernando.

"Here's to Brazil, mate, sensational memories and some of the most spectacular women in the world!

6

A Kettle of Fish and a Burnt Pudding

The sea
It smiles from afar,
Teeth of foam,
Lips of sky.

La Balade del Agua del Mar – Frederico Garcia Lorca
(1898-1936)

EARLY IN FEBRUARY 1978, fresh from my South American odyssey, I pitched up in my old stomping ground St Petersburg,

Florida, chomping at the bit to find a late ride in the SORC.

It was boom times for boat-builders, designers, sail-makers and spar manufacturers. Unlike cruising compatriots, whose attitude with their beloved boats was 'till death us do part', the new breed of Grand Prix owners and their quest to win at all costs went through their yachts like sheets of shit paper.

Out of ninety-three boats competing, only twenty-seven were more than two years old, and forty of them were less than a year old. Gone into moth-balls were many from the early generation of I.O.R yachts, where designers had manipulated the perimeters of the girth measurements by bumping them with micro-balloons to obtain a favourable handicap, often resulting in distorted shapes similar to a python that had swallowed a calf, and moving just as slowly.

At first glance some of these more radical debutantes had finer bows and broader arses, and appeared to have complicated tall skinny rigs and centreboards. Due to the way length was measured, displacement determined, and the way stability was penalized in I.O.R. rules, serious genetic issues would raise their ugly heads, wreaking absolute havoc in the downwind leg of the Boca Grande race.

On the evening of my arrival at the St. Pete's Yacht Club, any anxiety of scoring a ride for the series was kicked out of the back door when I ran into my old mate Captain Tits in the bar.

"Christ it's good to see you, I heard you were in town! What boat are you sailing on, you old bastard?" he asked as we shook hands.

"Nothing yet, still making up my mind," I bluffed.

"Well don't bother looking any further. You're sailing with us on *Fox Fire*. She's a spanking new 44' Scott Kaufman dagger-boarder," he stated in a gritty sandpaper rasp.

"Your voice sounds like a creaking door, mate, are you a bit under the weather?" I asked.

"Some bloody strap-hanger from up north gave me a dose of the flu, so you'll have to do the foredeck," he croaked.

"Ok, mate. I hope you've got a cracking helmsman to drive her. Dick Deaver from North Sails busted his jaw in a bad broach on the Shitty Britty (Britton Chance) dagger-boarder *Resolute Salmon*. He said she was a bitch to steer downwind."

"There's no worries there. Ed Lorence from Watts sails and a posse of his West Coast Warriors have done more Trans-Pacs than you can shake a stick at. Those guys will be taking care of her downwind," he reassured.

Fox Fire had been built up in Annapolis, Maryland, by the Crane brothers out of cold-moulded cedar. Her hull was white with a pair of bright red blazing flames painted along her top sides. Below decks was a near-naked stripped-out interior, dominated by the dagger-board case, a spacious chart table and a 70 HP Pathfinder engine. Beneath the floorboards, stacked and strapped to the bottom of the boat fore and aft of the centreboard case, were umpteen lead pigs used as internal ballast. *Fox Fire*, along with twenty-two other yachts, was in Class C, the largest and the one that comprised more bridesmaids than any other class.

After a sensational start to the race we kicked off in an eighteen-knot Northerly on a blazing reach across Tampa Bay, and by the time we passed under the Sunshine Bridge were at the head of our pack, closely pursued by the more proven Holland 44's *Marionette* and *Mandrake*. The majority of classes had started before us, and a row of white sails stretched out in front of *Fox Fire* towards the rounding buoy beyond Egmont Key, and we caught the first glimpse of the big boats already southbound towards the Boca Grande mark, with their multi-coloured spinnakers billowing out before them.

By the time our turn came we were still leading the chasing posse, with an ebbing tide pouring out from Tampa Bay and swirling around the weed-encrusted metal buoy and its tolling bell. As we bore away, the adrenaline kicked in after a lightning-quick hoist, and a clap of thunder heralded our big red and white kite bursting into life when the lads ground the pole's brace back and started trimming. *Fox Fire* shuddered as she took off down the back of the first wave, quickly gaining momentum on the surge downwind. Perhaps the bell's toll had been a forewarning. Little did we know what was about to occur, and that within a few hours this particular leg would be remembered in the annals of SORC history as the 'Demolition Derby' – or the 'Last Dance of the Debutantes'.

It may be said that at that time of go-fast new innovations, the foremost progress would have been in spar development, with a continuous refinement of fittings and improvement of the weight ratio and aerodynamic efficiency in each part of the mast. Stearns Sailing Systems had produced a variable-walled D type alloy section with a small bolt rope-groove for the mainsail.

Some of the two-tonners, which included the four Canada's Cup contenders, *Mia IV* and *Black Magic*, both Kaufman dagger boarders, and *Agape*, a Holland, sported three-quarter sections with triple spreaders, while the fourth Evergreen, a C & C dagger-boarder with a scow-like hull, had a four-spreader rig that was forty-five percent lighter than conventional double spreader spars, and two inches narrower athwart-ships.

Evergreen, due to her strange-shaped green hull with orange and white stripes running along her topsides, was known as the 'big green breakfast bowl'. A technological marvel of her time built out of carbon fibre and epoxy honeycomb, her Mylar sails and aft cockpit cluttered with more hydraulic controls than those high bullocks on a tower of bull giraffes, she could have been something from a NASA space programme.

However, there was one major hiccup with the latest Grand Prix yachts – they suffered from poor stability, flimsy rigs and advanced hydraulic systems where the spar bent more than two feet at its tip. As a result crews were temporarily overwhelmed by the new technology, which led to more complicated and less safe boats.

Although *Fox Fire* had a high ballast ratio, the power was distributed just below her centre of buoyancy, creating a ten to fifteen-degree rhythmic rolling motion that could cause her to get out of control before the hull became stiff enough to nullify it. This major design flaw became alarmingly apparent right from the onset of the downwind leg, and after a couple of near wipe-outs we set a blooper in an attempt to stabilize her. At first, having the chute choked down, and the blooper's broad shoulder pulling like a freight train out in front of the main, worked wonders and dampened the rolling. But by mid-afternoon we ran into trouble. The wind shifted to the east and began gusting over thirty knots. Boats began to gybe, and two of the more well-trialled keelers, *Marionette* with an international star-studded crew, and *Love Machine's* Tom Whidden with his Sobstad sails, managed to handle the manoeuvre unscathed, crossing over in front of us.

On board *Fox Fire* and the yachts behind us, a far different scenario was unravelling, with a series of heart-stopping knock-downs. No sooner had we dropped the blooper and cleared the baby stay away for the gybe, all stability was lost. Midway through the hairy operation, Captain Tits up on the bow snapped the lazy brace into the pole's beak, just as a strong gust of wind hit, sending us into a succession of death rolls, made even worse because the dagger-board was up. It was balls to the wall when the kite's wild oscillations sent the boat lunging off to leeward into the mama of all Chinese gybes, and the boom swished across the deck, catapulting most of the crew right through the leeward lifelines. The mainsail and semi-submerged spinnaker pinned *Fox Fire* down on her side, and we hung onto the lines treading water, trying to figure out what the fuck to do next. It took about five tense minutes to re-right the boat, having to release the halyards, while the beefiest of the crew clambered out onto the dagger-board that someone by this time had managed to push out.

Close by, *Evergreen*, the big green breakfast bowl, wasn't looking too good either. She broached to weather and lay flat on her side with the sails flogging. How the hell her mast didn't break was a mystery. However, they did have two great innovators on board, Tim Stearn and Lowell North. Lowell had not been nick-named 'The Pope' – that bloke in the Vatican that's meant to produce miracles – for no reason.

On *Fox Fire*, apart from a bunch of busted stanchions and a bent spinnaker pole, the mast had been twisted out of column. So we retired. Unbelievably, in the wild and raw weather the varnished hull of the fractional rig *Mr Jumpa* swept by us like a smoking locomotive on its last frontier, flying a full main and a kite with Kiwi legends Woody Woodroffe and Roscoe Guiniven on board. To add salt to the wound, some smart-arse sitting near its wide-open skiff-styled stern yelled back through cupped hands,

"When you get back to the boozer, don't drink all the cold piss, you west coast wankers!"

As they galloped on in a shower of flying spray, we watched totally bamboozled, like a bunch of out-of-luck buck-jumping riders on the wrong side of a winning streak. In actual fact, the damage we suffered could have been a lot worse. Five other yachts in our class were dismasted, and our smaller sister *Black Magic* was thrown into a horrendous broach that damn near capsized them, and dislodged a heavy tool-box down below with such a force that it punched a hole through the hull the size of a clenched fist.

Following the Boca Grande drama, we set off on the long-distance

Lauderdale race as apprehensive as kamikaze pilots. Fortunately providence was on our side, and with fair to medium air, reaching upwind and beating in sloppy seas, we finished a creditable second in class and fourth in the big fleet.

On the morning of the Miami to Nassau race it blew a strong northerly, and the first leg took us on a hard beat up to an offshore sea-buoy north of Fort Lauderdale, before peeling off east across the Gulf Stream towards Greater Isaac lighthouse. Halfway to Lauderdale, in 25 knots and a steep lumpy sea, under a reefed mainsail and the number 3 headsail, and heeled right over with half the crew hanging their legs over the weather rail, a sound akin to the deafening crack of a stockman's whip lashed through the wind.

"Hold on folks! We've lost the goddamn rudder!" screamed Ed Lawrence, our helmsman, and the boat crash-tacked as if hit by a mugger's fist.

Those of us riding the rail catapulted face first into the sea. Chaos ensued in the following minutes and scrambling bodies struggled to get out of harm's way. *Fox Fire* turned into a wild beast and careered all over the ocean. The boom's traveller had broken loose and become a lethal flailing weapon. After half-an-hour of frantic wrestling to get the sails down and securing everything above and below decks, we had to figure out how the fuck to steer the now rudderless boat. Maybe the spinnaker pole with a washboard could gain steerage, but by some fortuitous luck a coastguard cutter returning from another rescue mission spotted us. At first the captain wanted to tie us up fore and aft athwart the cutter amidships, but we unanimously revoked this idea as far too dangerous due to the rough conditions, not to mention the lightweight construction of the boat.

"No mate!" Captain Tits shouted through the blower quick as a flash. "If *Fox Fire's* hull gets hit by a rogue wave, the side strapped against the cutter will cave in like a peanut shell."

Thank Christ the cutter's captain saw reason. Although reluctant at first, he instructed one of his crew to heave us the end of a thick eye-spliced hawser. Fastening two of our longest dock lines to the hawser, we ran them down through a couple of snatch blocks on the bow and back through the genoa leads to the primary winches to form a bridle.

The situation didn't look too bad for a brief moment. The cutter motored dead ahead until the slack line tightened, and then the shit hit the fucking fan. The cutter captain thumped the throttles down hard, which had the undesired effect of lifting *Fox Fire* up onto a terrifying plane. To say what happened next was anything less than heart attack material would be an understatement. Suddenly the boat veered off to port on a 30 degree angle, ploughing her bow down so far that a wipe-out looked inevitable. Then on a violent rebound she surged across the cutter's stern like an out of control railway car, sliding sideways on a suicide mission into a monstrous broach. God knows how, but before we slewed up beam on ends, Captain Tits and a pommy blonde-headed bloke, Bobby Thompson, smoked the bridle's ends, saving us from certain catastrophe.

Now on tenterhooks after the shit-in-your-pants rollercoaster ride, we decided on a more prudent and scientific approach. Below decks we dragged back all the sails and any other heavy gear we could pull to the arse-end of the boat. This time, when the tow was up, we streamed out the spinnaker sheets attached to fenders and a few empty sail bags out behind us. With a couple of the crew on the primary winches trimming and paying out the bridle's tails at half the previous speed, we somehow managed to avoid any further screw-ups and made it back to the marina.

The fiasco left the *Fox Fire* program in tatters, and the crew scattered in various directions. Not before, however, Ed Lawrence and navigator Joe Buck offered some parting advice to the owner, Dr. Joe Stepka and his right-hand man Hank Burkhard, a wise old buzzard who owned a Peterson two-tonner, *Ricochet*, up in the Midwest. They suggested Stepka call up the designer and ask him to make some major modifications to the ballast ratio and rudder, as it had become apparent you couldn't steer the boat downwind in over 20 knots. And they added that unless he was on a suicide mission, never, ever to take her out on the open ocean again.

Once relocated to the Great Lakes she did alright for a while in the lighter airs and smooth seas. Apparently someone salvaged the rudder, which had twisted off the titanium shaft due to a lack of stainless steel webbing, and as for the ballast, 350 lbs of lead was removed forward of the dagger board, 150 lbs aft and 150 lbs added to the bottom of it.

But that wasn't the end of the story. Sometime in the early '80s *Fox Fire* changed hands and wound up in Seattle, where the new owner refitted her with a fixed keel and decided to take part in the Victoria-

Maui Race. True to form, not far from Maui, history repeated itself and the rudder fell off again. Once repaired with a new one and undeterred they set out to sail back to Seattle. This time the blow was a fatal one. Disaster struck somewhere between Ports Angeles and Townsend, before the entrance to Puget Sound. A rising 'deadhead' or 'sinker' as they're sometimes known, the size of a solid telegraph pole, drove a hole through her underbelly as big as a Spanish man o'war's cannonball. A coastguard managed to rescue the crew minutes before the old girl finally foundered and gurgled down into the deep depths.

After a couple of months sailing and messing about in Mexico's Yucatan and the Caribbean islands, I weighed anchor and headed north for a ride in the Newport-Bermuda race. The races always follow the sun and so too does the fun along with crowds of excited spectators. Sailors and friends gather in the bars and on the waterfronts as the atmosphere builds at the start of competitions. Wherever there are boats there are girls, West Coast babes from San Diego to Sausalito and East Coast honeys from steamy Miami to the summer heat in Marblehead, Massachusetts and not forgetting those real cool chicks you find around the Great Lakes in the Midwest. The possibility of a pirate's plunder was phenomenal. Armed with an Aussie accent, single and young, you could not help but be in demand.

The groupies had their own set-up known as the 'International Racer Chaser Association' and adopted the motto 'In Us They Thrust', which was the girl's version of the one we paid yacht hands used when referring to the boat owners 'In Us They Trust'. The members of the 'International Boat Nigel's Association' was mainly made up of Aussies, Kiwis, Poms, Yanks, Yarpies, Canucks and the odd Frog. The fly-in crews were often mates of the owners, known as 'Briefcase Barons' in the case of company men, or 'straphangers', a term used for the commuters who rode the U.S subways to work, apart from the sail-makers and rock stars, like Connors and Co.

At the beginning of June I fetched up in the small town of Essex, situated on the banks of the Connecticut River, after completing a long East Coast delivery on a vintage 50' wooden William Gardner ketch. I popped into a nearby watering hole the Griswold Inn, often frequented by yachties and known as the 'The Gris', where I ran into an old mate, a sail-maker from North's called Steve Prime. Before we'd sunk a second beer he scored me a berth on a brand new Holland two-tonner,

Circus Maximus: photographer unknown

Secret Affair, very similar to Imp, built out of composites with geodesic aluminium frames.

It seemed like a good idea to take up the offer, if Imp was anything to go by Secret Affair would be a rocket ship and after tuning up the boat in the feeder races we'd be competing in the Bermuda Blue Water Classic. But unfortunately disaster struck on the orange painted boat on our final hit out, three days before the start of the Bermuda Race. On a hell of a windy leg off Rhode Island during a gybe the lazy sheet got tangled around the end of our boom and we were pinned on our ear in a wipe-out. The mast inverted inside out and was damaged so severely that the owner Tom Greenawalt pulled the pin on the trip.

Worried at the thought of being land-bound, I drifted into the beer tent ready to drown my sorrows until late into the night, when I staggered out blind drunk and catapulted helter-skelter over the tent ropes and passed out. Next thing I knew, I woke up lying in a bunk on a boat on the way to the starting line of the race bound for Bermuda. My old mates Captain Tits and Tuxworth had found me unconscious and tangled up amongst the tent ropes the night before and thrown me on board *Circus Maximus*. I'd been press-ganged.

Circus Maximus was a wooden Yves-Marie de Tanton designed 68' cold-moulded west system epoxy and one of the early 'sledges', designed to be a downwind flyer. An ocean-going greyhound, this new breed of radical yacht was capable of speeds of up to twenty-five knots. Her sleek, varnished timber hull was long and tapered like a cigar and instantly caught one's eye. She displaced just 22,000lbs and was as sparse inside as a DC3 with no seats. Sailing her in big seas and strong headwinds your whole world would turn upside down, and it was a living hell of constant slamming and seesawing, while you prayed nothing would break.

Just after dusk I was up on the foredeck, a mixture of hard-working sweat and sea air slowly clearing a monumental hangover, when the yacht's owner John Raby called up from the navigation desk, where he was sitting in one of those big swivel barber-type chairs.

"Would you like some Mount Gay rum, Chas?" he asked, pulling out a couple of glasses.

"Sure," I replied, and gulped back the hair of the dog.

"I want you to steer, from now you can be one of the principal helmsmen," he said, while handing me several hundred green backs, "and this will help you out in Bermuda."

Raby desperately wanted to catch the rip-roaring northeaster wind that follows a cold front, hoping it would carry us at a scorching pace our competitors would not be able to match. However, it was not to be, and instead we found ourselves at the mercy of light headwinds that held us prisoner for about thirty hours of slow sailing. We crossed tacks with a couple of small forty-footers and were in bad shape. Deciding there was only one way out, we continued east of the rhumb line in an attempt to find a favourable Gulf Stream eddy. Gradually over the next forty-eight hours the wind freed us into a close reach down towards Bermuda.

During the night things improved, and the following morning under a rising sun we had clawed our way up amongst the leading boats. In the light conditions we were able to carry a half-ounce super-star cut spinnaker and *Circus Maximus* spread her wings, managing to squeeze like a pip from a water melon between the two big maxi yachts *Ondine* and *Tempest*. When darkness crept in, a breeze sprang up out of the night and we rounded the bottom of the island and steamrolled down past Kitchen Shoals, hearing over the radio that an unidentified vessel

Circus Maximus racing
photographer unknown

was approaching the finishing line. The unidentified vessel was us on *Circus Maximus*, or 'Circus Ridiculous' as she was often known. We entered St. George's Gap to the sound of the local crowds cheering us home. In a six hundred and twenty-mile race we had covered seven hundred and forty miles and still won. The circus had well and truly come to town.

At the dock stood the White Horse Inn, and waiting on the jetty were three cases of crisp cold beer donated by the portly landlord. It was a good finish for Tux, too, when a pretty waitress snared him and dragged him back to her den. The next day he was nowhere to be seen, still willingly trapped in her lair as we left to sail down the narrow, inner reef-strewn channel to Bermuda's capital, Hamilton. At the Royal Bermuda Yacht Club we found an expectant cluster of good-looking girls from Tux's harem, that he'd lined up to come over from the States, and with no further ado we happily cut his lunch.

When the racing finished it was time to look for work. I was commissioned to deliver the British yacht *Brother Cup* up to the States. She was a Peterson 44' built by Lallows on the Isle of Wight, owned by the larger-than-life, ex-RAF Ernie Dewar. 'Lock' Murray was on board, a big moustachioed man with a slow drawl and absolutely enormous feet on which he never wore shoes, Lou Varney, a Caulkhead from the Isle of White, and Karen, a peach from the Black Forest I'd met earlier in the year while sailing in the Gulf of Mexico. We provisioned for a long voyage and delicately stowed a couple of cases of Gosling's Black Seal Rum and a good supply of Amstel and Beck's beer to keep us going for a trip that would take us from Bermuda to Sturgeon Bay, Wisconsin.

It was rough but fast travelling, particularly in the Gulf Stream. In those days Loran was the principal navigational equipment, but you couldn't get a fix with this system unless within a couple of hundred miles of the mainland, so I fished out the sextant and steered by the stars. A strong south-westerly wind blew up and the decks were awash in a stormy sea, which poured in through the sliding hatch above the navigating area, making it a bitch to work out the celestial calculations with buckets of seawater raining down onto the chart table. And worse, the flood seeped into the storage lockers, liquidising emergency powdered rations into a mess of scrambled eggs and custard that escaped and ran everywhere.

In just under four days we sailed into New York. From there it would be a journey inland along the waterways up to the Great Lakes, which meant pulling the mast out at Minneford's boatyard and laying it out on the deck so we would be able to fit under the bridges further up the river. Rather than continue on down towards the Statue of Liberty against a floodtide, I took the shortcut through Harlem. There's always a risk going through there that kids will hurl opened cans of paint and bricks off the bridge onto whatever dares pass beneath, but we slipped by like a ghost-ship in the flickering light of an early dawn, and the only sign of life was a scull being rowed by four guys wearing T-shirts that read 'Harlem Boat Honkies' waving us on by.

We steamed on up the Hudson and under the George Washington Bridge. Just before West Point Military Academy we spotted a floating pontoon with a small figure standing on the end of it beckoning us in, and we drew up alongside to find a diminutive Englishman who had recognised our 'red duster' ensign and wanted to invite us all to a Sunday barbecue in the rickety tin shed he'd built named 'The Chelsea Yacht Club'. I gave him a couple of bottles of Black Seal rum, and along

with the beautiful Karen, joined the fiesta. Early next morning we refu-
elled and chugged towards Albany, upstate New York, passing the big
old mansions that lined the river banks before finally reaching the
entrance to the canals.

The canal waterways are built on a step system, going either up or
down with each lock one passes through. We hung chaff bags stuffed
with straw over the sides of *Brother Cup* to stop the hull being ripped
to shreds in the narrow holding channels. Karen would go up to meet
the lock-keepers in a bikini with her buns hanging out – we got through
a lot quicker with her help, otherwise you could wait around forever.

When the locks lifted the boat up forty feet or so we'd get a bird's-
eye view of the rolling countryside, full of Canadian geese and wild
deer, and sometimes found ourselves side by side with the great American rail system. Huge trains thundered down the track stuffed to the
gills with Cadillacs from Detroit, the drivers blowing their whistles and
waving base-ball caps as they steamed past us. We stopped for a while
in Tonawanda, a little town at the end of the waterway close to Buffalo,
to re-rig the boat so she could sail on across the lakes, and someone
gave us a car to go and explore on land for a while. We drove across
to Niagara Falls and listened to the roar and bellow of the water as it
crashed down from above. In later years I would be reminded of the
same sonorous boom when I was out in the North Pacific between
Taiwan and Japan, where the typhoons create a similar wild music.

It felt good to hoist the sails again, and under the auspices of a
favourable wind we journeyed past Cleveland and up to motor-city
Detroit, into Lake Huron and Thunder Bay. The bay lived up to its
name. Lightning and thunder blasted in from the prairies, and hail-
stones the size of pigeon's eggs tumbled onto the decks while we sailed
past the sweeping white sand dune beaches north of Michigan. We
arrived at Palmer Johnstone's yard in Sturgeon Bay. Lifting the boat
out of the water, foreman Chuff Wilman scratched his head and said it
was a miracle we hadn't lost the rudder on the trip, the bearing was
almost completely worn away.

With *Brother Cup* safely delivered, I jumped at the chance when
Chuff asked me to sail with him in the Chicago-Mac Race on a newly-
launched Peterson two-tonner, *Wizzard*. According to local sailors in
that neck of the woods you haven't really sailed until you've done the
big freshwater races. It didn't bother me much as I had already com-

peted in two Chicago-Mackinacs before, but old memories stirred when I thought to myself about the Port Huron 628-mile non-stop race to Chicago on a C & C, *Ranger*, a few years before.

It can be daunting, for sure. Out on the lakes the Native Spirits can toss down almost every type of weather imaginable. Conditions can change in a flash when the low pressure systems rush down from the Arctic, stirring up ferocious electrical storms, and fast-changing wind directions whip the water into a seething mass of waves and turmoil. After a bone-rattling gale had subsided and been replaced by a big high-pressure system which becalmed *Ranger* off Sleeping Bear Bay, a cast of a million swarming flies settled in a thick carpet on the boat. Those critters got into our ears, eyes, noses and mouths until we thought we'd go crazy. Down below, the conditions were just as horrendous. The owner Craig Welch, known as Ironsides, wheelchair-bound since suffering a severe stroke, was sitting at the saloon table frantically swatting the blood-loving flies away with a frayed Time magazine, which by now matched the colour of Mao's little red book.

"What do you reckon of the flies, Chas?" he asked, and I told him they made me homesick, for we had plenty of them in Australia.

The insect invasion lasted into the next day too when, after another storm shot across from Milwaukee, squadron after squadron of dragon flies descended on us like gossamer-winged biplanes and attached themselves to the mainsail while we reached in and out along the beach with our star-cut spinnaker. Each time we gybed, hundreds of them fell onto the decks and turned the surface into a slippery skating-rink, until finally the last of them was shaken off the sails in the breeze that filled in and carried us on to the finish in Chicago.

Meanwhile, back on *Wizzard*, passing under the Mackinac Bridge not far from the finish, I reminisced about the end of another Chicago-Mackinac Race. Bob Tway, a great jester of a character and the owner of a 67' blue Chance ketch, *Masker*, decided to settle a score with an old mate. The race finishes on an island where no cars are allowed and the local transport is horse and buggy. Standing outside the Pink Pony bar, Bob walked up to the nearest buggy driver ready to unleash a perfectly-formed plan he'd been hatching.

"I need several large bags of your horse manure for my wife's roses. Could you pour as much as possible down the forward hatch of that red boat over there in the morning?" he asked, pointing to a vessel tied up to the end of the dock.

Early the next morning, when Bob Tway was well on his way and making his escape on *Masker*, the buggy driver arrived to carry out his instructions. He tipped a monstrous load down the hatch of the boat on top of Bob's old foe and his girlfriend, who lay sleeping underneath, smothering them with piles and piles of horse shit.

After bidding my *Wizzard* shipmates farewell, I had to get going, and like a rolling stone that gathers no moss, from deep in the heart of the Midwest I boarded a kerosene canary bound for Honolulu. I arrived at the Waikiki Yacht Club to find it awash with yachties rushing around in preparation for the start of the maiden Pan Am Clipper Cup. The main bar was heaving with rivals from opposite parts of the Pacific spilling outside onto the lawn.

Enterprising Dick Gooch, a former Sydney petrol station proprietor who had seeded the idea of the Clipper Cup and was now in charge of promoting it, was deep in conversation with the vertically-challenged team manager Alan Brown and American Howard Hamstra, Vice President, General Council of Pan Am. Looking no further afield I spotted the portly figure of Monte Cristo, cigar-chomping Jack Rooklyn who controlled a vast poker machine empire and was owner of the lightly-constructed timber sloop *Apollo*. An entourage of seasoned sailors were sharing his company – the new owner of the C & C 61' *Sorcery*, Californian Jake Wood, who flashed horse-like teeth laced with gold and sported a piratical white goatee, Sydneysiders Don Mickleborough and ginger-haired 'Tweetie' Thompson, broad-shouldered Aucklander Syd Brown, and a tall long-legged fella 'Bamboo' Opperman. Big Syd waved and beckoned me over to where Jake was recounting a favourite line to Jack.

"My business might not be as lucrative as yours, but even so one of my plants supplies a lot of tooling for aerospace. It's the domestic airlines that are our bread and butter. I love the sight of vapour trails up in the sky when I'm sailing, there's 500,000 of my lock-nut fastenings in a Boeing 747. There are five companies in the free world apart from mine that make them, and we hold the patents and sell 'em the tooling." He paused to finish his drink.

"Fair bloody dinkum!" gawked Sydney butcher 'Tweetie'.

Jake's attention diverted from his lock-nut fastenings to Tweetie.

"Your buddy Mickleborough reckons you make some of the best

sausages in Sydney, he wasn't bullshitting was he?"

"Oh no, he's fair dinkum, mate. We supply truckloads down at Rushcutter's Bay for fundraising breakfasts at the Australian Naval Association and the twilight barbecues next door at the CYC. And what's more, we sell shitloads of snags to the yachts competing in the Sydney-Hobart race."

Jake Wood, with a practical engineering background, had a mind like a mathematical calculator. He toyed with his beard for a moment before resuming.

"Well, Tweetie, it sounds like you're my man. The plan is to take *Sorcery* Down Under next year for the Hobart Race, and I'd sure like to sample some of your sausages, but I need to know a bit more about them so my cook doesn't screw up the order."

"No worries, Jake. For the sailors we keep it nice and simple. Three flavours of lamb, pork and beef. They're our standard size, six inches long, and we sell 'em garnished with sprigs of parsley and wrapped by the foot or the fathom – whatever tickles your fancy, we'll deliver them down to the dock on Boxing race day."

Jake, feeling hungry by now, was almost licking his lips before he replied.

"That sounds sensational, it's a neat idea with the parsley, although I don't eat that shit myself. You can forget about the beef, but I like pork and the crew will go for the lamb. Do you have a name for them?"

"Yeah, Morning Glories," Tweetie replied.

Jake didn't miss a beat and with a wolf-like grin came back with,

"What a name! I bet the ladies at the CYC love 'em too. If your pork and lamb Morning Glories taste half as good as pussy, I'd like to order five fathoms of the fuckers for the race."

The motley assembly whooped with laughter before Big Syd's gruff voice intervened to sound out Bamboo.

"Talking of fathoms, Bamboo, it's got me wondering what sort of depths you encounter around here when setting the offshore markers for the Olympic triangles."

"Well, it's pretty deep. They used my fishing boat to lay them and it has its moments setting the outer marks in at about 350 fathoms."

"I'll be buggered, that's three and a half times deeper than the Australian continental shelf," Mickleborough croaked.

220

"Hey Tweets, that's well over the length of four thousand of your Morning Glories," Jake chipped in.

"Fair bloody dinkum," Tweetie mumbled to himself.

"What type of gear do you attach to the buoys," asked Big Syd.

"To anchor them we use a bunch of those cinder building blocks bound up tight with quarter-inch manila rope attached to a length of monofilament line that's shackled on to one end of an eye-spliced polyurethane strop which straddles a cheeked sheave hanging from the buoy." Bamboo paused to catch his breath. "Can you follow me?" he asked. A general nodding of heads bobbed up and down, so he went on.

"It takes about fifteen minutes for the cinder blocks to drop onto the ocean floor. Now, here's the secret of the exercise – it's imperative that you keep the cocksucker taut, so we tie the bitter end of the polyurethane line onto a counterweight that hangs like a pendulum in one of those grand-daddy clocks, and it undulates to the tides and the waves, so the marker is always bolt upright."

I was just about to make a move on some good-looking girls when Jake collared me, interrupting my mission.

"Hold your horses, sailor, have you got a minute? Rumour has it you sailed on *Sorcery* in the Miami-Montego Bay and Fastnet Race, including a Transatlantic crossing – is that correct?"

"Oh yeah, I reckon I covered a lot of miles on her a few years ago."

"Well in that case Chas, maybe you come close to knowing the old girl pretty well, and that's exactly what I need. How about you come and sail with us?" he asked, sticking out a big bear-paw of a hand.

I thought about it for a couple of seconds and threw my hat into the ring.

"You got yourself a deal, mate!" I replied.

"Great!" he beamed back with a piratical gleam in his eye.

It occurred to me that it had been some five years since I'd trod *Sorcery's* decks. The old warhorse was longer in the tooth now and no match on handicap against her latest rivals specifically designed to I.O.R. However, between Jake and myself we'd covered at least 25,000 miles on C & C 61's, and as the saying goes, 'Old age and treachery will overcome youth and skill'.

My most vivid recollections are of a dead downwind run under spinnaker from Kauai across to the steep basalt cliffs of Nihau and their fallen boulders that had formed bastion borders to the breaking seas beneath them. Near on twilight we gybed, clearing the northernmost part of the sparsely Polynesian-populated island, and set out on a three-hundred-mile blast reach down the westward side of the islands under the arc of the glittering Milky Way.

Midway through the second day we crossed the leeward side of the twenty-six-mile-wide Alenuihaha Chanel. Here the trade winds get squeezed like a concertina, accelerating in force as they funnel down between the two magnificent volcanic sentinels, Maui's Haleakala and Hawaii's Mauna Kea. The sun rose high above the yard arm and spread its rays out across the sea like a vast oriental fan.

Jake lumbered up onto deck armed with an aviation bubble sextant and his radio direction finder, and after waving them around in the air for a short time he quickly made some calculations before announcing,

"Goddammit, we're too close to the Kona coast. Set the big yellow chute, we've gotta haul our arses outta here before we get trapped under Mauna Loas's lee."

But his words were wasted and all too late. The breeze deserted us and we ground to a halt, firmly ensnared in the wind-shadow cast from the gigantic ten-thousand-foot volcanic peak. From its base beneath the sea the volcano is taller than Mount Everest, or as Mickleborough quipped, 60,000 Morning Glories high. The afternoon was sheer hell. A short, wretchedly steep sea pummelled us relentlessly, sending *Sorcery* into a wicked rolling motion, punctuated at regular intervals by a sickening lurch that slammed the sails and tested tempers with short fuses. To make matters worse, a spreader pierced a terrible rip in the light No. 1 headsail, and no sooner had we replaced it with the big 'drifter' than it suffered the same fate. Merl Peterson, Mickleborough and I stitched repairs faster than a flock of hard-working seamstresses mending sailors' pants.

Thankfully, when the sun began to set, the faintest tickle of wind slowly gained momentum, and hoisting a reaching chute we made our way out towards a cluster of cauliflower-headed cumulus clouds that had been gradually forming. Some time before midnight a large thunderstorm rolled over us, and for hours we tore along the highway in teeming rain, lit by sheets of lightning serenaded by growling thunder. By the time we reached the graveyard watch, we were well past South Head as the storm dissipated. Out off our bow the Halemaumau firepit,

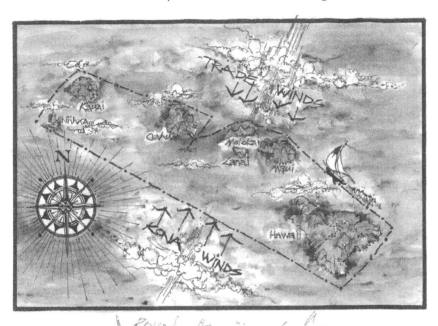

The Royal Hawaii Cup Race
Art: Douglas Hawkins

five thousand feet above the sea, spat forth great licks of fire, flashing across Mona Loa's flanks, while Pele, the goddess of fire, played games with her molybdenum shovel, tossing molten lava high into the sky as she danced. When the first bold rays from the rising sun started streaming in from the east, the tracks of molten lava flowing down to the ocean were revealed, resembling the outstretched fingers of an ogre's reaching hand surrounded by swirling spent fumes. And there, just beyond, to everyone's disbelief, side by side in a windless zone, appeared the two mighty ketches, *Kialo III* and *Ondine* – two of the greatest blue-water racing boats in the world.

This day was ours, however. We crossed a mile or more in front of the ketches five hundred miles into the race. When the first wind gusts hit the big boats, they took off like a pair flying fortresses in full pursuit of us. We pounded on into the full force of the trade winds with a solid 25 to 30 knots dead on the nose as we beat up the coast towards the Cape Kumukahi, the most eastern part of Hawaii, crashing through enormous white-crested seas rolling towards us in majestic lines, until they thundered into the base of towering rock formations and broke into a foaming mass of spray against the basalt pillars. High above us streams cascaded out of the volcanic rock tumbling down giant cliff faces, creating iridescent emerald, sapphire and saffron rainbows in their rushing descent into the ocean.

It was a raw and wild environment we were witnessing that few people have ever seen. Captain Cook may have been killed on the other side of the island, and many have visited his monument, but for a sailor it is to wonder how he and his men managed to chart the area in such precise detail. Although – compared with the ancient Pacific navigators and the astonishing journeys these great voyagers made in this part of the world with such extraordinary accuracy, and whose unique art is sadly nearly lost – one can only marvel at their skill and knowledge.

By the time we rounded Cape Kumakahi and headed towards Hilo flats the race was near done, but for one last incident at the end of a fast spinnaker run from Molokai to Diamond Head. As we gybed *Sorcery* one last time, the lazy brace wrapped tight as a boa constrictor around Juice's leg and hoisted him high off the deck. Yelling for help he dangled hopelessly, buffeted around in the wind and flying meters out from the boat until he was hauled in. We ditched the kite after crossing the finishing line.

Lay day brought its fair share of drama, too. On our way to the big party we watched in horror as two cars ploughed into each other with an almighty bang. The guy that had been crashed into leaped out of the pulverised remains of his vehicle in furious pursuit of the other driver. While the band in the square played lilting tropical songs on their ukuleles, he pulled out a gun and shot a round of bullets into the other guy. The poor bastard fell into the fountain and the water ran red with blood as he died.

Pushing on to the presentation, we were adorned with fragrant stems of Frangipani and Hibiscus given to us by beautiful local girls at the door, maitais flowed freely, and a feast of suckling pig was cooked in the smouldering heat of the local earth oven hangis. It was long before videos became the name of the game, and American photo journalist Phil Yule, along with a bunch of other marine photographers from all over the globe, did the next best thing, projecting sensational shots of the race taken from sea and air onto a huge screen. It was a bullroarer of a night and the show brought the house down. As the evening wore on a couple of buses arrived to carry the crews that wanted to kick on downtown to the 'Korean Cultural Centre', which in actual fact was a well-known establishment called the Spotlight Bar. The word soon spread, and a fleet of coaches packed full to the brim took off, rattling and honking down the road. Like a flood tide we poured into the bar until it was absolutely chock-a-block and the bouncers slammed the doors.

The bell rang, and to cheers and wolf whistles the show began. Ruby Rose and Suzy Q dropped their knickers, exposing fuzzy maps of Tasmania, as Big Syd, along with a well-known Sydney yachtie, aka Don Juan, perched on stools in the front of the stage. Suzy Q bent over with her long sleek black hair running down her back stopping an inch from her twitching tattooed buttocks, from which she was puffing halos on a large cigar. Big Syd with his ham-sized fists plucked the cigar out neat as a whistle and jammed it into his chuckling Balmoral mate's mouth, and slippery as an eel it fell out, tumbling down to burn on the floor.

Meanwhile, Ruby Rose had a couple of hard-boiled eggs on the go; neatly she arched her back and, with her legs apart, fired them off with the force of a double-barrelled shotgun. Macready the Rigger had placed a schooner of beer on fellow Victorian 'Budgerigar's' head, and it was the girl's plan to hit the glass, but for poor 'Budgie' it went embarrassingly astray, much to the amusement of fellow spectators. While the eggs shot off like missiles, one of them ran out of steam and hit Budgie, broke open and slid slowly down his spectacles and beakish nose, straight down his gaping, pelican-like throat. The second egg knocked the glass off his head, and beer streamed out of the glass all over his face. Macready's grinning face turned to masked horror as Budgie regurgitated, as Pelicans often do, everything he had semi-digested from the day's events, depositing it all over the rigger's trousers, with the remnants trickling down into his brand new suede dock-sider shoes. The girls danced to shouts of 'we want more' and the show rolled on into the early hours of the morning.

It was shortly after the 'Korean Cultural Centre' fling that I spotted the Doug Peterson-designed *Magic Pudding* for the first time, although she began life with the rather unprepossessing name of the B195. In order to get her built in the first place, Tommy 'Terrific' Stephenson, Australian Yachtsman of the Year, who had also won the world Half

Tons in Chicago in 1975 skippering *Foxy Lady*, became Doug Peterson's agent Down Under, and with the help of his mate John Karrasch, stalked Pioneer Electronics for B195's sponsorship, and at the end of the chase the company rose to the bait.

It was decided that dedicated and talented timber-boat builder Bruce Keir would be asked to construct the yacht. An outstanding dinghy sailor, Bruce surrounded himself with a team of guys with similar sailing experience and who also shared his enthusiasm for wonderful workmanship. His boatyard specialised in constructing Flying Dutchmen and Fireball dinghies, and the centre of operations was in Seaford, a southern bay-side town near Melbourne. Bruce got hold of a stack of Tasmanian King Billy pine along with a sprinkling of Mahogany, Spruce Pine and Cedar, and set about building the finest One-Tonner in the world.

The technical stuff went as follows: the B195 was 11.2 metres long, 3.73 metres across the beam and displaced 1854 kgs. Compared to the new Farr One Ton centreboarders it had a slightly narrower stern, was a fraction fuller in the bow, and the virtually un-ballasted centreboard drew 2.4 metres. The mast was built by Stearns in Sturgeon Bay, Wisconsin, and made of an extremely light and narrow alloy in fabricated sections. It had triple spreaders and a set of 'hounds', or 'diamonds' as they're sometimes known, was fractional-rigged and stepped into the deck with a compression post below decks to support it, accompanied by a complicated state of the art hydraulics that controlled everything. The B195 was without doubt the forerunner of a revolution in yacht design, and destined to have a huge impact on the way the sport's future was sponsored and advertised. In the boat's brief history some amazing sailors trod her decks, and the list reads like a yachting hall of fame. From the Aussie sailing world Tommy Stephenson, Bill Lawler, Hugh and Ian Treharne, John 'Steamer' Stanley, Dick 'Sightie' Hammond, John Bertram, Jamie Wilmot, Ian Perdriou, Russel 'Budgie' Evans, and from New Zealand 'Macca' McCready, Roscoe Guiniven – and, of course, Bruce Keir.

The B195 sponsors, Pioneer Electrics, were about to open a can of worms. The International Yacht Racing Union (IYRU) contained a certain idiosyncrasy in Rule 26. The precept referred to advertising and it read:

'The hull, crew or equipment of a yacht owned or sponsored wholly

or in part by a group or organisation shall not display any wording or emblem that specifically relates to such owner or sponsor.'

It would seem, reading this, that the door was firmly closed on any sponsorship proposal, and in order to comply with this state of affairs, companies seeking publicity in return for their investment had something of a razor's edge to walk. Inevitably the company demanded its pound of flesh, and although they agreed not to interfere with any aspects of sailing, they certainly extended interest to the choice of a boat name, and so the merry dance began in figuring out how to comply both with Rule 26 and their own requirements.

Some bright spark came up with the idea of christening B195 *Pioneer Sound*, an appropriate name on all counts, for she was certainly a pioneer thanks to Doug Peterson's brilliance, and 'sound' is a seafaring term that means ' inlet from the sea or deep bay over which soundings can be taken'.

After considerable head-scratching an idea developed which would avoid any possible controversy over sporting bylaw and obvious exploitation of the company name 'Pioneer'. There was only one thing for it. Somewhere in the world, a place called Pioneer Sound had to be found. The search was on, from the Azores to Zanzibar. Believe it or not, there was nowhere on earth bearing this name, and so an ingenious ploy was hatched and the plot thickened with further intrigue.

"We have to have our own Pioneer Sound. If one doesn't exist, we'll create it. No one can argue with that!" Karrasch resolutely decided.

Over on the West Coast of Australia lived the fabulous eccentric, self-styled 'His Royal Highness Prince Leonard of Hutt River Province'. The Prince had applied to the United Nations for his own self-governed principality. It was a terrific joke to everyone, and passports and visas were supplied to all Prince Leonard's subjects, although the taxation department did not consider the idea remotely amusing. Nevertheless, the prince's kingdom would serve B195's sponsorship issues perfectly, and it was put to him that perhaps he could officially name a watering-hole in his territory 'Pioneer Sound'. The magnanimous ruler agreed to the proposition, and to this day a letter exists saying a lake in the Hutt River province is so called. As a result, Pioneer was able to officially involve itself with the boat, and Rule 26 remained unviolated. The launch became quite a famous affair, and in September 1977 the Prime Minister's wife, Tammie Fraser, smashed a bottle of champagne on the yacht's bow during the official naming ceremony at Melbourne's Brighton Pier. As for the Prince, his invitation to the shindig was written but not posted. Pioneer Electrics got cold feet at the last minute in case of a diplomatic incident.

With no further ado the yacht was trucked to Sydney, and her career got off to a flying start. She won the Australian One Ton Championships and in October was shipped over the Tasman Sea to Auckland for the World Championships free of charge on Australia National Line's newest and biggest container ship, *Australia Venture*. She did not fare quite so well in the series against the new breed of Bruce Farr centreboarders, who were faster to windward, although the B195, whose centre of gravity doesn't change whether the board is up or down, was more stable downwind, and it was here that she kept pace with her rivals; and she was the best by far of the Australian boats, coming fourth in the final standings.

Doubts were raised that maybe the B195 might not be strong enough to handle really heavy conditions, but nevertheless she was selected to sail for the state of Victoria in the 1977 Southern Cross Cup, where she scored a third in the middle distance race. The last race of the series, the Sydney-Hobart, was beset by a rampage of dirty weather. Fifty-nine yachts retired, and sadly, B195 cracked her hull about eighty miles off Gabo Island, and diverted to Gippsland Lakes and Bull's shipyard for repairs.

It was at this point that John Karrasch decided to rename the B195 to *Magic Pudding* after Norman Lindsay's immortal character, and it's true to say she displayed more than a hint of Don Quixote's character. Her white hull sported blue stripes to match Pioneer Electrics colours, and she was further decorated with pictures of Lindsay's magic pudding on either side. Once some ballast had been added to her centreboard to improve her upwind performance in rugged weather, she was ready to rock, and got selected to represent the Australian National Team along with Syd Fischer's *Ragamuffin* and another Peterson designed boat, the two-tonner *Big Schott*. The yachts were shipped over to Pearl Harbour and won the Pan Am Series, and best of all, *Magic Pudding* rose triumphant to win the Around the State race.

Whether it was the luck of the draw or fate, meeting *Magic Pudding* in Hawaii changed the course of my career considerably, and would give me the reputation of being one of the only guys loco enough to sail fractional rigs on long-haul deliveries. At the end of the Pan Am Clipper race I shared a cab to the Yacht Club with Budgie and McCready, who asked me what my immediate plans were.

"Well fellas, I've got none for the time being," I told them.

Word spreads fast on the yachting grapevine, and the next day I was confronted by the pair of them along with John Karrasch and Tommy Stephens.

"If you're at a loose end, Chas, how would you feel about delivering *Magic Pudding* over to the States?" asked Tom.

"Sure, no worries," I replied.

And with that we struck a deal, and Macca and Budgie showed me around the boat before they shoved off for the airport.

"She's got a wee bit of damage up forward that you'd best check out while we're still here," Budgie mentioned hesitatingly.

Crawling over a stack of sails to have a closer look, I soon got his drift.

"Shit, fellas, she's not in the best of shape!" I ruminated, taking stock of the busted frames and a couple of floor-boards that were jammed as braces between the wire tire-rod holding the deck down and up against the hull to prevent it panting.

Fortunately, I ran into Butch van Artsdalen not long after, the legendary surfer who'd been one of the first to conquer the pipeline, and he introduced me to a mate of his, Morey, a well-known local guru for repairing big boards. In fact, he was related to Tom Morey who invented the Boogie-Woogie belly-board. They were good blokes, and considering I was just about broke, but for a couple of slabs of beer and a bottle of bourbon, Morey skilfully reinforced the whole front section of the boat until it was almost bullet-proof, and we all went out to north beach for a barbecue to celebrate.

Apart from me and Juicehead, two girls came along for the trip, one of which was a well-known sailor and a motor mechanic from Auckland, who I put in charge of the engine. She might have been shaped like a plump partridge but she was as hard as bloody nails. We provisioned *Magic Pudding* with two big boxes of passion fruit, given us by some kind person, and sixteen dozen eggs, a few tins of spaghetti, a sack of Spanish onions to keep scurvy at bay, and some fishing gear. It's about all we could get – not that we'd be doing much cooking. Down below was a real Spartan affair, the galley consisting only of a two-burner metho stove. And someone who worked at the Kaiser Hospital came up with some medical gear for free, which included a supply of antibiotics that came in useful for a dose of the clap Juice reckoned his girlfriend left him with, although she said it was the other way round. Anyway, that shit we had on board solved the problem.

It's two thousand three hundred miles if you take a straight line from Hawaii to Los Angeles, but we were travelling against the wind, which meant our journey would cover over three thousand miles, and it wasn't about to be an easy trip. You have to head north of the islands on the starboard tack for about six or eight hundred miles before tacking over. Then there's a choice of either going over the top of the high pressure system or straight through it, so you always carry a lot of fuel when you take the windless highway, and maybe have to motor through a boundless blue world of sea and sky.

Setting off on our ocean trek, it was imperative that we completed some sort of shakedown. As mad as it seemed, we set sail via the Kaiwi Channel, a notorious stretch of water separating Oahu from Molokai – a tough assignment, but a calculable risk; after all, if we ran into trouble and suffered some mishap, hopefully we could run off down to Maui and lick our wounds in Lahaina.

By the time we passed Koko Head at the bottom of Oahu it was dark, and the wind strong enough to blow the milk out of your coffee. Around midnight, under a high-cut storm jib and a fully-reefed main, conditions were getting uglier by the minute. Low clouds skimmed under a resplendent silver fish moon and the gathering gale-force wind could have torn a poacher's lurcher off its leash.

We had reached the end of the ocean corridor, where a tidal gate teetered on the outer rim of Molokai's underwater volcanic precipice which sheers off into the pacific blue. Here two mighty forces clash: the wind-driven ocean rollers and a wicked adverse local diurnal current. The roar of the waves sounded like a locomotive drowning out the whine of the wind and the rattling leeward rigging. A formidable and furious Kanaloa, Hawaiian god of the ocean and custodian of the dead, had risen from his dark squid-inhabited depths frequented by the spirits of his angry warriors, and was about to let loose.

The confrontation was relentless. Under the guise of fifteen-foot steep seas with fuscous faces and white-crested heads, the spirits from the deep set upon us in savage thrusts like rows of ragged, gleaming

Magic Pudding B195
Photo: photographer unknown

shark's teeth. Hour after hour Juice and I interchanged back and forth from the tiller to mainsheet, trying to keep our bold little boat out of harm's way. Rogue monsters rolled in like a bombora, breaking right over the deck, flooding the cockpit and sending a deluge of water cascading down below where the girls bailed for their lives. Come dawn, Kanaloa decided to let us pass, withdrawing his ferocious mates back down to the ocean bed so we could break free of the shackles holding us back and begin clawing away from Molokai's lee shore and out into sea swells.

Maybe the sea god decided to test us one more time just for the hell of it. Calamity struck several days later somewhere north of Kauai. Slogging our way uphill in tough conditions, the front face of the centreboard broke loose. Down below, the situation had become diabolical. Each time *Magic Pudding* rose and pitched forward when she rode over a pacific roller, a torrent of swirling seawater spilled into her overflowing bilges. Ditching the main, we feathered her into the wind. On board was a stout bit of six foot 4" x 2", and I jammed it into a deep slot which was inserted through the top of the dagger-board and cranked it back with a winch to ease its forward pressure. A major problem on the damaged casing was largely due to the machined stainless screws. Their threads were either stripped, or the backing nuts had fallen off and gone tumbling down to the devil's kitchen beneath us.

While the girls chucked and bucketed the incoming deluge, I managed to scavenge six king-size screws, extracted from various parts of the galley sink and chart table. With a tube of 5200 marine sealant I refastened the front of the dagger-board box. Perhaps on purpose, or some idiot's lack of foresight when installing the engine, its crank handle was about as handy as a set of tits on a Brahmin bull – it fitted out, but you couldn't swing it. Instead it found some purpose when we wrapped the spare dock lines around the centreboard trunk and tightened them up, using it as a Spanish windlass – good enough to get us to San Diego, so we kept pressing on.

One pitch-black night Loo-Loo, the roly-poly mechanic, shouted out,

"What in the hell's that?" stabbing her hand towards a mammoth silhouette looking out of the darkness dead ahead.

"Christ, its bloody close!" I hollered, and in a second slammed the tiller extension to bear away just in the nick of time. The week before we left, a fleet of yachts had set off on a similar course, and it was quite conceivable that one of them may have suffered a serious mishap. A fresh NE wind still blew, and six hundred miles from land it was all hands on deck with little time to dawdle or consider any other options than the daunting decision of running back on a reciprocal course into an area fraught with danger to take a closer look.

Luffing up into the wind as close as we dared go, Juicehead shone the twelve volt spotlight into the night to reveal a long, low, semi-submerged shape with white spume foam from the breaking seas swirling around it. Heaving a sigh of relief, one thing was for sure: it wasn't a yacht or a shipping container. Perhaps with its cylindrical shape, the fuselage of a red Chinese rocket ship, god knows, it could have been anything, and judging by the state of its waterline and the flotsam around, it had been adrift for quite a while. We quickly got under way again, thanking our lucky stars we hadn't run into the thing.

Far enough north by the morning, we flopped over onto the opposite tack and started sailing eastwards towards the Pacific high. Gradually, over the next couple of days, our wind died away and a new breeze tilled in from the southeast, so we shook out the reefs and changed to a larger headsail. We were now within the outer boundaries of what has become known in recent times as the North Pacific gyre, a vast area of ocean bigger than the state of Texas, where the currents and winds slowly rotate in a clockwise motion, carting and pushing along with them tons of junk that's been thrown carelessly into the ocean. Eventually this accumulated shit ends up at its centre, like the grate in a kitchen sink. Environmental scientists call it the world's biggest plastic rubbish dump. The pollution is now visible from satellites, and when you peer down into the depths, it's a mass of endless suspended plastic as far as you can see. And since the Japanese tsunami it can only get worse. Back then we'd never heard of it, only the North Pacific high acts like this, as it fluctuates with the changing seasons with the middle perimeters of the gyre.

Saving hundreds of miles, we took the shortcut, chugging away hour after hour as we traversed a tranquil mirror-calm sea. Suddenly, plumb in the eye of the Pacific high, the monotonous drone of the motor was drowned out by a clattering metal clanging. Shutting the iron genoa down and raising the engine's cover, I was devastated to discover the casting supporting the alternator's bolted bracket had completely sheared off. It was serious situation. We were a thousand miles away from the nearest landfall, and Davey Jones' locker lay thirty thousand feet beneath us. With no wish to die a slow death from dehydration or starvation, a plan of attack had to be swiftly hatched.

Juicehead came up with the possible lifesaving solution of mounting the alternator to the bottom of the boat. It sounded preposterous at first, but his idea held some merit. Rolling up our sleeves, we sawed up a couple of floor-boards and bolted the alternator to them, then fastened it to the limber holes in a pair of stringers that conveniently ran as reinforcements across the bilge in front of the engine. After a lot of fucking about, the alignment was okay, but the belt still too slack for comfort. Amongst her paraphernalia Catherine, the long-legged Seattle chick, found half a jar of Hawaiian honey, and to give it a bit of extra grip I buttered the belt with some of the stuff, and thankfully it stuck like sheep-shit to the sole of a stockman's Blundstone leather boot.

Somehow we made it out the other side. Bursting from our atmospheric bubble, we encountered a brisk nor'wester and a lumpy sea which brought a 'shiver me timbers' chill, as Long John Silver would have said. *Magic Pudding's* wooden hull began to flex, our makeshift alternator went crazy and threatened to rip the stringer out of the boat, or worse, tear someone's hand off, so we hastily dismantled it and stowed the lethal weapon away in a safe place.

Under cold steely skies we rolled on for the rest of the week, and by the time we closed the Californian coast, the batteries were dead as dodos – no lights, no instruments. We were down to our last can of spaghetti and a few eggs, and the fish had stopped biting. Morale lifted somewhat when the wind shifted and *Magic Pudding* hooked into the hot, dry Santa Anna blowing off the land, often called the Devil's Breath for its ability to fan up fierce forest fires that occur at that time of year. With San Diego a couple of hundred miles over the horizon, we set off on a screaming reach in crystal clear blue waters and the next morning sighted Point Loma. By noon we rounded its big beacons and buoys adorned with sleeping sea lions which heralded the harbour entrance. We passed Dennis Connors, of America's Cup fame and the then current world Star champion, out practising for the next World's in San Francisco later in the year.

"Where have you come from?" he shouted out.

"Honolulu," we called back.

"Jesus, on a fractional rig, I don't believe it!" he hollered.

We got all the way up to San Diego Yacht Club under sail, and while we dropped the main to park right under the main bar, a crowd came out clapping and cheering. Doug Peterson was there on the dock with a case of beer.

"You're a braver bunch than me," he said shaking his head, wondering how the pudding and her crew were still more or less in one piece.

We had navigated much of the trip with a hundred dollar second-hand plastic Davis sextant which melted in the hot sun so you'd have to bend the thing back into shape to use it, and which meant all the sightings had to be double-checked – a bent sextant is not so good on accuracy; and we'd only had a pilot chart to plot our way across the Pacific. It had taken us eighteen days in all, and although an insurance policy had been taken out before the journey started it wasn't needed. But Christ, it was a hard trip!

On top of surviving the voyage the unexpected welcoming reception was all too much for our girls. They grabbed their gear and bolted off to the showers to repair their bedraggled condition. All Juice and I wanted was a fucking cold drink, and we didn't emerge from the bar until several six-packs of Peterson's cold crisp beer had been poured down our parched throats. As a consequence of the hours and days spent at the tiller steering, both of us, apart from losing weight, were suffering from the sailor's curse – 'gunwale bum'. It's a painful pox-marked ailment resulting from a saltwater-saturated arse. The yacht club's shower facilities felt pretty luxurious after the conditions on *Magic Pudding* – piping hot running water is sheer ecstasy after time at sea. Checking out the state of our bodies in the big mirrors, Juice-head's hideous strawberry-scaled hindquarters with his testicles hanging down between them was a gruesome sight, and with a mask of horror on his face he hightailed it out of there like a scalded cat.

Peterson's Shelter Island two-storey office wasn't hard to locate. You could hear the blaring music emitting from it a country mile away. Doug's designs were in worldwide demand and his drawings flew off the drafting board, the telephone never stopped ringing and the guys burned the midnight oil to keep on top of things. John Reichel, Jim Pugh and Billy Tripp assisted Doug and churned out I.O.R. custom designs at a phenomenal rate. Doug was beginning to rake in royalties from the mass-production of fibreglass cruising yachts, including the Peterson 44 built in Kaohsiung, Taiwan, and commissioned by San Diego yacht broker Jack Kelly, who sold over two thousand of them.

Magic Pudding was plucked out of the water and shored up on land where Billy and I could remove the rudder to check its carbon stock and both sets of the bearings. Billy was simply astounded to discover no wear and tear, both of us amazed that she was one of the few yachts that hadn't suffered some major failure in this area, considering others with a lot less miles under their keels had experienced real problems.

A baseball's throw across the way was Carl Eichenlaub's boatyard where *Magic Pudding's* modifications would be carried out. Billy pointed out one of their racing boats being built of aluminium, and mentioned some of the names of others constructed out of alloy in the yard: *Pied Piper, High Roller* and *Champagne* amongst them. Carl had been a former national Lightning dinghy champion, and a teenage Dennis Conner had often crewed with him. Now Carl was famous for the hundreds of lightweight wooden racing dinghy hulls he had turned out over the decades – Snipes and Stars and Lightnings being some of them. He'd become so successful he referred to himself as a 'bare-bone boat builder', supplying the hulls and leaving his clients to deal with the final fitting out. We found him under a tarpaulin-shaded boat, and he emerged speckled in powdered sawdust with his ruffled hair streaked in marine paint. Like his other boatbuilding contemporaries, Bob Derecktor and Chuff Wilman at PJ's, his workpants were hitched up high by a pair of bright-coloured braces.

Seeing Billy, Carl lit up like a match, and the two of them dived into a rap about the repairs and modifications for *Magic Pudding*. Some of their technical conversation simply flew over my head, but that's hardly surprising. Carl was a genius and Billy super-smart. Nowadays Billy is regarded as one of the finest naval architects around, regularly having his yacht designs launched by some of the most renowned boat yards in the world. And Carl became an absolute legend in his lifetime, partly due to his dedicated services to many American Olympic campaigns. In the year of the millennium he received the Nathaniel G Herreshoff trophy, the highest sailing award for service to yachting in the U.S.

That weekend I got word from Tux and the boys on *Circus Maximus* over on the East coast asking me to join them in an attempt to break the 175' three-masted schooner Transatlantic sailing record. Early Monday morning a distant haze signalled a scorching day, and I stood on the balcony outside the yacht club contemplating my next move. It was the 25th September, three months till Christmas. Suddenly there was an almighty bang that brought everyone to a standstill and broke the early morning quiet, and clouds of black billowing smoke spiralled into the sky. Someone mentioned the Mexican bushfires and another thought it may have been an exploding oil terminal. But in fact, it was America's worst aviation tragedy. An incoming Southwest Airlines Boeing 727 had collided with a Cessna 172 in mid-air and crashed down into North Park, a San Diego residential neighbourhood.

A couple of days later I slung the hook and boarded a paraffin pelican bound for the Big Apple to join *Circus Maximus* in a bid to take a shot at breaking the speed record from New York to France. Holed up in a hideous Winnebago that looked like a gigantic horse-float in Bob Derecktor's boatyard in Larchmont, a message came through that *Magic Pudding* had gone up in flames, and the fire had left only a remnant of her bow and stern. The only other bit saved was the rudder. So they stuck it into another boat, called *Brown Sugar*, her near sistership. They said it had been an electrical fire, but that completely bamboozled me as I knew the batteries had been flat as a pancake. The theory was, maybe it had been deliberately torched.

Down in San Diego, just short of the Mexican border at Doug Peterson's house, the remains of *Magic Pudding's* bow section sits in the front yard. And the only part of her that ever felt the tickle of a badger's brush and the slick swish of varnish was her transom, which is now a bar in the bespectacled and bearded designer's house; and hopefully the drinking station is adorned with the four big green barnacled glass fish-balls we salvaged from far out in the Pacific on the yacht's longest and final voyage. I guess many an anecdote is reminisced over a few beers at the Magic Pudding Saloon, a memorable monument for sure.

As for the Circus Ridiculous caper, I waited with former shipmates Tucks, Woody and Captain Tits while she was beefed up for the Transatlantic record attempt. We sat around for a month drinking piss at Jonathon Livingstone Seagull's bar, holding on for the ultimate autumn storm which would give us the wind and speed needed to try and break the record; but it never came, so we shelved it until the following spring.

The course of events changed once more when a band of Frenchmen bought the yacht in order to take a crack at it themselves, although it was a move they nearly didn't survive. Somewhere way out northeast of Sable Island, a graveyard of the Atlantic, hunting the Gulf Stream's warm waters on a wild and windy night, the *Circus* was running downhill like a bitch on heat with the howling hounds from hell chasing her rooster tail. Whatever happened next is anyone's guess. But when their mast sheared off at the deck and came crashing down, its spreaders stoved in her topsides, punching holes the size of cannon balls into the old girl. The frantic French crew spent a few hours desperately trying to stem the incoming torrent of water, to no avail. By the time dawn broke, a Frog freighter bound for Marseilles recued them from the life-raft, so they got a free ride back to France.

But that wasn't all. Several months later, *Desperado*, another down-wind flyer built in the same boatyard as *Circus Maximus*, also took a crack at the record and suffered a similar fate somewhere near Bermuda in the Devil's Triangle. The final scoreboard read: North Atlantic 2, Yves-Marie de Tanton 0.

In the year of the millennium I met up with Tommy Stephens where he was supervising the completion of a marina at the Subic Bay Yacht Club in the Philippines. We ended up sailing together on a Mumm 36, *Suicide Blonde*, that had been shipped from Honolulu to participate in the President's Cup and had a half-naked woman painted on her top-sides that raised a lot of smiles.

At one of the parties over a couple of San Miguels, I asked Tom,

"Whatever happened to Karrasch, the bloke that owned *Magic Pudding*, when she went up in smoke?"

He looked back at me slightly startled.

"Hell, I didn't realize you hadn't heard. The poor bastard got hooked up in some shady business deal that went sour and they tossed him in prison to cool his heels for a couple of years. But he was a smart bugger, and before he went into the slammer he bought a couple of shark cats and started a fish and chip shop that sold the shark they caught as flake, and it kept him solvent while he was banged up." Tom paused and took a swig of his beer, and with a grin went on,

"It's strange you mentioned his name, I hadn't heard of him in donkey's years. And then right out of the blue late last year he called me up on the dog and bone, saying he was contemplating taking another shot at a racing boat, and if he did, would I put the project together for him. So we sort of let it sit there and I haven't heard from his since."

But the spirit of *Magic Pudding* didn't end there.

In 2005, when I was in England for the '85 'Roll Upside Down' reunion on Simon LeBon's *Drum*, I ran into Billy Tripp at the Chequers Tavern in the south coast town of Lymington, who told me:

"You wouldn't believe it Chas, the old boat's rudder is in *Brown Sugar* to this day and they're still sailing with it."

"Fair dinkum: you've got to be bloody kidding!" I exclaimed.

"No, no, it ain't bullshit. What's more, wait till you get a drift on this! You remember an American guy, Bill Green, who used to work with Jeremy Rogers back in the '70s before they went into liquidation?"

"Oh, shit yes. He was a bloody good sailor. Wasn't he on *Gumboots* when they won the One Ton Cup?"

"Yeah, that's the guy. Well, he's moved on now and runs a big show down the road, Green Marine, where they're building a shitload of boats out of composites, including one of my designs. Yesterday we were rapping about carbon, and I mentioned the phenomenal longevity of the magic *Sugar* stock, and blow me down, but Bill looks back at me without batting an eyelid and tells me it was built down the road at Roger's old place!"

Before he left, Billy asked me if I still had the half-model of *Brown Sugar* he gave me all those years ago in San Diego.

"I sure do, it's hanging up on a wall looking out at the Iron Pot on the Derwent in my dear old mother's house back in Tassie," I answered.

"Well, you'd better hang on to it, it's a bit of a collector's item now. Back in '79 the bad boys on *Brown Sugar* got blackballed from the Big Boat series in San Francisco. It was a dubious distinction, the only time it's ever happened. The committee said it was 'for conduct unbecoming gentlemen,' " he grinned.

Time is a traveller…

To be continued…